John Quincy Adams

BOOKS BY HARLOW GILES UNGER

American Tempest

Improbable Patriot

Lion of Liberty

Last Founding Father

The Unexpected George Washington

Lafayette

John Hancock

Noah Webster

America's Second Revolution

The French War Against America

HARLOW GILES UNGER

John
Quincy
Adams

Da Capo Press
A Member of the Perseus Books Group

Designed by Trish Wilkinson
Set in 11.5 point Adobe Garamond by The Perseus Books Group

Library of Congress Cataloging-in-Publication Data
Unger, Harlow G., 1931–
    John Quincy Adams / Harlow Giles Unger.
        p.   cm.
    Includes bibliographical references and index.
    ISBN 978-0-306-82129-5 (hardcover : alk. paper) — ISBN 978-0-306-82130-1
(e-book) 1. Adams, John Quincy, 1767–1848. 2. Presidents—United States—
Biography. 3. United States—Politics and government—1789–1815. 4. United
States—Politics and government—1825–1829. I. Title.
E377.U57 2012
973.5'5092—dc23
[B]   2012009399

Published by Da Capo Press
A Member of the Perseus Books Group
www.dacapopress.com

Da Capo Press books are available at special discounts for bulk purchases in the U.S. by corporations, institutions, and other organizations. For more information, please contact the Special Markets Department at the Perseus Books Group, 2300 Chestnut Street, Suite 200, Philadelphia, PA 19103, or call (800) 810-4145, ext. 5000, or e-mail special.markets @perseusbooks.com.

10 9 8 7 6 5 4 3 2

Who but shall learn that freedom is the prize
  That nature's God commands the slave to rise,
Roll, years of promise, rapidly roll round,
  Till not a slave shall on this earth be found.

—JOHN QUINCY ADAMS, 1827.[1]

Contents

List of Illustrations ix

Acknowledgments xi

Chronology xiii

             Introduction 1

CHAPTER 1   *A First Son for a Founding Father* 5

CHAPTER 2   *The Seeds of Statesmanship* 29

CHAPTER 3   *The Land of Lovely Dames* 47

CHAPTER 4   *"He Grows . . . Very Fat"* 63

CHAPTER 5   *Never Was a Father More Satisfied* 87

CHAPTER 6   *A Free, Independent, and Powerful Nation* 107

CHAPTER 7   *A Profile in Courage* 123

CHAPTER 8   *Diplomatic Exile* 145

CHAPTER 9   *Restoring Peace to the World* 159

CHAPTER 10   *Stepladder to the Presidency* 179

CHAPTER 11   *The Great and Foul Stain*   *199*

CHAPTER 12   *The End of the Beginning*   *229*

CHAPTER 13   *A New Beginning*   *259*

CHAPTER 14   *Freedom Is the Prize*   *285*

Notes   *315*

Bibliography and Research Resources   *339*

Index   *349*

List of Illustrations

Maps

No. 1. Boston Bay and Quincy Bay   15
No. 2. Louisiana Purchase   127
No. 3. The "Adams Strip"   134
No. 4. Missouri Compromise   214

Illustrations

1. Abigail Adams   9
2. The Adams farm and birthplace of John Quincy Adams   10
3. John Adams   13
4. Battle of Bunker's Hill   16
5. Benjamin Franklin   35
6. Palace of Versailles   36
7. John Quincy Adams at sixteen   45
8. Panoramic view of St. Petersburg   48
9. Francis Dana   49
10. Abigail Adams II ("Nabby")   57
11. Harvard College   64

12. Edmond Genet   76
13. President George Washington   81
14. John Quincy Adams at twenty-nine   91
15. Louisa Catherine Johnson (JQA's fiancée)   100
16. President John Adams   104
17. President Thomas Jefferson   130
18. Retirement home of John and Abigail Adams   141
19. Emperor Napoléon I   151
20. Secretary of State James Monroe   172
21. Agreement at Ghent   175
22. Cows graze near the Capitol   197
23. Secretary of State John Quincy Adams   201
24. Secretary of the Treasury William H. Crawford   222
25. Secretary of War John C. Calhoun   230
26. Andrew Jackson   233
27. George Washington Adams   234
28. Speaker Henry Clay   237
29. President John Quincy Adams   240
30. Marquis de Lafayette   242
31. First Lady Louisa Catherine Adams   248
32. John Adams II   249
33. Going to the White House levée   251
34. Charles Francis Adams   265
35. James K. Polk   275
36. Henry Adams at Harvard   287
37. Killing of the captain of the *Amistad*   288
38. Congolese chief Cinque   290
39. President John Tyler   295
40. Daguerreotype of John Quincy Adams   297
41. Bunker's Hill Monument   304
42. Congressman Abraham Lincoln   307
43. Death of John Quincy Adams   309

Acknowledgments

My deepest thanks to Sara Georgini, an assistant editor of *The Adams Papers*, at the Massachusetts Historical Society in Boston, for vetting the finished manuscript of this book. Her encyclopedic knowledge of the life and times of the Adams family saved me weeks, probably months, of research and checking. My thanks, too, to Kelly Cobble, curator, and Patty Smith, museum technician, at the Adams National Historical Park, Quincy, Massachusetts, for their gracious and most generous help in providing illustrations for this book. Also very helpful in obtaining illustrations were Richard Sorenson of the Smithsonian American Art Museum, Smithsonian Institution, Washington, DC; Jessica Blesso, of the Library of Congress duplication services; and Anna J. Cook, assistant reference librarian at the Massachusetts Historical Society.

I know of no words that can express my gratitude to all the great folks at Da Capo Press and the Perseus Books Group, which published this book—the fourth they've published with my byline. If this were a newspaper or magazine, all their names would appear on a masthead. I have no idea why book publishers don't print mastheads in books, but, to try to thank those responsible for the publication and sale of this volume, I am breaking with tradition and not only displaying a masthead but dedicating this book to all the people listed.

Da Capo Press
A Member of the Perseus Books Group
John Radziewicz, Publisher, Da Capo Press
Robert Pigeon, Executive Editor
Lissa Warren, Vice President, Director of Publicity
Kevin Hanover, Vice President, Director of Marketing
Sean Maher, Marketing Manager
Jonathan Crowe, Editor
Cisca Schreefel, Project Editor
Trish Wilkinson, Designer
Jennifer Kelland, Copy Editor
Cathy Armer, Proofreader
Marie Maes, Indexer

My most sincere thanks to you all and to the entire sales team of the Perseus Books Group.

* * *

NOTE: Spellings, punctuation, and grammar in the eighteenth- and nineteenth-century letters, manuscripts, and publications cited in this book have, where appropriate, been modernized without my knowingly altering the intent of the original author. Readers may find the original spellings in the works cited in the notes.

Chronology

July 11, 1767—John Quincy Adams (JQA) born in Braintree (later re-named Quincy), Massachusetts, the first son of John and Abigail Adams.

1775—Sees Battle of Bunker's Hill from hillside near home across Boston Bay.

1778—Sails for France with father, the emissary of Congress seeking French financial aid for the Revolutionary War.

1779–1781—Attends school in Paris, then the University of Leyden.

1781—Goes to St. Petersburg as secretary for American minister Francis Dana at the Russian court.

1783—Rejoins father in The Hague, then Paris; resumes studies.

1785–1787—Returns to the United States; earns degree from Harvard College.

1787–1790—Studies law; admitted to Massachusetts Bar.

1791–1793—Practices law in Boston; publishes newspaper articles assailing French Revolution and defending Washington policy of neutrality.

1794—Appointed U.S. minister to Holland by President George Washington; hones skills as a diplomat and undercover observer of political trends.

1797—John Adams elected second President of the United States; JQA appointed minister to Prussia; marries Louisa Catherine Johnson.

1800—Father loses bid for reelection and recalls son from Prussia; JQA's first child, George Washington Adams, born; resumes law practice.

1802—Federalists elect JQA to state senate.

1803—Elected to U.S. Senate; second son, John Adams II, born.

1804–1808—Abandons Federalist Party; votes as independent representative of "the whole nation"; votes for Louisiana Purchase; third son, Charles Francis, born in 1807; Federalists force him to resign from Senate.

1809—President James Madison appoints him minister to Russia.

1811—Refuses appointment to U.S. Supreme Court.

1813—Appointed head of commission to negotiate end to War of 1812.

1817—President James Monroe appoints him secretary of state.

1818—Negotiates historic treaty with Britain, fixing northern boundaries with Canada; declares support for Latin American revolutions against Spain; mother, Abigail Adams, dies.

1819—Negotiates U.S. acquisition of East and West Florida from Spain; extension of western U.S. border to Pacific Ocean.

1820—Missouri Compromise; embraces abolition.

1823—Rejects military alliance with Britain; writes key passage of Monroe Doctrine.

1824—Runs in presidential election; Electoral College vote is inconclusive.

1825—House of Representatives elects him sixth President of the United States after Henry Clay shifts votes and is named secretary of state; Andrew Jackson charges "corrupt bargain."

1826—John Adams and Thomas Jefferson both die on July 4.

1828—Loses presidential election to Jackson, after four years of congressional obstructionism.

1829—Firstborn son, George Washington Adams, dies.

1830—Massachusetts voters elect him to House of Representatives; rejects party allegiance; renews pledge to represent "the whole nation."

1831—Presents petitions from Pennsylvania Quakers for abolition of slavery; debates over tariffs.

1832—Begins struggle against nullification; snubs Harvard ceremony for Jackson.

1834—Supports Jackson demands for French compensation; middle son, John Adams II, dies.

1835–1836—Presents petitions for abolition in Washington, DC; guards Smithson bequest for national scientific institution; leads abolition movement in Congress; House passes Gag Rule to stifle abolition petitions; attacks Gag Rule as unconstitutional.

1839—House turns to JQA to organize committees.

1841—Wins Supreme Court decision freeing black prisoners of the *Amistad*; becomes first president ever to be photographed.

1842—Momentous House speech provides basis for Emancipation Proclamation; southern House members charge him with treason and demand censure; wins ban on dueling in Washington, DC.

1843—Leads unsuccessful struggle to prevent annexation of Texas; promotes construction of astronomical observatories and expanded scientific studies.

1844—Defeats Gag Rule.

1846—Suffers stroke; makes startling recovery and returns to House.

February 23, 1848—Dies in House of Representatives.

Introduction

He served under Washington and with Lincoln; he lived with Ben Franklin, lunched with Lafayette, Jefferson, and Wellington; he walked with Russia's czar and talked with Britain's king; he dined with Dickens, taught at Harvard, and was American minister to six European countries. He negotiated the peace that ended the War of 1812, freed the African prisoners on the slave ship *Amistad,* served sixteen years in the House of Representatives, restored free speech in Congress, led the antislavery movement . . .

. . . and . . .

He was sixth President of the United States.

John Quincy Adams was all of these things—and more.

A towering figure in the formative years of the United States, John Quincy Adams was the only son of a Founding Father and President to become President himself, and he was the first President to serve in Congress after his presidency. The oldest son of John and Abigail Adams, John Quincy Adams seemed destined for greatness from birth. His mother's Quincy forebears had stormed ashore in the Norman landings at Hastings in 1066 and rode to Runnymede in 1215 to force King John to sign the Magna Carta. His father not only served as the nation's first vice president and second President but helped draft the Declaration of Independence, enlisted George Washington to lead the Continental Army, secured the foreign aid that won the Revolution, and drafted nine of thirteen state constitutions after independence.

Pushed by his parents to climb the heights of their ambitions for him, John Quincy Adams surpassed their expectations—not, ironically, as President of the United States but as American ambassador to six European nations, a fearless secretary of state, a powerful voice before the Supreme Court, a fighting senator and congressman, and America's first champion of human rights and foe of injustice. He served the American people for two-thirds of a century under ten Presidents—besides himself.

Sent to Europe by President James Madison, John Quincy Adams negotiated the Treaty of Ghent that ended the War of 1812. Later, as President James Monroe's secretary of state, he engineered the seizure and annexation of Florida and wrote the core provision of the Monroe Doctrine ending foreign colonization in the Americas. An eloquent lawyer, he argued brilliantly before the Supreme Court to prevent Congress from criminalizing political dissent. In another case before the high court, he won freedom for kidnapped Africans on the slave ship *Amistad*, saving them from a life of bondage. A strong supporter of scientific advances, he was the first American President to have his face and figure impressed for posterity by a startling new process called photography.

As an independent congressman, John Quincy Adams scorned party affiliations, helped found the Smithsonian Institution, defeated state efforts to nullify federal laws, and forced the House of Representatives to restore free speech and citizens' right to petition Congress. During his sixteen years in the House, he was argumentative and politically unpredictable but consistent in his fierce and constant defense of justice, human rights, and the individual liberties that his father and other Founding Fathers had fought for and won in the American Revolution. With support from Illinois freshman congressman Abraham Lincoln, John Quincy Adams forced the House of Representatives to repeal the so-called Gag Rule that banned debate over slavery. He then stunned Congress—and the nation—by demanding that Congress extend constitutional liberties to Americans of African descent by abolishing slavery.

A witness to sixty-five years of critical American history, John Quincy Adams bequeathed to the nation one of its most important literary and historic treasures—his diary. Started when he was only ten, his eyewitness account remains the most complete, personal, day-to-day record of events and life in the New World and Old, from the 1770s to the 1840s—14,000 pages in all, dating from the eve of the Revolutionary War to the eve of the Civil War. A sweeping panorama of American history from the Washington era to the Lincoln era, the story of John Quincy Adams follows one of the greatest, yet least known, figures of the early republic, beginning with a boy's-eye view of the slaughter on Bunker's Hill and a precocious teenager's dinner conversations with Franklin, Jefferson, Lafayette, and other eighteenth-century luminaries. From age ten to his late seventies, Adams describes his adventures crossing the Atlantic through storms and British cannon fire; his travels across Europe; his life as a Harvard student and professor; his early romances; his marriage and warm family life; and his contacts with an incredible number of giants in American and European history: John Hancock, George Washington, Thomas Jefferson, Benjamin Franklin, the Marquis de Lafayette, James Madison, James Monroe, John Marshall, Henry Clay, Andrew Jackson, Napoléon, the Duke of Wellington, Czar Alexander I, King George III, and many others—including his own illustrious father and mother, John and Abigail Adams. His diary reveals the surprising twists in negotiations that ended the War of 1812; the vicious, behind-the-scenes machinations of the "barbarian" Andrew Jackson to undermine the John Quincy Adams presidency; and his tragic loss of two beloved brothers, two sons, and a cherished infant daughter.

And near the end of his life, John Quincy Adams risked death to lead the antislavery movement in the House of Representatives. With a roar that still echoes under the Capitol dome, he demanded passage of the first federal laws to abolish slavery in the United States. He died on the floor of the House of Representatives, fighting for the rights of man.

John Quincy Adams was one of the most courageous figures in the history of American government, ranking first among the nine great Americans whom John F. Kennedy singled out in his Pulitzer Prize–winning book *Profiles in Courage*. He will almost certainly rank first in the minds of readers of the pages that follow.

CHAPTER 1

❧❦❧

A First Son for a Founding Father

"Mr. Adams!" the old lady shrieked. "You're embarking under very threatening signs. The heavens frown, the clouds roll, the winds howl, the waves of the sea roar upon the beach."[1]

Ten-year-old John Quincy Adams looked up at his father, who nodded to the lady, smiled and excused himself, then whispered reassurances in his son's ear: the woman, was "a good lady . . . an Adams with very delicate health . . . much afflicted with hysterical complaints . . . often a little disarranged in her imagination."[2] With that, father, son, and their servant boarded the barge and bounded over the angry waters toward the twenty-four-gun frigate *Boston* that waited in the bay to take them across the Atlantic to France. All but echoing the lady's warning, the waves lapped the sides of the barge—slapping passenger faces, stinging John Quincy's eyes with salty spray, and filling him with fear of impending disaster at sea.

Several days later, the captain of the *Boston* confirmed the boy's fear—shouting to crewmen and pointing to the horizon: three British navy frigates had climbed into view. Heeling over with sails full, the *Boston* fled and lost sight of two ships, but the third stayed in sight, pursuing the entire day,

night, and all next day, intent on capturing the American ship and its famous passenger.

"Our powder, cartridges and balls were placed by the guns," John
Adams recalled, "and everything made ready to begin the action."[3] As night
fell, the enemy "was gaining on us very fast," and John Quincy knew that if
the British captured them, his father faced summary hanging from the
yardarm, while the boy himself faced impressment and a life of servitude in
the British navy.

Nightfall only added to their danger as winds picked up and swelled
into a hurricane. The Adamses went below to their cabin, where "it was
with the utmost difficulty that my little son and I could hold ourselves in
bed with both our hands . . . bracing ourselves with our feet."

Then, "a sudden, tremendous report" rocked the ship. Adams and his
boy had no way of knowing "whether the British frigate had overtaken us
and fired on us or whether our guns had been discharged."[4]

As they waited for the sea to smash through the door and rush into
their cabin, John Adams held his frightened little son in his arms, but said
nothing, as the last-minute thoughts and regrets of every man facing death
raced through his head. Of all his regrets, he rued his decision to take his
boy on the Atlantic crossing—a foolhardy decision for an adult, let alone a
child, in midwinter. But Adams and his son had been apart for nearly two
years; John Quincy needed paternal attention, and John Adams missed the
joys of nurturing his oldest son. On learning he would have to go to
France, he thought the trip a perfect opportunity for the two to grow close
again—and to expose "Johnny" to the glories of French and European culture, with their history, art, music, architecture, and languages. The American Revolution had deprived the boy of most educational and cultural
advantages, not to mention his father's attention. Now the boy and his father faced death together at sea in each other's arms.

John Quincy Adams had been born a decade earlier, when the first seeds of
the Revolution were sprouting; periodic riots erupted in Boston, New York,
Philadelphia, and other American towns. Britain's Parliament had raised

taxes on goods shipped to the colonies, then it shredded the Magna Carta and ordered admiralty courts in Canada to try American smugglers—without juries of their peers.

"And this sequence of events," John Quincy explained, "was to affect the fortunes of no single individual more than those of the infant then lying in his cradle in the little village of Braintree, in the Massachusetts Bay."[5]

That infant was the second child and first son of John and Abigail Adams, of Braintree, Massachusetts, a farming community about six miles south of Boston, later renamed Quincy. At birth, John Quincy was the most recent in a long line of illustrious forebears who helped shaped the destiny of the English-speaking world. The first recorded Quincy sailed with William the Conqueror across the English Channel from Normandy in 1066 to crush English forces at Hastings. A century and a half later, in 1215, Saer de Quincy, Earl of Winchester, rode to Runnymede and helped force King John to sign the Magna Carta, which guaranteed English freemen the right to trial by a jury of their peers.

Subsequently, the Quincy and Adams clans* produced a host of distinguished noblemen, churchmen, physicians, and scientists—among the last, Thomas Boylston, a renowned English surgeon who emigrated to Massachusetts with his son, Zabdiel Boylston, who pioneered smallpox inoculation in the New World. The Adams family also included ordinary craftsmen, of course—among them, John Alden, who may have been the

---

*Although there is no etymographic or etymological basis for it, the Adams and Quincy families and natives of Massachusetts have, for generations, pronounced "Quincy" as "Quin-zee." In fact, the origins of the Quincy family lie in Cuincy (now pronounced "Kahn-see" but probably "Ku-whan-see" in old French) in northwestern Normandy, France, where a knight named "de Cuincy" (literally: "from Cuincy") joined the 1066 invasion of Britain. Some of the "Quincys" evidently intermarried with Scots, whose burr may have corrupted the spelling of "Cuincy" to "Quincy" and its pronunciation to "Quin-zee." By 1203, nine years before he appears at the signing of the Magna Carta at Runnymede, Saer de Quincy (tr.: "sieur" or "sire"—i.e., master—of Quincy/Cuincy) appeared as co-commander of a fortress in Normandy with his Scottish cousin Robert Fitzwalter.

least significant until Henry Wadsworth Longfellow rhymed him into poetic immortality in *The Courtship of Miles Standish*. A cooper on the *May-
flower*, Alden caught Longfellow's odic fancy by wedding Priscilla Mullins.
John and Priscilla Alden's granddaughter would marry Joseph Adams Jr.,
great-grandfather of John Quincy Adams. His son, Joseph Adams III, tied
his family's academic future to Harvard College, becoming the first of a
long line of Adamses to study there. The second was John Adams, John
Quincy's father, who graduated in 1755 at the age of twenty.

Harvard was the first college established in the New World, and within
a decade of its founding in 1636, it had evolved into more than a mere
college: it was a "school of prophets"—a divinity school engaged in "a noble and necessary work"[6] to create and lead a new sort of nation conceived
in liberty. From the first, its students and graduates were extraordinaries—
and Americans recognized them as such.* Their motto was "Veritas"—a
"truth," enhanced by the divine, that gave Harvard men the wisdom of
both God and man to transform America's wilderness into a Paradise.

Although John Adams's parents hoped he would enter the ministry after Harvard, the school broadened its curriculum to include secular studies, and he opted for teaching at first, then law. After winning admission to
the bar, he settled in Braintree to practice law, fell in love, and, on October
25, 1764, married Abigail Quincy Smith. Abigail was the second of three
daughters of the Reverend William Smith of nearby Weymouth and
granddaughter of Colonel John Quincy, longtime Speaker of the Massachusetts colonial legislature. Unlike the illustrious Quincys, many of the
Smiths lived in the shadows of humanity—victims of genetically transmit-
ted mental illnesses, including alcohol abuse, that usually led to premature
death. Abigail Smith's brother, William Smith Jr., suddenly and inexplica-
bly abandoned his wife and children to poverty and plunged into humanity's gutter—whoring, drinking, and finally dying at an early age. In raising

---

*Harvard graduates included more state governors, state legislators, state and federal
judges, congressmen, Supreme Court justices, and Presidents than any other American institution of higher learning.

*Abigail Adams, wife of John Adams, America's second
President, and mother of John Quincy Adams,
America's sixth President. Her family's roots stretched
back to the Battle of Hastings in 1066 and the signing
of the Magna Carta in 1215.* (NATIONAL PARKS
SERVICE, ADAMS NATIONAL HISTORICAL PARK)

her own children, Abigail Adams resolved to instill in them principles of
self-discipline and prayer to protect them from alcohol and other sins.
"Nothing," she believed, "bound the human mind but religion."[7]

Deprived of formal education as a woman, she more than compensated
by devouring the books in her father's huge library of religious and literary
works, including Shakespeare's plays, the English poets, and a wide range
of classical tales that gave her a broader education than that of most men.
Indeed, Harvard's young John Adams found Abigail more than an intellectual equal as well as a romantic match. Nine months after she married John
Adams, she gave birth to their first child, a daughter they named Abigail

The ninety-five-acre Adams family farm, in Braintree (now Quincy), Massachusetts, with the birthplace of John Quincy Adams on the left, the birthplace of his father, John Adams, to its immediate right, and John and Abigail Adams's retirement "mansion" on the far right. In the rear is Penn's Hill, where Abigail Adams took seven-year-old John Quincy to witness the Battle of Bunker's Hill. (NATIONAL PARKS SERVICE, ADAMS NATIONAL HISTORICAL PARK)

but called "Nabby" to distinguish her from the senior Abigail. Two years later, on July 11, 1767, Abigail's second child was born—a son they named John Quincy Adams, after the infant's father and maternal grandfather.

At John Quincy's birth, his father's reputation had spread far beyond Braintree. "The disputes [with Britain] grew," John Quincy explained, and "agitated no household more than that in which this boy was growing up. My father, from pursuing a professional life, began to feel himself impelled more and more into the vortex of controversy. . . . My mother's temperament readily caught the rising spirit of popular enthusiasm and communicated it to me."[8]

A move from Braintree to Boston put John Quincy's father close to the state's most influential clients—and at the center of popular anger over British rule. "America is on the point of bursting into flames," Boston's

Sons of Liberty warned,[9] and on March 5, 1770, two years after John Quincy's family had settled in town, an angry mob transformed the Sons of Liberty's warning into the Boston Massacre, with British troops killing two men and wounding eight, two of whom quickly died from their injuries.

To prevent disorder from spreading, the royal governor ordered the soldiers and commanding officer arrested and charged with murder. He thwarted accusations of favoritism by naming John Quincy's father and his mother's cousin Josiah Quincy—two outspokenly anti-British lawyers—to defend the soldiers in an out-of-town trial before a jury of farmers, none of them Tories. Motivated in part by political ambition, Adams gambled that, win or lose, the case would show him as a man of stature who eschewed hatred in favor of the law and the right of every free Englishman to a trial by a jury of his peers. Fearing reprisals against his family, he sent his wife, who had just given birth to their second son, Charles, to the safety of their Braintree farm with their children. He need not have worried. After his brilliant summation, the jury unanimously acquitted the soldiers, saying they had legitimately defended themselves against unprovoked mob assault.

His courtroom triumph gained John Quincy's father national and international fame—and election as Boston's representative in the Massachusetts House of Representatives. The trial also ended mob protests; the troops retired, and with Boston at peace, the Adams family moved back to town, where Abigail gave birth to their third son, Thomas Boylston Adams.

Although street disorders ended for a while, new import duties provoked more smuggling, and by the end of 1773, protests against a British tea tax climaxed with a mob boarding three ships in Boston Harbor and dumping more than three hundred chests of tea, worth about $1 million, overboard. British troops returned to Boston, declared martial law, and closed the city to commerce, threatening to keep it closed until Bostonians either repaid the East India Company for the vandalized tea—or starved.

"Boston became a walled and beleaguered town," John Quincy recounted. "Among the first fruits of war, was the expulsion of my father's family from their peaceful abode in Boston to take refuge in his and my native town of Braintree."[10]

Outraged by the British threat to starve the innocent with the guilty, colonial leaders elsewhere convened a Continental Congress in the fall of 1774 to respond, and after ensuring his family's safety in Braintree, John Quincy's father rode off to Philadelphia with four other Massachusetts delegates. Although the First Continental Congress ended indecisively in late October, orders arrived in the spring for British troops to crush the rebellion and "arrest the principle actors and abettors in the Congress,"[11] including John Adams. John Quincy never forgot the terror he felt when he heard of the threat to arrest his father: "My mother with her infant children, dwelt every hour of the day and of the night liable to be butchered in cold blood, or taken and carried into Boston as hostages by any foraging or marauding detachment of men."[12]

In May 1775, John Quincy's father again left for Philadelphia and a Second Continental Congress, where forty-three-year-old George Washington arrived in uniform dressed for war. At six foot three, he towered over other delegates—especially forty-year-old John Adams, who, even his wife Abigail conceded, was "short, thick and fat."[13] Nonetheless, their mutual interest in farming gave Adams and Washington common ground to form a firm friendship that often included dining and attending church services together.

On June 2, a letter from Dr. Joseph Warren, a close family friend of the Adamses and president of the Massachusetts Provincial Congress, urged the Continental Congress to take control of disorganized New England militiamen laying siege to Boston by appointing a commander in chief. "The sword should, in all free states, be subservient to the civil powers," Warren argued. "We tremble at having an army (although consisting of our own countrymen) established here without a civil power to provide for and control them."[14]

In a more dire letter, Abigail Adams wrote to her husband of the chaos engulfing Braintree, with their home a "scene of confusion—soldiers coming in for lodging, for breakfast, for supper, for drink, &c. &c."

Sometimes refugees from Boston tired and frightened seek an asylum for a day or night, a week—you can hardly imagine how we live. . . . I wish

John Adams, second President of the United States and father of John Quincy Adams, the nation's sixth President. He had been a prominent lawyer before attending the first two Continental Congresses, and his Thoughts on Government *served as the basis for constitutions in nine of the thirteen states after independence.* (AFTER A PORTRAIT BY JOHN SINGLETON COPLEY; NATIONAL PARKS SERVICE, ADAMS NATIONAL HISTORICAL PARK)

you were nearer to us. We know not what a day will bring forth nor what distress one hour may throw us into.[15]

Visibly upset by Abigail's letter, John Adams replied by return, "Oh that I was a soldier! I will be. I am reading military books. Everybody must and will and shall be a soldier. . . . My dear Nabby and Johnny and Charley and Tommy are never out of my thoughts. God Bless, preserve and prosper them."[16]

A few days later, John Adams reacted to Dr. Warren's warning and asked Congress to draft patriot forces besieging Boston into a Continental Army and appoint a supreme commander. Congress agreed, and again Adams rose to speak. He had mingled discreetly with delegates from middle and southern colonies and discovered "a jealousy against a New England Army under the command of a New England General," who, if he defeated the British, might give law to the other states.

"I had no hesitation to declare," he responded, "that I had but one gentleman in mind for that important command, and that was a gentleman from Virginia . . . whose skill and experience as an officer, whose independent fortune, great talents, and excellent universal character, would command the approbation of all the colonies better than any other person in the Union."[17] Two days later, Boston's John Hancock, the president of Congress, wrote to Dr. Joseph Warren, "The Congress here have appointed George Washington, Esq., General and Commander-in-Chief, of the Continental Army."[18] As Hancock penned his inimitable signature, however, Warren already lay dead on the field of battle at Breed's Hill, on the Charlestown peninsula opposite Boston.

Like Boston, Charlestown sat in Boston Bay on what was nearly an island, connected to the mainland by a narrow neck. Two hills dominated the neck, Bunker's Hill, as it was then called, near the mainland, and the smaller Breed's Hill, nearer the water. Warren had gone to Bunker's Hill to warn the commander of ammunition shortages and joined the troops behind a makeshift fortification on Breed's Hill.

When she heard the first cannon blasts, Abigail Adams shuddered, then suppressed her fears of running into British soldiers and took seven-year-old John Quincy to a hilltop behind their home in Braintree, where they watched a battle unfold across the bay. By day's end, the battle had turned into a slaughter. The first British troops to land had set Charlestown aflame, while 2,400 of their comrades swarmed up the hillside like ants— only to topple by the hundreds under a rain of American fire from above.

"The town all in flames around them," Abigail wrote to her husband, "and the heat from the flames so intense as scarcely to be borne . . . and

An 1830 map of Boston Harbor shows Quincy Bay at the bottom, with the site of President John Quincy Adams's home indicated in small print.

the wind blowing the smoke in their faces . . . the reinforcements not able to get to them."[19]

Seven-year-old John Quincy and his mother watched a second wave of British troops surge upward over their fallen comrades—only to fall back again, regroup, and charge a third time, tripping over lifeless bodies, sprawling to the ground into pools of blood and torn flesh, then crawling upwards on their hands and knees until enough reached the summit to silence the few patriot arms not out of ammunition. One thousand dead

Seven-year-old John Quincy Adams witnessed the Battle of Bunker's Hill with his mother from a distant hilltop. Nearly 270 patriots perished, including Dr. Joseph Warren, the Revolutionary War leader and the Adams family's physician, seen in the throes of death in an engraving by Gotthard von Muller, after the painting by John Trumbull. (NATIONAL PORTRAIT GALLERY, SMITHSONIAN INSTITUTION)

British soldiers covered the hillside; 100 dead patriots and 267 wounded lay on the hilltop. John Quincy said the battle and the carnage it left made "an impression in my mind" that haunted him the rest of his life.

"I saw with my own eyes the fires of Charlestown," he exclaimed, "and heard Britannia's thunders in the battle . . . and witnessed the tears of my mother and mingled them with my own at the fall of Dr. Joseph Warren, a dear friend of my father, and a beloved physician to me."[20] Only days before his death, Warren had devised an ingenious array of splints to save John Quincy's forefinger from amputation after the boy had suffered a bad fracture.

John Quincy watched his mother sob as she described Warren's death to her husband: "Our dear friend . . . fell gloriously fighting for his country—saying better to die honorably in the field than ignominiously hang upon the gallows."[21]

When the last patriot lay still on Bunker's Hill and the British had ceased firing, Abigail led her frightened seven-year-old home, and together they recited the Lord's Prayer. "My mother was the daughter of a Christian clergyman," John Quincy explained, "and therefore bred in the faith of deliberate detestation of war."[22] Abigail made John Quincy promise to repeat the Lord's Prayer each morning before rising from his bed—a promise he kept for the rest of his life. The memory of Bunker's Hill, he said, "riveted my abhorrence of war to my soul . . . with abhorrence of tyrants and oppressors . . . [who] wage war against the rights of human nature and the liberties and rightful interests of my country."[23]

A few days later, Abigail and John Quincy were still shaken by the slaughter at Bunker's Hill. "We live in continual expectation of hostilities," she wrote to her husband. "Scarcely a day that does not produce some, but like good Nehemiah . . . we will say unto them, 'Be not afraid. Remember the Lord who is great and terrible, and fight for your brethren, your sons, and your daughters, your wives, and your houses.'"[24] Her sorrow over Warren's death soon turned into fury, however, and Abigail declared a personal war against the British. With John Quincy at her side, unwrapping each piece and handing it to her, she melted all her prized pewter spoons in molds to make musket balls for patriot soldiers.

In the days that followed, John Quincy lived "in unintermitted danger of being consumed with my family in a conflagration kindled by a torch in the same hands which . . . lighted the fires of Charlestown."[25] As dangerous as the threat of fire was that of disease. Eight neighbors died of dysentery, distemper, and other maladies that raged through Braintree and nearby hamlets. Hunger spared no one; soldiers and refugees alike plundered kitchen gardens and root cellars of whatever food they could find, often stealing into the Adams house and terrifying Abigail and the children as they searched.

"Does every member feel for us?" Abigail pleaded to her husband about his colleagues in Congress. "Can they realize what we suffer?"[26]

Despite the disorder, Abigail and John maintained their regular correspondence, each addressing the other as "My Dearest Friend," with Abigail
always conveying their children's love and "duty" to their father. Whenever
his letters arrived, she told him, "You would laugh to see them run upon
the sight of a letter—like chickens for a crumb when the hen clucks."[27]

With schools closed and her husband absent, Abigail Adams took
command of John Quincy's education, encouraging him to read ever
more books from his father's library and calling in John Thaxter, a cousin
who was studying law in John Adams's office, to tutor the boy in mathematics and science. When she discovered her son turning pages of some
prose or poetry without reading, the resourceful mother complained
aloud about her eyes and asked John Quincy to read to her. After writing
to her husband about her ruse, John Adams replied that he was "charmed
with your amusement with our little Johnny. Tell him I am glad to hear
he is so good a boy as to read to his Mamma for her entertainment and to
keep out of the company of rude children."[28]

John Adams went on to provide a complete curriculum for "our little
Johnny."

I am under no apprehension about his proficiency in learning. With his
capacities and opportunities he can not fail to acquire knowledge. But let
him know that the sentiments of his heart are more important than the
furniture of his head. Let him be sure that he possesses the great virtue of
temperance, justice, magnanimity, honor, and generosity, and with these
added to his parts, he cannot fail to become a wise and great man.

Does he read the newspapers? The events of this war should not pass
unobserved by him at his years.

As he reads history, you should ask him what events strike him most.
What characters he esteems and admires? Which he hates and abhors?
Which he despises?

Treachery, perfidy, cruelty, hypocrisy, avarice, &c &c should be
pointed out to him for his contempt as well as detestation.[29]

Adams insisted that his son master Greek, "the most perfect of all languages," and that he read the original text of Thucydides's *History of the Peloponnesian War*. Besides pressing him to meet his father's academic demands, Abigail constantly reminded John Quincy of his family heritage and his father's achievements as a scholar, lawyer, and legislator, as well as his courage in defying British rule and risking death by serving in the Continental Congress. John Quincy responded with bold displays of his own courage that added to his mother's pride.

"Master John," Abigail reported to her husband, "cheerfully consented to become 'post-rider,'" venturing alone on horseback past British troop encampments to carry family news between Braintree and Boston.

"As the distance was not less than eleven miles each way," John Quincy boasted, "the undertaking was not an easy one for a boy barely nine years old."[30]

Abigail's demands, discipline, expectations, and hectoring—along with fears generated by war—took a toll on the boy, however, often leaving him depressed and convinced he would never match the achievements of his "Pappa." Abigail read and reread her husband's letters from Philadelphia exhorting his son to achieve "great and glorious deeds." The letters insisted that scholarship be central to the boy's life to ensure his achieving his father's ambition to "become a wise and great man."[31]

"At ten years of age," John Quincy recalled later, "I read Shakespeare's *Tempest, As You Like It, Merry Wives of Windsor, Much Ado About Nothing*, and *King Lear*."

> There was also a small edition of Milton's *Paradise Lost*, which I believe I attempted ten times to read and never could get through half the book. . . . I was mortified, even to the shedding of tears, that I could not even conceive what it was that my father and mother admired so much in that book, and yet I was ashamed to ask them an explanation. I smoked tobacco and read Milton at the same time, from the same motive—to find out what was the recondite charm in them which gave my father so

much pleasure. After making myself four or five times sick with smoking, I mastered that accomplishment . . . but I did not master Milton. I was thirty when I first read *Paradise Lost* with delight and astonishment.[32]

Following his success placing George Washington in command of the military, John Adams's erudition and quick legal mind raised him to leadership in Congress—perhaps higher than he wanted. By summer's end in 1775, he was sitting on ninety committees, serving as chairman of twenty-five, and by his own admission, he was "worn out"—and longed for his wife and children.

"My dearest friend," he wrote to Abigail. "I have some thoughts of petitioning for leave to bring my family here. I am a lonely, forlorn creature. . . ."

I want to walk with you in the garden—the Common—the Plain—the Meadow. I want to take Charles in one hand and Tom in the other and walk with you, Nabby on your right and John upon my left, to view the corn fields, the orchards, &c. Alas, poor imagination. How faintly and imperfectly do you supply the want of originality and reality.[33]

Abigail longed for John as much as he longed for her. She too began her letters "My Dearest Friend."

My anxiety for your welfare will never leave me but with my parting breath. 'Tis of more importance to me than all this world contains. The cruel separation to which I am necessitated cuts in half the enjoyments of life; the other half are comprised in the hope that what I do and what I suffer may be serviceable to you and the little ones and our country.[34]

In August, John Adams learned that his thirty-four-year-old brother, Elihu, had died of dysentery at his army camp, and reports from Boston about troop outrages left him worried about his family's safety. He pleaded with Abigail to "fly to the woods with our children" in the face of danger.

John Quincy tried assuaging his father's fears with a pledge to defend the family and the family home.

"John writes like a hero," Adams wrote back to Abigail, "glowing with ardor for his country and burning with indignation against her enemies."[35]

Adams surprised his wife in December by appearing at the farm unexpectedly—only to surprise her even more, four days later, by leaving for Watertown, Massachusetts, to report to the Provincial Congress. He returned home three weeks after that—then left for Philadelphia almost immediately, with hardly a moment for John Quincy and the other children.

By then, Abigail was so lonely for her husband that she grew angry, asking bluntly, "Shall I expect you or do you determine to stay out the year?" After he left, she decided to cease writing him after one last message. "I miss my partner," she admitted. "I have not felt in a humor to entertain you with letters. If I had taken up my pen perhaps some unbecoming invective might have fallen from it. . . . Our little ones whom you so often recommend to my care and instruction shall not be deficient in virtue or probity if the precepts of a mother have their desired effect, but they would be doubly enforced could they be indulged with the example of a father constantly before them."[36]

"I cannot leave Congress, without causing injury to the public," her husband snapped,[37] but then reiterated his loneliness for her and his family. "I never will come again without you if I can persuade you to come with me," he promised. "Whom God has joined together ought not to be put asunder so long with their own consent. We will bring master Johnny with us."[38]

In the spring of 1776, Adams and the Continental Congress learned that George Washington's Continental Army had forced the British to evacuate Boston on March 17. Adams and the others cheered as Virginia's Richard Henry Lee then resolved that the United Colonies "are, and of right ought to be, free and independent states." Congress postponed voting on the resolution until July 1 to permit Adams, Benjamin Franklin, Thomas Jefferson, Robert Livingston, and Roger Sherman to prepare a formal Declaration of Independence. Congress approved it without dissent on July 4.

Adams subsequently achieved still greater prominence by writing a document he called *Thoughts on Government*, which, by the end of the year, had served as the basis for constitutions in nine states. Adams's *Thoughts on Government* called for establishment of republican governments, each with an executive and a bicameral legislature with separate, clearly defined powers.

In June 1777, a month before his tenth birthday, John Quincy wrote to his father, whose long absence and exalted position had transformed him into a distant, godlike fantasy in the boy's imagination. Although he was ahead of most students twice his age, his mother's hectoring convinced him he was falling short of his father's expectations.

Dear Sir: I love to receive letters very well; much better than I love to write them. I make a poor figure at composition, my head is much too fickle, my thoughts are running after birds eggs, play and trifles, till I get vexed with myself. Mamma has a troublesome task to keep me steady, and I own I am ashamed of myself. I have but just entered the 3d volume of Smollett, tho' I had designed to have got it half through by this time.

John Quincy pledged to devote more time to reading and promised to write again in a week "and give a better account of myself."

I wish, Sir, you would give me some instructions with regard to my time & advise me how to proportion my studies & my play . . . and I will keep them by me & endeavor to follow them. I am, dear Sir, with a present determination of growing better, Yours.[39]

Early in winter 1778, the French government became the first foreign nation to recognize the United States' independence. By then, John Adams was chairman of Congress's Board of War and Ordnance—in effect, the nation's secretary of war. Shortly thereafter, he wrote to Abigail of his intention to retire from government and return home "to my practice at the bar." After four years in Congress, he realized, he had left too many debts unpaid, and, with money depreciating, "I was daily losing the fruits of seventeen years' industry."

> My family was living on my past acquisitions which were very moderate. . . . My children were growing up without my care in their education, and all my emoluments as a member of Congress for four years have not been sufficient to pay a laboring man upon my farm. Some of my friends . . . suggested to me what I knew very well before, that I was losing a fortune every year by my absence.[40]

With her husband gone for all but four of the previous twenty-four months, Abigail had taken a dominant role in the Adams household. When a smallpox epidemic swept into Boston, she confronted the dreaded disease by taking her children and sixteen relatives to Boston to submit to inoculation with live infected serum. Although she and John Quincy emerged unscathed, the vaccine left eleven-year-old Nabby ill for several days and six-year-old Charles so sick he needed weeks to recover. She also oversaw the farm, farmhands, and household servants, as well as the buying and selling of lands.

"I have supported the family!" she complained to her husband.

Late in 1777, John Adams arrived home before Christmas to what he called "a blissful fireside, surrounded by a wife and a parcel of chattering boys and girls"—and a stack of letters from potential clients promising lucrative fees to take their cases. After he had left for Portsmouth, New Hampshire, to take one such case, a letter from Congress staggered Abigail: Congress had appointed her husband a commissioner to France to replace Connecticut's Silas Deane and to join Benjamin Franklin and Virginia's Arthur Lee in soliciting financial aid from the French government.

"Dr. Franklin's age alarms us," explained Massachusetts congressman James Lovell, and because they suspected Arthur Lee of spying for England, "We want one man of inflexible integrity on that embassy."[41] As for

Deane, Congress had recalled him after receiving an accusation that he had embezzled congressional funds intended for arms purchases.

Abigail was furious and tried to reverse the appointment with an irate letter to Lovell: "How could you contrive to rob me of all my happiness?" she demanded.

> You who so lately experienced what it was to be restored to your family after a painful absence from it. . . . I have often experienced the want of his aid and assistance in the last three years of his absence, and that demand increases as our little ones grow up, three of whom are sons and at this time of life stand most in need of the joint force of his example and precepts. And can I, Sir, consent to be separated from him whom my heart esteems above all earthly things and for an unlimited time? My life will be one continued scene of anxiety and apprehension, and must I cheerfully comply with the demand of my country?[42]

The prospect of another long separation from her husband terrified her. Even if he survived the dangerous transatlantic winter voyage, he faced summary hanging for treason, without trial, if a British ship captured his vessel. Who would support their family if he failed to return, she demanded to know. With their family's finances already in a "very loose condition," John Quincy and her other children, she wailed, faced "growing up in poverty without ever knowing their father."[43]

Knowing her husband would never refuse his country's call, Abigail decided to ask him to take the entire family with him to France. And when he returned from Portsmouth, he surprised her by agreeing enthusiastically— only to learn a few weeks later that Congress lacked funds for the family's passage and living expenses overseas.

John Adams was no more eager to leave his family than Abigail was to see him go, and to John Quincy's dismay, his parents decided he should accompany his father on the voyage. His presence would not only ease some of his father's loneliness for his family but allow John Adams and his firstborn to reforge father-son bonds and give John Adams greater influence over his son's development. Foreign travel would also enhance John Quincy's education and accelerate his evolution into the "wise and great man" his parents expected him to become. John Quincy hated the idea at first. Instead of romping with friends at school, he faced possible drowning at sea or capture and impressment in the British navy—or worse, by pirates. Just as dismal were the prospects of endless days of incessant study under constant watch and criticism by his scholar-father, whom he hardly knew and whose impossible success his parents expected him to emulate or surpass.

"My dear son," Abigail tried to console him, "It is a very difficult task for a tender parent to bring her mind to part with a child of your years going to a distant land nor could I have acquiesced in such a separation under any other care than that of the most excellent parent and guardian who accompanied you."

> Let me enjoin it upon you to attend constantly and steadfastly to the precepts and instructions of your father as you value the happiness of your mother and your own welfare. You are in possession of a natural good understanding and of spirits unbroken by adversity and untamed. Improve your understanding by acquiring useful knowledge and virtue such as will render you an ornament to society, an honor to your country, and a blessing to your parents.[44]

Preparations for an eighteenth-century transatlantic voyage were not simple and, indeed, needed all the efforts of John and Abigail Adams and their children. In the absence of passenger ships, travelers usually had to bribe captains of cargo or naval vessels to take them aboard, then pay more bribes to obtain sheltered sleeping quarters. Congress, however, had ordered—and agreed to pay—the captain of the frigate *Boston* to transport John Adams to Europe. Like passengers on other ships, however, Adams still had to bring his own provisions for a voyage of unpredictable length and hardships. Transatlantic crossings could last thirty to sixty days, depending on prevailing winds and possible detention by enemy naval vessels or privateers. Apart from the clothes they would need at sea and in France, John and John Quincy Adams bought and carried aboard

> a bushel of corn meal, thirty pounds of brown sugar, two bottles of mustard, two pounds of tea, two pounds of chocolate, six live chickens, a half-barrel of "fresh meat," five bushels of corn, a barrel of apples [a precaution against scurvy], six small barrels of cider, "a fat sheep," a ten-gallon keg of rum; three dozen bottles of Madeira wine, thirty bottles of port wine [water and milk were unsafe to drink], fourteen dozen eggs, seven loaves of sugar, a box of wafers, and a pound of pepper . . . and . . . three reams of paper, two account books, twenty-five quills; a dozen clay pipes; two pounds of tobacco, two mattresses, two bolsters [as pillows], and £100 in silver currency of various denominations stuffed in shoes.[45]

Not making preparations easier or more pleasant were warnings from well-meaning relatives, friends, and neighbors about everything from sea-sickness to pirates, privateers, and English gunboats. All knew that if the British captured John Adams, they would hang him and impress young John Quincy.

On the day of departure, family members and friends escorted Adams and his son from their door to water's edge on Quincy Bay, where a barge bobbed about under thickening clouds, waiting to take them to their ship.

On February 13, 1778, John Adams and his son John Quincy ignored the ominous warnings of a hysterical relative who shrieked of "threatening signs" in the sky and sea; with their servant, they climbed aboard the *Boston* and set sail for France. Six days out, John Quincy and his father saw the three British frigates materialize on the horizon, speeding under full sails to capture the *Boston* and its famous passenger. The captain told John Adams that "his orders were to carry me to France . . . to avoid fighting if he could, but if he could not avoid an engagement he would give them something that should make them remember him. . . . Our powder, cartridges and balls were placed by the guns and everything made ready to begin the action."[46]

John Quincy watched his father "encourage the officers and men to fight to the last." He knew his father intended "to be killed on board the *Boston* or sunk to the bottom in her rather than be taken prisoner."[47]

By nightfall on the second day of the chase, the British frigate chasing the *Boston* was no closer, and as the winds picked up and reached hurricane force, John Quincy and his father went to bed. Suddenly, they heard a thunderous crash above as the hurricane's wind rocked the ship. John Adams clasped his boy in his arms and prayed: he was ready to die for his country, but asked God to spare his little son.

CHAPTER 2

The Seeds of Statesmanship

From the first, the *Boston* seemed doomed.

"The wind was very high," John Adams noted as they lost sight of the Massachusetts coastline. "The sea very rough . . . the snow so thick the captain thinks he cannot go to sea. . . . All is yet chaos on board. His men are not disciplined."[1] With British gunboats poised on the horizon, the *Boston* rolled almost helplessly and threatened to send Adams sliding across the deck. He kept a tight grip on the rail with one arm and wrapped the other around his ten-year-old son.

"I confess," he said to himself, "I often regretted that I had brought my son, [but] Mr. Johnny's behavior gave me a satisfaction that I cannot express. Fully sensible of our danger, he was constantly endeavoring to bear it with manly patience, very attentive to me and his thoughts constantly running in a serious strain."[2]

Adams looked at the oncoming gunboats and wondered how they would survive if the British overtook them—until the sting of a crashing wave made him question how they would survive if the British *did not* overtake them. "The constant rocking and rolling of the ship made us all sick. Half the sailors were sick. I was seized with it myself this forenoon.

29

My servant Joseph Stevens and the captain have both been very bad." Adams waxed philosophic for a moment and analyzed the causes of "mal de mer" as stemming from "the effect of agitation combined with a variety of odors from coal, stagnant water, and those parts of the ship where sailors slept—often unwashed for days. There is the same inattention to the cleanliness of the ship and the persons and health of the sailors," Adams complained, "as there is at land of the cleanliness of the camp and the health and cleanliness of the soldiers. The practice of profane cursing and swearing . . . prevails in a most abominable degree."[3]

Adams and his son slept together in a small space in the "'tween decks" on the double mattress he had brought aboard, beneath their own sheets and blankets and using bolsters for pillows.

As the main deck was almost constantly under water, the sea rolling in and out at the ports and scuppers, we were obliged to keep the hatchways down—whereby the air became so hot and so dry in the 'tween decks that . . . I could not breathe or live there. Yet the water would pour down whenever a hatchway was opened, so that all was afloat.[4]

Although the *Boston* was "overmetalled"—that is, the weight of her guns (five twelve-pounders and nineteen nine-pounders) was too great for her tonnage—the captain ordered her "to sail with the guns out," Adams explained, "in order to be ready, and this . . . made the ship labor and roll so as to oblige us to keep the chain pumps as well as the hand pumps almost constantly going." The weight of the gun barrels extending off the sides made the ship "wring and twist in such a manner as to endanger the masts and rigging."[5]

Father and son had sought shelter in their bunk, when the storm slammed the ship with explosive wind bursts and they heard the terrifying crash from above. An officer appeared almost immediately "and told us that the ship had been struck with lightening and the noise we had heard was a crash of thunder . . . that the large mainmast was struck. . . . We lost sight of our enemy, it is true," John Adams's shaky hand penned his diary the next morning, "but we found ourselves in a dreadful storm. . . .

> It would be fruitless to attempt a description of what I saw, heard and felt during these next three days. To describe the ocean, the waves, the winds, the ship, her motions, rollings, wringings and agonies—the sailors, their countenances, language, and behavior is impossible. No man could keep his legs, and nothing could be kept in its place. A universal wreck of everything in all parts of the ship, chests, casks, bottles &c. No place or person was dry. On one of these nights, a thunder bolt struck three men upon deck and wounded one of them. . . . He lived three days and died raving mad.[6]

Just as calm settled over the surrounding sea, a boy about John Quincy's age—the son of Connecticut merchant Silas Deane—approached John Adams with a note that startled Adams by asking him to "take care of the child in his situation as you would wish to have done to a child of your own. It is needless to mention his youth and helplessness."[7] In effect, the note told Adams he was now the boy's guardian. Although taken aback, Adams was well aware of the bonds that tied members of New England's Christian elite to each other—especially their minor children. Even if unrelated and unacquainted, all felt a deep kinship through their common ties to Puritan founders, whose intermarriages left many, if not all, somewhat related—even when they did not know it.

Silas Deane's brother, Barnabas, saw Adams's departure as a good opportunity to divest himself of responsibility for raising his brother's son Jesse, and he simply put the boy on board with a note charging Adams to deliver him to his father in France.

John Adams had no sooner read Deane's presumptuous letter when another boy—eighteen-year-old William Vernon—handed him an even more presumptuous missive from a member of the Continental Navy Board. "I presume it is unnecessary to say one word in order to impress your mind with the anxiety a parent is under in the education of a son. . . . Therefore I have only to beg the favor of you, Sir, to place my son with such a gentleman whom you would choose for one of yours." He asked Adams to find a merchant "either at Bordeaux or Nantes, of Protestant principles," to teach him "general and extensive business," and he enclosed "a gratuity of one hundred pounds sterling that may be given to a merchant of eminence to take him for two or three years."[8]

"Thus," Adams puzzled in his diary, "I find myself invested with the unexpected trust of a kind of guardianship of two promising young gentlemen, besides my own son." It was fortunate for all the boys that Adams had started his professional life as a teacher and found "few things that have ever given me greater pleasure than the tuition of youth."[9] As it turned out, Jesse Deane was only a year older than John Quincy, and the two, each grateful to have found someone his own age, became inseparable shipboard companions.

Between storms and other crises at sea, Adams himself read French literature and put his son and Jesse Deane in the hands of the ship's French surgeon, Nicholas Noël, who agreed to teach the boys French. To ease tension among the seamen, the captain allowed them to stage "frolics," with all the men dousing each other with flour then dancing on the main deck. Adams suspected the captain ordered such "whimsical diversions in order to make the men wash themselves."[10]

A more prized diversion came a month after they left Massachusetts, when "we spied a sail and gave her chase . . . and came up beside her." To Adams's shock, "She fired upon us . . . so that the ball went directly over my head." Adams's ship immediately turned broadside with her big guns aimed squarely at the other ship, which immediately surrendered, yielding a prize Adams estimated at £80,000. Half went to the owner of the *Boston*, 12 percent to the captain, and shares ranging from 1 to 6 percent to the ship's officers and crew, depending on rank.

On March 29, 1778, six weeks after they had left Massachusetts, John Adams and his son sailed into the estuary leading to Bordeaux, when a pilot came aboard and announced that France and England were at war. On April 1, the Adamses set foot on shore with Jesse Deane, eighteen-year-old William Vernon, and Dr. Noël. Two American merchants, who regularly checked incoming cargoes, took the famed John Adams and his friends for a sumptuous lunch and a tour of the town, a visit to theater before tea and the opera in the evening. Adams marveled at the splendor of French grand opera. "The scenery, the dancing, the music," he gasped. "Never seen anything of the kind before."[11]

Adams placed young Vernon with one of the merchants, and on April 4, he set off with his son by carriage for Paris, along with Jesse Deane and a small retinue. Covering 150 miles in only two days, they reached Poitiers in west-central France. "Every part of the country is cultivated," Adams remarked. "The fields of grain, the vineyards, the castles, the cities, the parks, the gardens, everything is beautiful. Yet every place swarms with beggars."[12]

From Poitiers, they rode north to Tours, then east to Orleans and finally Paris, where they checked into an expensive hotel and John Adams put two tired little boys to bed. "My little son," he wrote in his diary, "has sustained this long journey of nearly 500 miles at the rate of an hundred miles a day with the utmost firmness, as he did our fatiguing and dangerous voyage."[13]

After meeting Benjamin Franklin in Paris, John Adams learned to his distress that Jesse Deane's father, Silas, had left for America to present himself to Congress and dispute the charges made about him. Adams would now have to care for Jesse indefinitely.

Putting servants in charge of the boys, Adams followed Franklin on a whirlwind tour of diplomatic receptions at the Palais de Versailles and the châteaus of the ruling French nobility—the Duc de Noailles, the Marquis de Lafayette's father-in-law; Prime Minister Comte de Maurepas; and Minister of Foreign Affairs Comte de Vergennes, who took Adams to meet King Louis XVI.

To eliminate the high cost of lodging, Adams moved into a furnished apartment in the Hotel Valentois, a château that Franklin was renting in

Passy, then a small town between Paris and Versailles.* Franklin charged Adams no rent and gave him the use of his nine servants as well as his elegant carriage and coachman. Adams enrolled his son and Jesse Deane with Franklin's grandson, nine-year-old "Benny" Bache, in a private boarding school that was near enough to allow John Quincy to spend Sundays with his father. Hardly an intimate occasion, Sunday dinners chez Franklin saw a small army of celebrated figures in the arts and government feasting on a galaxy of delicacies and fine wines from Franklin's cellar of more than 1,000 bottles from renowned French vineyards.

"He lives in all the splendor and magnificence of a viceroy," John Adams wrote of Franklin after one Sunday feast, "which is little inferior to that of a king."[14]

In addition to Latin and French, the boys learned music, dancing, fencing, and drawing, and within a few weeks, John Quincy spoke fluent French, the universal language of the European upper classes and diplomats everywhere. Not as harsh as many such schools, Monsieur Le Coeur's *Pension* began the school day at 6 a.m. and ended at 7 p.m. but included frequent periods for play to ease the strain of academic discipline.

"It was then that the idea of writing a regular journal was first suggested to me," John Quincy recalled. As he wrote to his mother at the time, "My pappa enjoins it upon me to keep a journal or diary of the events that happen to me, and of objects that I see and characters that I converse with from day to day." All but breathing his father's thoughts and words, he told his mother,

> I am convinced of the utility, importance & necessity of this exercise . . . and although I shall have the mortification a few years hence to read a great deal of my childish nonsense, yet I shall have the pleasure and advantage of remarking the several steps by which I shall have advanced in

---

*Today, Passy is a largely residential area adjacent to the heights of the Chaillot neighborhood overlooking the Seine on the Paris Right Bank opposite the Eiffel Tower.

*Benjamin Franklin invited John Adams and his eleven-
year-old son, John Quincy Adams, to live in his château
on the outskirts of Paris after Adams's arrival as one of
the American commissioners soliciting financial and
military aid from the French government.* (LIBRARY OF
CONGRESS)

taste and judgment and knowledge. I have been to see the palace and gardens of Versailles, the Military School at Paris [École Militaire] . . . &
other scenes of magnificence in and about Paris. . . .

I am, my ever honored and revered Mamma, your dutiful & affectionate son John Quincy Adams[15]

His father's mission to Paris would prove short-lived, however. After
barely a month, John Adams wrote to Congress urging the appointment

The Palais de Versailles, where Benjamin Franklin took John Adams to meet French foreign minister Comte de Vergennes.

of Franklin as sole American envoy to France, saying that commissions inevitably generate too many internal frictions to make them effective in international diplomacy.

"The public business has never been methodically conducted," he grumbled, "and it is not possible to obtain a clear idea of our affairs."[16] He found his fellow commissioner Arthur Lee argumentative, sharp-tongued, and disagreeable, with a violent temper, and he considered Franklin a dissipated "charlatan," posing as a philosopher without ever having studied philosophy or the great thinkers. Although Franklin was exceptionally generous, he was a confirmed sybarite, rising late in the morning and, according to Adams, "coming home at all hours." Franklin, Adams concluded,

> has a passion for reputation and fame as strong as you can imagine, and his time and thoughts are chiefly employed to obtain it, and to set tongues and pens, male and female, to celebrating him. Painters, statuaries, sculp-

tors, china potters and all are set to work for this end. He has the most affectionate and insinuating way of charming the woman or the man that he
fixes on. It is the most silly and ridiculous way imaginable, in the sight of
an American, but it succeeds to admiration, fulsome and sickish as it is, in
Europe.[17]

With Franklin pursuing his rich social life, few diplomatic reports had
flowed from Paris to Congress, and Adams assumed the burden of comb-
ing through hundreds of accumulated documents and condensing them
into a series of reports that left him with too little time to enjoy Paris or,
for that matter, get enough sleep. All but dismissed by a loyalist acquaintance as "a man of no consequence," the work-oriented Adams seemed
"out of his element" in the world of diplomacy—especially in Paris.

"He cannot dance, drink, game, flatter, promise, dress, swear with the
gentlemen and talk small talk or flirt with the ladies. In short, he has none
of the essential arts or ornaments which constitute a courtier," one of his
friends remarked.[18] Adams himself admitted, "I am wearied to death with
gazing wherever I go at a profusion of unmeaning wealth and magnificence. Gold, marble, silk, velvet, silver, ivory, and alabaster make up the
show everywhere."[19]

In March 1779, eleven months after they had arrived in France, John
Quincy and his father were elated to begin their trip home to America,
taking a coach from Paris to Nantes, where the Loire estuary empties into
the Bay of Biscay and the Atlantic Ocean. Franklin agreed to care for
Jesse Deane and relieve John Adams of that responsibility.

Few ships sailed or docked on schedule in a world at war, and their ship,
the *Alliance,* was not in port. The two Adamses spent the next seven weeks
seeing the countryside, reading books, writing letters, attending theater,
concerts, and operas, and visiting the castlelike home of Maryland merchant Joshua Johnson, his English wife, Catherine, and their three little
girls. Adams had befriended Johnson's brother, Maryland governor Thomas
Johnson, at the Continental Congress, establishing a tie that would bind
the two families for the rest of their lives.

On April 22, the *Alliance* arrived at Nantes, and the Adamses all but leaped aboard—only to be told to disembark. The vessel would not sail to America because the French government had assigned it to John Paul Jones's squadron to harass British shipping in the English Channel. "This is a cruel disappointment," Adams railed in his diary.

A few days later, the Adamses traveled westward along the southern shore of Brittany to the port of Lorient, where they were told they were more likely to find a ship bound for America. What they found were weeks of boredom in a town devoid of culture. The highlights of their stay were several dinners with John Paul Jones and a visit to his ship, the *Bonhomme Richard*—once a decrepit French ship that Jones had refitted with forty-two guns and renamed in Franklin's honor.*

On June 17, three months after leaving Paris, John Quincy and his father boarded the French frigate *Sensible* in Lorient, along with the first French ambassador to the United States, the Chevalier de la Luzerne, and his aide, the Marquis François de Barbé Marbois. In what proved a smooth, uneventful crossing, John Quincy Adams displayed both his language skills and his pedagogical skills absorbed from teachers at his French school, as he succeeded in teaching the two French diplomats to speak serviceable English—in just eight weeks.

"The Chevalier de la Luzerne and Mr. Marbois," John Adams beamed, "are in raptures with my son."

> I found them this morning, the ambassador seated on a cushion in our state room, Mr. Marbois in his cot at his left hand and my son stretched out in his at his right—the ambassador reading out loud in *Blackstone's*

---

*Bonhomme Richard was the French form of Benjamin Franklin's pseudonym. Later that summer, Jones would have to abandon the *Bonhomme Richard* in a sea of flames off the English coast after attacking the British *Serapis,* which was escorting a fleet of thirty-nine merchant ships. In the ensuing battle, the British commander struck his flag to surrender, and as flames consumed the *Bonhomme Richard,* Jones transferred his men to the *Serapis* and sailed it back to Lorient.

Discourse . . . and my son correcting the pronunciation of every word and syllable and letter. The ambassador said he was astonished at my son's knowledge; that he was a master of his own language like a professor. Mr. Marbois said "your son teaches us more than you. He shows us no mercy. We must have Mr. John."[20]

The *Sensible* reached Boston at the beginning of August 1779, and John Adams had no sooner stepped ashore than his friends, neighbors, and family elected him to a special convention to draft a constitution for Massachusetts. The convention, in turn, asked him to draft the document himself, and drawing from his brilliant *Thoughts on Government*, he wrote most of the Massachusetts Constitution of 1780. Beginning with a bill of rights, it placed all political power in the hands of the people and guaranteed such "natural, essential, and unalienable rights" as free speech, a free press, and free assembly. It also guaranteed free elections and the right of freemen to trial by jury and to protection against unreasonable searches and seizures, the right to keep and bear arms, the right to petition government for redress of grievances, and "the right of enjoying and defending their lives and liberties" and "of acquiring, possessing, and protecting their property."[21]

When John Adams had blotted the ink at the end of his draft, word arrived from Congress that, based on his recommendations, it had dissolved the commission in Paris in favor of a single ambassador, but instead of Franklin, it voted unanimously to appoint him, John Adams, to fill the post.

Seventy-one days after landing in Boston, Adams and his son boarded the same ship that had brought them home, the *Sensible*, and sailed for France for the second time in a year.

"My habitation, how disconsolate it looks!" Abigail raged at her husband. "My table, I set down to it but cannot swallow my food. O why was I born with so much sensibility and why possessing it have I so often been called to struggle with it?"[22]

Adams, however, had not hesitated to accept the appointment, which he believed would allow him to negotiate peace with England and recognition of American independence. "Let me entreat you," he pleaded with

Abigail, "to keep up your spirits and throw off cares as much as possible. . . . We shall yet be happy. I hope and pray and I don't doubt it. I shall have vexations enough. You will have anxiety and tenderness enough as usual. Pray strive not to have too much."[23]

Knowing he would no longer live in Franklin's orbit and being more familiar than before with Parisian life, John Adams brought his middle boy, ten-year-old Charles, as a companion for John Quincy, and Abigail's cousin John Thaxter as a tutor and part-time guardian for both children. Thaxter had tutored John Quincy once before, while studying law at John Adams's Boston law offices. Also traveling with Adams aboard the *Sensible* was the new legation secretary, Francis Dana, a Harvard graduate like Adams and a successful Boston lawyer. A Revolutionary War veteran, he had served five months at Valley Forge with George Washington. All were elated by the prospect of life in Paris except John Quincy, who had wanted to prepare for Harvard. Setting aside her own disappointment, Abigail tried to lift her son's spirits: "These are the times in which a genius would wish to live," she told him. "It is not in the still calm life . . . that great characters are formed. . . . When a mind is raised and animated by scenes that engage the heart, then those qualities which would otherwise lay dormant wake into life and form the character of the hero and the statesman."[24]

Having only just turned twelve, John Quincy saw no advantages to being either a hero or a statesman, but his parents were raising him to be both, and he knew he had little choice but to try to fulfill their ambitions. Although he had made several false starts at keeping a diary, he now began again in earnest. He had no way of knowing then, but his new diary would become an addictive, lifelong pastime and evolve into one of the greatest personal histories of the times ever recorded by an American. He left no doubt of its design on the title page:

A
Journal by Me
JQA

His journal's opening words were far more prophetic than either he or his mother could realize at the time: "1779 November Friday 12th. This morning I took leave of my Mamma."[25]

Three days of savage storms in the North Atlantic split the ship's seams, and as water seeped through the hull, the captain ordered all adults to take turns working pumps, each of them enduring four hour-long shifts per day. Even twelve-year-old John Quincy manned a pump until he fell to the floor exhausted. On December 9, 1779, the ship came within sight of the northwestern coast of Spain, and abandoning plans to sail to Bordeaux, the captain put into the tiny port of Ferrol. Less than an hour after the men stopped pumping, seven feet of water had filled the hull of the ship.

"One more storm would very probably have carried us to the bottom of the sea," John Quincy wrote to frighten his mother and demonstrate his heroism in having manned the pumps.

Although they were safely ashore, gale-force winds and relentless rain made further travel by sea impossible—on any ship. They now faced crossing the all-but-impenetrable Pyrenees to reach France, over dangerous roads and mountain trails where highwaymen lurked behind every bend, ready to assault unsuspecting travelers. John Adams organized a mule train with thirteen mules and three old carriages that John Quincy said had been "made in the year one." Adams hired two local muleteers, one to guide them, the other to take up the rear, and he bought himself a set of pistols.

"We set out like so many Don Quixote's and Sancho Panza's," John Quincy scrawled in his diary at the end of the first day. When they reached Coronna near the base of the Pyrenees, they dined at the house of the French consul, then lodged at a local inn. Heavy rains pinned them down until the day after Christmas, when they began their trek through the Pyrenees and what John Quincy called "the worst three weeks I ever passed in my life."

The roads in general are very bad. . . . The streets are filthy and muddy. . . . The lodgings I will not try to describe, for it is impossible . . . chambers in which anybody would think a half dozen hogs had lived there six months. . . . As for the people, they are lazy, dirty, nasty, and in short I can compare them to nothing but a parcel of hogs.[26]

Making their trip even worse, they all contracted "violent colds," developed fevers, and, according to John Adams, "went along the road, sneezing, coughing in all that uncomfortable weather . . . and indeed were all of us more fitted for the hospital than for travelers. . . . The children were sick. Mr. Thaxter was not much better. . . . I was in a deplorable situation. I knew not where to go or what to do. . . . I had never experienced anything like this journey. . . . In my whole life, my patience was never so near being totally exhausted."[27]

Although rain and snow slowed travel, it apparently discouraged highwaymen as well as ordinary travelers. The Adamses encountered none and escaped the Pyrenees on Sunday, January 15, 1780, when Adams, his sons, and his aides reached the Spanish port city of Bilbao—and the luxurious home of merchant Joseph Gardoqui. After several days recuperating, they set off in comfortable carriages and reached Paris on February 9, settling into the posh Hotel de Valois on the rue de Richelieu, in the heart of the city. A day later, Adams enrolled both boys in a boarding school, where John Quincy resumed his studies of Latin and Greek, geography, mathematics, drawing, and writing. To his delight, he reunited with Jesse Deane, whom Franklin had taken under his care while the boy's father, Silas Deane, was in America.*

Once Abigail Adams learned that her son was safe and in school, she wrote pleading for a word from him.

---

*Deane returned to France later in 1780 and lived the rest of his life in exile, taking his son Jesse with him to Ghent, then London. Jesse Deane sailed home to America to stay in 1783, and Silas Deane died under mysterious circumstances aboard a Boston-bound ship in Deal, England, in 1789.

My dear Son,

Writing is not *a la mode de Paris*, I fancy, or sure I should have heard from my son; or have you written and have I been so unfortunate as to lose all the letters which have been written to me for this five months. . . . Be dutiful my dear son.[28]

John Adams, meanwhile, took up his duties as American ambassador, writing Foreign Minister Comte de Vergennes at Versailles, "I have now the honor to acquaint you that . . . the United States Congress did me the honor to elect me their Minister Plenipotentiary to negotiate a peace with Britain and also to negotiate a treaty of commerce with that kingdom."[29]

To Adams's consternation, Vergennes responded to his every effort to promote peace negotiations with objections couched in diplomatic niceties. Although Adams could not know it at the time, Vergennes had no intention of fostering peace between the Americans and their former overlords. Intent on weakening Britain enough to permit French reconquest of Canada, Vergennes planned on providing the Americans with enough military aid to prolong the American Revolution indefinitely and sap the military strength of both sides—without allowing either to win. As an autocratic monarchy, France had no interest in promoting the rights of man or independence for Adams's self-governing republic.

Frustrated by Vergennes's diplomatic obstructions, Adams decided to go to Amsterdam to enlist financial help from the Dutch government "to render us less dependent on France," as he explained to Congress.

Once there, Adams enrolled the boys in the city's famed Latin school, but the headmaster found their inability to speak Dutch too great an impediment, and Adams withdrew them. At the suggestion of a friend who was studying medicine at the University of Leyden, Thaxter took John Quincy and Charles to that city, rented lodgings, then enrolled in the university himself and took the boys with him to lectures. He tutored them intensively until each of them—first John Quincy, then Charles—acquired enough knowledge to enroll in the university as full-time students, despite their ages.

"You have now a prize in your hands indeed," the proud father told his older son, who had turned thirteen. "If you do not improve to the best advantage," he cautioned the boy, "you will be without excuse. But as I know you have an ardent thirst for knowledge and a good capacity to acquire it, I depend on it, you will do no dishonor to yourself nor to the University of Leyden."[30]

Abigail was equally proud. "What a harvest of true knowledge and learning may you gather from the numberless varied scenes through which you pass if you are not wanting in your assiduity and endeavors. Let your ambition be engaged to become eminent, but above all things, support a virtuous character and remember that 'an honest man is the noblest work of God.'"[31] Still a mother, however, she did not neglect maternal concerns: "I hope, my dear boy, that the universal neatness and cleanliness of the people where you reside will cure you of all your slovenly tricks and that you learn from them industry, economy, and frugality."[32]

Slovenly though he may have been, thirteen-year-old John Quincy was scholarly to a degree that astonished many accomplished university professors and caught the attention of Jean Luzac, a prominent lawyer, history scholar, and editor of the influential *Gazette de Leyde*. He became great friends with the boy, who scored his first diplomatic triumph by introducing Luzac to his father. Their encounter turned Luzac into Holland's most outspoken advocate of Dutch financial aid to the Americans and produced substantial loans to the Americans and eventual recognition of American independence.

In early summer 1781, Congress appointed Francis Dana minister to the court of Empress Catherine II in St. Petersburg to seek Russian recognition of American independence. Though a fierce autocrat, Catherine pretended to embrace social progress, when, in fact, she had reduced Russia's free peasantry to serfdom. Some members of Congress hoped commercial interests might encourage her to establish diplomatic ties to the New World and encourage other neutral nations to follow suit. Oddly, the otherwise brilliantly educated Dana spoke no French, which was the language not only of international diplomacy but of everyday social inter-

John Quincy Adams, seen here at sixteen, a year after having gone to St. Petersburg, Russia, as American minister Francis Dana's translator and legation secretary. (NATIONAL PARKS SERVICE, ADAMS NATIONAL HISTORICAL PARK)

course among the Russian aristocracy. Taken by John Quincy Adams's erudition, social maturity, and language skills, Dana invited the boy, who was still fourteen, to serve as his secretary and interpreter, and John Quincy, eager for independence and in awe of working with a veteran of Valley Forge, accepted. It was an incredible choice, but Dana—like most people who talked with John Quincy—often forgot he was talking to a mere boy. John Quincy was remarkable, and Dana believed it would take too long to find and transport to Europe another American—of any age—to serve as a more effective secretary of legation.

"This morning, brother Charles and I packed up our trunks," John Quincy wrote in his diary on June 28, 1781, "and I went to take leave of our riding master." Unlike his older brother, Charles had been unhappy in

Europe and was returning to his mother in America. John Quincy Adams was about to turn fifteen and begin life on his own—in the service of his country as a foreign diplomat. A devoted scholar by then, he would not leave without copying some of his favorite works to take with him. In the days before his departure, he copied Alexander Pope's "Ode for Music on St. Cecilia's Day" and "Universal Prayer," as well as "Mr. Addison's *Tragedy of Cato*." American patriots—none more than George Washington—cherished the Roman statesman Cato's noble sentiments: "What pity is it that we can die but once to serve our country."*[33]

On the day of his departure, John Quincy made this entry in his diary: "Saturday, July the 7th, 1781: This morning we packed up everything to go on a journey." The boy diplomat closed his journal, slipped it into his coat, and embarked on the beginning of what would be a lifelong adventure of service to his country.[34]

---

*American Revolutionary War hero Nathan Hale is said to have paraphrased Cato as he was about to be hung by the British as a spy: Hale's last words were said to have been, "I only regret that I have but one life to lose for my country."

CHAPTER 3

The Land of Lovely Dames

For the first time during his extensive travels, John Quincy found his 2,000-mile midsummer journey from Holland to St. Petersburg free of threats to life or limb. Although he missed his father and brother, he seemed composed, wore a pleasant expression, and proved an amiable companion to Francis Dana, who, at thirty-eight, was twenty-four years older than his "secretary." The journey proved instructive for both.

"The tradesmen always ask the double of what a thing is worth," John Quincy complained, "and if you have anything made, you will certainly get greatly cheated if you do not make the bargain beforehand." In Catholic Palatine, he found that "Protestants can not own houses or farms," and across the Rhine from Cologne, he fell on "a village inhabited by Jews. A nasty, dirty place indeed. . . . In Frankfurt am Mein . . . there are 600 Jewish families who live all in one street which is shut up every night and all day Sundays, when the gates are shut."[1]

On July 25, he reached Berlin, which he called "the handsomest and the most regular city I ever saw,"[2] but he criticized the king, who "treats his people like slaves." They found conditions worse when they crossed into Poland, where, for the first time in his life, John Quincy encountered

Panoramic view of St. Petersburg, where fifteen-year-old John Quincy Adams spent the winter of 1782 as secretary and translator for American minister Francis Dana. The palatial buildings in the center include the famed Winter Palace and the then new Hermitage, in which Catherine the Great housed her art collection. (LIBRARY OF CONGRESS)

slaves. "All the farm workers are in the most abject slavery," he noted with disgust. "They are bought and sold like so many beasts, and are sometimes even changed for dogs or horses. Their masters have even the right of life and death over them, and if they kill one of them they are only obliged to pay a trifling fine. [The slaves] may buy [their freedom], but their masters . . . take care not to let them grow rich enough for that. If anybody buys land, he must buy all the slaves that are upon it."[3]

On August 27, 1781, John Quincy and Dana reached St. Petersburg and settled in the luxurious Hotel de Paris, near the Winter Palace. "The city of Petersburg," he wrote to John Thaxter in Paris, "is the finest I ever saw. It is by far superior to Paris, both for the breadth of its streets, and the elegance of the private buildings."

To Dana's dismay, Russian foreign ministry officials refused to receive him or even recognize his presence. His notes went unanswered, and sentries refused him entry through the palace gates. In frustration, he turned to the French chargé d'affaires for help, but Foreign Minister Comte de Vergennes at Versailles had sent instructions not to aid the Americans. The

Massachusetts-born and Harvard-educated Francis Dana served at Valley Forge with George Washington before becoming an American diplomat and the first American envoy to Russia. (LIBRARY OF CONGRESS)

French diplomat exuded warm words and pledged to help, but stunned Dana by suggesting that the American's reliance on a child as his secretary and interpreter might compromise his status.

Not long thereafter, stunning news arrived of George Washington's remarkable victory at Yorktown. Although Dana was certain the American triumph would open doors at the Winter Palace, weeks passed without success. As winter's paralyzing deep freeze enveloped the Russian capital, John Quincy had nothing to do but study. Although their lodgings were warm enough, temperatures outside dropped to levels that made venturing into the fresh air foolhardy. "The thermometer at night," John Quincy noted in early February 1782, "was 15 degrees below freezing." It fell to twenty-five below, then twenty-eight below. "Stayed at home all day."[4]

By then, his diary entries had shrunk to a sentence or two, noting only the temperature and his decision to remain inside and read. Both he and Dana were idle most of the time, with no diplomatic work or contact with Russian authorities. It was fortunate that St. Petersburg had at least one bookshop with English-language works, and both John Quincy and Dana purchased an enormous quantity. Before the end of winter, John Quincy had read—among other things—all eight volumes (more than five hundred pages each) of David Hume's *History of England*, Catherine Macaulay's eight-volume *The History of England from the Accession of James I to that of the Brunswick Line*, William Robertson's three-volume *The History of the Reign of Charles V*, Robert Watson's two-volume *The History of the Reign of Philip the Second, King of Spain*, Thomas Davies's *Memoirs of the Life of David Garrick*, and the two-volume landmark work in economics by Adam Smith, *An Inquiry into the Nature and Causes of the Wealth of Nations*. He also restudied Cicero's *Orations* and John Dryden's *Works of Virgil*, copied the poems of Dryden, Alexander Pope, and Joseph Addison—and learned to read and write German.

"I don't perceive that you take pains enough with your hand writing," his father growled in response. "When the habit is got, it is easier to write well than ill, but this habit is only to be acquired in early life." Adams ended his letter more warmly, however: "God bless my dear son and preserve his health and his manners from the numberless dangers that surround us wherever we go in this world. So prays your affectionate father, J. Adams."[5]

Crestfallen at his father's response to his studies, John Quincy did not reply for a month, and when he did, he wrote in French to make it difficult for the elder Adams to read. Adams answered acerbically, "It is a mortification to me to find that you write better in a foreign language than in your mother tongue." Adams was, however, worried about his son—an adolescent, all but alone in a foreign land, with no companions but a middle-aged man and a pile of books.

"Do you find any company?" John Adams wrote. "Have you formed any acquaintances of your own countrymen? There are none I suppose. Of Englishmen you should beware. . . . My dear boy, above all preserve your innocence."[6] He grew more anxious as the winter progressed without John Quincy's gaining any substantial diplomatic experience. "I am . . . very uneasy on your account," he wrote in mid-May. "I want you with me. . . . I want you to pursue your studies at Leyden. . . . Your studies I doubt not you pursue, because I know you to be a studious youth, but above all preserve a sacred regard to your own honor and reputation. Your morals are worth all the sciences."[7]

John Quincy finally admitted to himself—and to his father—"I have not made many acquaintances here." Although he had "as much as I want to read," he longed for companions his own age. In addition, the crushing poverty, deprivation, and lack of freedom in Russian life—and the oppressive slavery he witnessed—left him depressed. "Everyone that is not a noble," he lamented, "is a slave."[8]

His father responded by urging John Quincy to return to Holland. Adams had succeeded in winning Dutch recognition of American independence and had moved to The Hague as American minister plenipotentiary.

Although eager to rejoin his father, John Quincy was enjoying his independence and took a long, circuitous route back to Holland through Scandinavia and Germany. After three weeks exploring Finland (then a part of Sweden), he reached Stockholm, and ignoring his father's exhortations on the importance of preserving his innocence, John Quincy Adams plunged into Swedish life for nearly six rapture-filled weeks.

"I believe there is no country in Europe," he exulted, "where the people are more hospitable and affable to strangers or more hospitable . . . than the Swedes. In every town, however small it may be, they have these assemblies [dances] . . . to pass away agreeably the long winter evenings. . . . There, one may dance country dances, minuets or play cards, just as it pleases you, and everybody is extremely polite to strangers." Years later, he recalled, that "the beauties of the women . . . could not be concealed. . . . The Swedish women were as modest as they were amiable and beautiful. To me it was truly the 'land of lovely dames,' and to this hour I have not forgotten the palpitations of heart which some of them cost me."[9]

While he was sampling Sweden's wine and women, his parents grew frantic. "I hope our dear son abroad," Abigail fretted to John, "will not imbibe any sentiments or principles which will not be agreeable to the laws, the government and religion of our own country. He has been less under your eye than I could wish. . . . If he does not return this winter, I wish you to remind him that he has forgotten to use his pen to his friends upon this side of the water."[10] John Adams feigned nonchalance in replying to Abigail but sent inquiries to French consuls in Germany and Scandinavia about his son's whereabouts.

John Quincy had reached Göteborg on the west coast of Sweden with every intention of remaining, when the French consul reported his father's anxieties and set the boy scrambling to make travel arrangements to Holland. He took a final fling at a masquerade ball where "the men dressed as sailors and the women [as] country girls. . . . I stayed there till about 4 o'clock this morning. When I returned to my lodgings, I threw myself upon the bed and slept till about 7 o'clock, then packed my trunks and set away."[11]

In the weeks that followed, John Quincy traveled to Copenhagen, Hamburg, and Bremen, finally rejoining his father in The Hague on July 22—noticeably more mature than when he had left.

"John is every thing you could wish," Adams explained to Abigail without revealing the obvious changes in his personality or probable causes. "Wholly devoted to his studies, he has made a progress which gives me entire satisfaction. . . . He is grown a man in understanding and stature as well. . . . I shall take him with me to Paris and shall make much of his company."[12] Even Abigail was impressed after reading John Quincy's first letter to her upon his return to Holland. "The account of your northern journey," she conceded, "would do credit to an older pen."[13]

Adams was more than delighted with his son, and early in August, the two left The Hague for Paris, where John Adams joined Benjamin Franklin and John Jay in negotiating a peace treaty with England—and elated John Quincy by recruiting him as a secretary to edit and transcribe documents. John Adams now accepted his precocious sixteen-year-old son as a man, a friend, and a pleasant, sophisticated companion, not only at concerts, the opera, and museums but at luncheons, dinners, and other functions with some of Europe's most distinguished figures. They, in turn, also accepted the young man as an equal. "Dined at . . . the Dutch ambassador with a great deal of company," John Quincy reported in his diary in mid-August 1783. "Dined at the Duke de la Vauguyon . . . the French ambassador at the Hague . . . the Baron de la Houze . . . the minister of France at the court of Denmark."[14] With each encounter, he listened carefully, gradually learning the language of diplomacy in which spoken words seldom matched their literal meanings. An "interesting concept" often meant "unacceptable," while a "different approach" could well mean war.

With France a center of scientific advances, John Quincy also witnessed astounding new processes and inventions and developed a deep interest in science. "My Lord Ancram," he recounted in his diary, "has undertaken to teach people born deaf and dumb not only to converse . . . fluently but also to read and write." Another entry described his having witnessed "the first public experiment . . . of the flying globe."

> A Mr. Montgolfier has discovered that if one fills a ball with inflammable air much lighter than common air, the ball of itself will go up to an immense height. It was . . . 14 foot in diameter . . . placed in the Champs de Mars.* At 5 o'clock, two great guns fired from the École Militaire. . . . It rose at once, for some time perpendicular and then slanted. . . . If it succeeds it may become very useful to mankind.[15]

The launch of the first balloon set off a mania in France, with Joseph de Montgolfier and his brother Étienne sending balloons into the atmosphere in Versailles and elsewhere. "The enthusiasm of the people of Paris for the flying globes is very great," John Quincy noted with excitement. "Several propositions have been made from persons who, to enjoy the honor of having been the first travelers through the air, are willing to go up in them and run risks of breaking their necks."[16]

---

*This large, rectangular stretch of open parkland reaches today from the front of the École Militaire to the Eiffel Tower but ran to the Left Bank of the Seine at the time John Quincy Adams describes.

In the midst of the whirlwind of social and scientific activities, John Adams worked out the final stages of treaty negotiations with Britain, with John Quincy helping prepare copies of the final documents. On September 3, Adams, Franklin, Jay, and British minister David Hartley met on the rue Jacob, on the Left Bank, to sign a treaty of peace between Britain and the United States, with Britain recognizing the United States of America as a free and independent nation.

In the months that followed, John Quincy and his father traveled back and forth between France, England, and Holland. They spent the autumn of 1783 in Britain, where John Quincy visited London's wonders—Westminster Abbey, St. Paul's Cathedral, and so on. He tramped through great museums and libraries, attended opera at Covent Garden, and saw productions of *Hamlet* and *Measure for Measure* at the Drury Lane Theatre, where the legendary Sarah Siddons starred each night. Benjamin West, the Pennsylvania-born Quaker artist who had moved to London, took him to see the art collection at Buckingham Palace and several art galleries, and he went to the opening of Parliament to hear the King's Speech from the Throne and the debates between Edmund Burke, Lord North, William Pitt, Charles Fox, and other great figures in the House of Commons.

At the end of the year, the Adamses returned to The Hague, where John Adams sought new loans for the United States, while John Quincy resumed his studies. In the spring, Abigail announced that, after a separation of four years, she was coming to Europe "in the joyful hope of soon holding to my bosom the dearest, best of friends."[17] John Adams was elated, saying his wife's letter "has made me the happiest man upon earth. I am twenty years younger than I was yesterday." And he signed it, "Yours, with more ardor than ever."[18]

A month later, Abigail arrived in England with her daughter, Nabby. Not long after they checked into their London hotel, a servant knocked at the door to announce, "Young Mr. Adams is come."

"Where, where is he?" Abigail and Nabby screeched in unison. Abigail described the scene in a letter to her sister: "Impatient enough I was, yet when he entered . . . I drew back not really believing my eyes—till he cried out, 'Oh, my momma! And my dear sister.' Nothing but his eyes at first sight appeared what he once was. His appearance is that of a man."[19]

Moved to tears as she wrote, Abigail told her sister she felt "exceedingly matronly with a grown up son on one hand and daughter upon the other."[20] And to husband John she wrote, "I was this day made very happy by the arrival of a son in whom I can trace the strongest likeness of a parent in every way dear to me."[21]

John Quincy rented a coach and took his mother and sister for a reunion with his father in Paris, where the whole family moved into a luxurious home in Auteuil, six miles west of the city in the Bois de Boulogne. Thomas Jefferson and his daughter—both lonely for family life after the death of his wife two years earlier—frequently came to dinner. Following Paris custom, Jefferson enrolled his daughter in a convent school, and he compensated for her absence by bonding with John Quincy, taking him to theater, concerts, and museums, and becoming an important figure in the young man's life. The two formed such close ties that John Adams remarked to Jefferson that John Quincy "appeared to me to be almost as much your boy as mine."[22]

The Adamses also spent time with the Lafayettes, who entertained Americans with huge buffet dinners at their home every Monday. After Queen Marie Antoinette gave birth to her first son and heir apparent, France rejoiced, and Adrienne Lafayette invited the Adamses to accompany her to the Te Deum at the cathedral of Notre Dame de Paris, where both King Louis XVI and the Marquis de Lafayette were to participate. "What a charming sight," John Quincy wrote in his diary, "an absolute king of one of the most powerful empires on earth and perhaps a thousand of the first personages in that empire adoring the divinity who created them and acknowledging that he can in a moment reduce them to the dust from which they sprang."[23]

By now, John Quincy was as much a celebrity in Paris as his father— treated as an equal by the likes of Jefferson and Lafayette, addressed as "Mr. Adams," and referred to as "young Mr. Adams" to differentiate him from his father. He had seen more of Europe than many of them and knew more of the social conditions and politics of distant lands—Germany, Poland, Russia, and Scandinavia. When artist Benjamin West arrived, he went to see John Quincy Adams, not his father, to arrange introductions to Jefferson and Lafayette. John Quincy's diary describes his winter in Paris: "Dined at the Marquis de la Fayette's . . . dined with Mr. Jefferson [and] Captain John Paul Jones . . . Dined at Dr. Franklin's. . . . Walked into Paris to the Marquis de la Fayette's to go with him to Mr. Jefferson's upon the subject of importation of our whale oil into this country."[24]

The Swedish ambassador, who had known John Quincy in Stockholm, invited him to bring his family to dinner. "Mon dieu que mademoiselle vôtre soeur est belle," he whispered of Nabby's beauty to John Quincy, saying he had seen few as lovely as she. "J'ai vu peu d'aussi jolies femmes qu'elle."* John Quincy apparently did not translate for Nabby. "He thought doubtless that I should tell her what he said," John Quincy noted in his diary later. "He is a very agreeable man."[25]

Abigail was less sanguine about dining with celebrities, saying she was "astonished" when "this lady I dined with at Dr. Franklin's . . . gave him a double kiss one upon each cheek and another upon his forehead. . . . She carried on . . . at dinner, frequently locking her hand into the Dr.'s . . . then throwing her arm carelessly upon the Dr.'s neck. . . . I must say I was highly disgusted and never wish for an acquaintance of this cast."[26]

In the course of the winter, John Quincy drew close to his mother and sister as never before, taking them to theater, concerts, operas, and museums—and introducing them to such celebrities as the heroic Jean-Pierre Blanchard, who only two weeks earlier had been the first person to cross from Dover to Calais in an air balloon.

The following spring, John Adams received word that Congress had named him America's first ambassador to Britain. By then, John Quincy recognized that he could no longer "loiter away my precious time in Europe"—that the time had come for him to enroll full time in university, finish his formal education, and choose a profession.[27]

---

*"Dear God, your sister is beautiful. I've seen few women as beautiful as she."

*Abigail Adams II ("Nabby"), the oldest child of John
and Abigail Adams, came with her mother to join her
father and younger brother John Quincy in Paris in the
summer of 1784.* (NATIONAL PARKS SERVICE, ADAMS
NATIONAL HISTORICAL PARK)

Although Harvard seemed a backward country school compared with the
University of Leyden or England's great institutions at Oxford and Cambridge, the pathway to professional and political leadership in America began
in Cambridge, Massachusetts, not Cambridge, England. "Harvard rendered
her sons fit to serve their country," historian Samuel Eliot Morison explained,
"not by practical courses on politics and government, but by a study of an-
tique culture that broadened their mental vision, stressed virtue, and promoted . . . the character appropriate to a republican. . . . American
revolutionary leaders, both North and South . . . could never have rendered
their distinguished services to the young republic without that classical learning which is denied to most Americans today."[28]

Intent on his son's rising to American leadership, John Adams wrote to Reverend Joseph Willard, who had awarded John Adams an honorary LL.D. at Willard's first commencement as Harvard's president in 1781. Adams assumed Willard would automatically admit John Quincy, given the boy's studies at Leyden, his mastery of two classical and three modern languages, and his command of an enormous body of classical and modern literature, philosophy, and science. As Adams described his son, "He has translated Virgil's *Aeneid* . . . the whole of Sallust and Tacitus'[s] *Agricola* . . . a great part of Horace, some of Ovid, and some of Caesar's *Commentaries* . . . besides Cicero's *Orations*. . . ."

> In Greek his progress has not been equal; yet he has studied morsels of Aristotle's *Politics*, Plutarch's *Lives*, Lucian's *Dialogues*. . . . In mathematics I hope he will pass muster. . . . We went with some accuracy through the geometry in the *Preceptor*, the eight books of Simpson's *Euclid* in Latin. . . . We went through plane geometry . . . algebra, and the decimal fractions, arithmetical and geometrical proportions . . . the differential method of calculations . . . and Sir Isaac Newton.[29]

Under no circumstances, Adams told the Harvard president, would he permit his son to enter Harvard as a freshman or sophomore, but if Willard admitted him as a junior or senior, "I should choose to send him to you rather than to Leyden." Adams also suggested that his own services to the nation warranted Harvard's waiving all expenses other than tuition.

Willard responded curtly, saying he would admit the boy subject to examination.

On May 12, 1785, a cabriolet* pulled up to the Adams home in Auteuil to take John Quincy to Lorient and a ship bound for America. He embraced his family and "took leave of my parents and my sister . . . at half after twelve with such feelings as no one that has not been separated from

---

* A two-wheel, one-horse carriage with a folding top for two people.

persons so dear can conceive."[30] He had said his good-byes to Lafayette and Jefferson the previous day and carried letters from each to deliver to America, along with a pack of hunting dogs that Lafayette asked him to take as a gift to George Washington. He also carried jars of whale oil that Jefferson had asked him to offer New York merchants as a commercial opportunity for illuminating the streets of Paris. For Jefferson, John Quincy's departure was wrenching, and when the rest of the Adams family left Paris for London, Jefferson lamented in a letter to John Adams, "The departure of your family has left me in the dumps." Without John Quincy's companionship, he admitted, "My afternoons hang heavily on me."[31]

Nine days later, on May 21, 1785, John Quincy Adams boarded one of the first four passenger ships to sail the Atlantic between France and America—the ninety-six-foot-long *Courier de l'Amérique*. "Every passenger pays five hundred livres* for his passage. . . . You live at the captain's table and have a small apartment on board to yourself. You must provide whatever refreshments you may be in need of and must bring your own sheets and pillows and napkins [towels]."

On the morning of July 18, the ship reached New York—the American capital at the time—and Adams went directly to Secretary of State John Jay's magnificent Broadway residence, where he was to stay. Recognized as a celebrity in New York as much as in Paris, John Quincy dined with Jay, then went with him to meet Elbridge Gerry and Rufus King, the two Massachusetts delegates to Congress. "I was introduced to the President of Congress [Richard Henry Lee]," he wrote of his first evening in New York, "and Mr. [James] Monroe of the Virginia delegation. I went to [New York] Governor [George] Clinton, but he was not within."[32] The next morning, he breakfasted with Gerry and King. "The President of Congress who was there was so kind as to offer me a room in his house."[33] As president of the Confederation Congress, Richard Henry Lee was, in effect, President of

---

*About $1,200 in today's money.

the United States, and he invited John Quincy to the weekly formal dinners he gave for American notables and visiting dignitaries.

After his experiences in Scandinavia and the long trip across the Atlantic, John Quincy was quick to note the characteristics of every attractive young lady he met. "Miss Jarvis," he remarked in his diary, "is very
fair, but Miss Ogden is a beauty. . . . There are five or six young ladies in
the family, one only is handsome."[34] And on another afternoon, John
Quincy went to see the eighteen-year-old widow of the nearly seventy-
year-old British officer Jacob Wheate. Lady Wheate, as he called her, "is
one of the most reputed beauties in the town. I own I do not admire her
so much as I expected to before I saw her. She is like too many of the
handsome ladies here: very affected."[35]

In mid-August, John Quincy set off for Boston, stopping in New
Haven, where Yale College president Ezra Stiles—a hero in the defense of
New Haven against the British—greeted the boy on what was then a tiny
hilltop campus. Adams was unimpressed, writing Nabby that the Yale library "is neither as large nor as elegant as your pappa's." His comment on
Yale was but one installment of a letter written over a ten-day span that
began in New York, where, he reported to Nabby that one afternoon, "I
dined in company with Mr. [Thomas] Paine, the author of *Common
Sense*, and [Rev.] Dr. [John] Witherspoon* . . . I have been introduced at
different times to almost all the members of Congress." Young Adams
was apparently tiring of his celebrity status, however, and told Nabby that
"wherever I go I hear a repetition of the same questions[:] . . . 'How do
you like Europe?' What country do you like best?' . . . and a hundred
other such. I am almost wearied to death with them, and I sometimes

---

*Scottish-born president of the College of New Jersey (now Princeton) and the only
clergyman and only foreign-born delegate to sign the Declaration of Independence,
Witherspoon was the most influential educator of his time. His students included
one president (James Madison), one vice president (Aaron Burr Jr.), sixty members
of Congress, and three Supreme Court justices.

think of writing a list of the questions with the answers, and whenever a person begins to make any questions, I would give him the paper. . . . Since my arrival here, every moment of my time has been taken up and yet I have had little or nothing to do."[36]

From New Haven, he went to Hartford and, finally, to Boston and his childhood home at Braintree. "No person who has not experienced it," he told his diary, "can conceive how much pleasure there is in returning to our country after an absence of six years, especially when it was left at the time of life that I did when I went last to Europe. The most trifling objects now appear interesting to me."[37] His aunt Mary, Abigail's sister, and her family greeted him in what proved a deeply emotional reunion for them all.

"We sat and looked at one another," John Quincy wrote to his mother. "I could not speak. . . . How much more expressive this silence than anything we could have said." After dinner, John Quincy and his uncle went to Cambridge to see John Quincy's brother Charles, who had enrolled in Harvard six weeks earlier. In the days that followed, John Quincy visited his grandparents, aunts, uncles, cousins—as well as such illustrious family friends as former Massachusetts governor John Hancock. He impressed them all—with his height as much as his erudition. He had left Massachusetts as a boy and returned a young man of five feet seven and a half inches—a half inch taller than his father and far thinner.

"Cousin John is come," his Aunt Mary wrote to her sister Abigail after his visit, "and brought with him in his own face such a resemblance of his papa and mama as I never before saw blended in one. And I am happy to perceive that it is not only in his person that he bears such a likeness to his parents. I have already discovered a strength of mind, a memory, a soundness of judgment which I have seldom seen united in one so young. His modesty is not the least of his virtues. . . . If his application is equal to his abilities, he cannot fail of making a great man."[38]

Eventually, John Quincy had to face the inevitable, and on August 31, 1785, he went to Harvard to see its president, Reverend Joseph Willard. Although Harvard boasted America's largest library, with 12,000 volumes, the jaded young Adams found the latter only "good, without being magnificent."[39] He had, after all, studied in the Bibliothèque du roi, in Paris, with its more than 1 million books and 80,000 manuscripts. He was less than impressed, as well, with the president's office and, indeed, with President Willard himself.

Raised in poverty after losing his father at the age of two, Willard was a mathematician with little appreciation for the romance of opera, music, and the grand arts that had formed so much of John Quincy's education. He was a serious man—dour, with a deep distaste for the boy's elegant clothes, his confident, worldly ways, and the ease with which he addressed older men as if they were social equals. Willard ran Harvard like a military institution, demanding that all who approached him—tutors and students alike—doff their hats when they passed. He banned wearing silk and limited student dress to coarse brown, olive, or black cotton jackets and pants called "homespun." From the first, he resented John Quincy's effervescent demeanor, enthusiasm, and joy. Even more, he resented the boy's assumption that, as John Adams's son, his admission to Harvard was a mere formality.

After asking John Quincy a few questions in Latin, then Greek, Willard scowled, then stunned the boy by telling him he was ineligible for admission to Harvard. It was the harshest blow he could possibly have delivered to the son of a Founding Father. Every man of note in Massachusetts history had gone to Harvard since its founding in 1634; eight of the fifty-six signers of the Declaration of Independence were Harvard graduates, including John Quincy's father and his cousin Sam Adams Jr. And now, with a few words, an undistinguished pedagogue, who had contributed nothing of note to his nation's freedom, had shattered the hopes of a Founding Father's son to complete his higher education, obtain a law degree, and assume the leadership of his country. He had crushed John Quincy Adams's career before it could begin.

CHAPTER 4

"*He Grows . . . Very Fat*"

Harvard president Joseph Willard so infuriated and humiliated John Quincy Adams that the boy would not even write about the interview in his diary, noting only that Willard "advised me to wait till next spring." In fact, Willard had arbitrarily declared the boy unprepared for Harvard and urged him to study with a tutor over autumn and winter and to re-apply in the spring. Willard told John Quincy that if he then passed the examinations, he could join the junior class in time for the last trimester of the academic year in April 1786.

John Quincy had never confronted arbitrary power before. Willard's was not the face of evil as much as it was the face of unbridled authority over men's lives, and John Quincy Adams despised it, would never forget it, and would fight it for the rest of his life. "Few men live long in the world," he concluded, "without having suffered from baseness and wicked-ness in others."[1]

Recognizing his impotence, Adams knew he had no choice but to obey Willard's directive if he wanted to study at Harvard, and he went to live and study with his uncle, Reverend John Shaw, the Congregational minis-ter in Haverhill, Massachusetts. Married to another of Abigail's younger

*Harvard College, the "school of the prophets," where John Quincy Adams, his
father, grandfather, brothers, and sons received their higher education. Founded
in 1636 as America's first college, the original buildings burned and were
replaced by Harvard Hall in 1675 (left), Stoughton Hall in 1699 (center),
and Massachusetts Hall in 1720.* (LIBRARY OF CONGRESS)

sisters, Shaw was a recognized scholar and approved tutor who had prepared many students for Harvard.

"My journal till now," John Quincy realized, "has almost entirely consisted in an account of my peregrinations. . . . The events for the future
will probably be a continual repetition . . . and will contain nothing that
even I myself may desire to remember, but I shall surely have observations
to make upon diverse subjects which it may be proper to commit to paper. And I can again employ the resource of sketching characters."[2]

After years in Europe's marbled halls, John Quincy found small-town
New England social life unimpressive. "The way we have here of killing
time in large companies appears to me most absurd and ridiculous," he

scrawled in his diary. "All must be fixed down in chairs, looking at one another like a puppet show and talking some common-place phrases to one another."³ After dinner one day, the shallow conversations left him particularly annoyed:

> I wonder how it happens that almost every kind of conversation that may be of any use to persons is excluded from polite company everywhere. Is it because the children of ignorance and folly are so much more numerous than those of thought and science that these must submit to imitate them?

"By the tyrannical law of custom," he concluded, otherwise intelligent people "were obliged to talk nonsense."⁴

John Quincy divided his time during the six months that followed between making notes in his diary about the girls he met and rereading Latin and Greek classics he had already studied in Europe. "I began this day to translate the *Ecologues* of Virgil," he noted one evening—then added, "Peggy is about 20 years old and is called a beauty. Her face has a great deal of dignity . . . but when adorned with a smile is extremely pleasant."⁵ A few days later: "Miss Williams is tall and pretty . . . ," and "Nancy is only 17. . . . Her shape is uncommonly fine and her eye seems to have magic in it. . . . Her heart is kind, tender and benevolent, and was she sensible of the pain she causes she would be the first to condemn herself." He apparently dismissed all thoughts about girls the next day, spending "the whole day at my studies. . . . I read Watt's *Logic*." There was little in the curriculum—Latin, Greek, English, or French—that he did not absorb: all the available works of Homer, Plato, Virgil, Cicero, Horace, Juvenal, and Terence, as well as John Locke and Alexander Pope—and the Bible.

As the end of his stay in Haverhill approached, he plunged into his first political controversy, confronting a group of Baptists and their minister who sought to end the town's assemblies, or dances. "Superstition of some kind will prevail with mankind everywhere," John Quincy raged.

Mr. Smith, the minister of the Baptist Society in this town, is violently opposed to dancing. It is in his mind of itself a heinous sin . . . and there are
many people here so warped in prejudice that they are really persuaded
they should incur the divine displeasure, as much by dancing as by stealing
or perhaps committing murder. . . . How one of the more innocent and
rational amusements that was ever invented can find so many opposers is
somewhat mysterious. . . . There are many who are envious to see others
amusing themselves. . . . However, the subscribers wisely take no notice . . . but go on their own way and despise all these senseless clamors.[6]

Several days later, he made a point of attending an assembly of more
than twenty couples, all but daring the Baptist minister to interfere. "I
might make a number of sarcastic reflections upon the manner of dancing," John Quincy reflected, "but I do not think it a matter of sufficient
importance . . . to laugh at a person who cannot show the elegance of a
dancing master."[7]

On March 14, 1786, John Quincy left Haverhill to take his entrance examinations at Harvard. Three professors, four tutors, and the librarian—
the entire Harvard faculty—joined President Willard in examining Adams
to eliminate presidential prejudice as a factor. After he displayed his skills in
Latin, Greek, mathematics, and philosophy, the frowning Willard conceded, "You are admitted, Adams."

John Quincy Adams spent the next fifteen months at Harvard learning little he did not already know from a faculty he found haughty and
"hard for me to submit to."

It seems almost a maxim among the governors of the college to treat
students pretty much like brute beasts. There is an important air and
haughty look that every person belonging to the government assumes,
which, indeed, it is hard for me to submit to. But it may be of use to me,
as it mortifies my vanity and, if anything in the world can teach me hu-
mility, it will be to see myself subjected to the commands of a person that
I most despise.[8]

His father had a much different perspective on Harvard: "Give me leave, my dear son, to congratulate you on your admission into the Seat of the Muses, our dear Alma Mater, where I hope you will find a pleasure and improvements equal to your expectations. You are now among magistrates and ministers, legislators and heroes, ambassadors and generals; I mean among persons who will live to act in all these characters. If you pursue your studies and preserve your health, you will have as good a chance as most of them, and I hope you will take care to do nothing now which you will in any future period have reason to recollect with shame or pain."[9]

Harvard students did not impress John Quincy, however. One afternoon, he watched a group of sophomores turn wild from drink, then smash their tutors' windows. "After this sublime maneuver," he remarked, "they staggered to their chambers. Such are the great achievements of many of the sons of Harvard. . . . About two-thirds of the class are behind hand, and the rest are obliged to wait for them till they come up."[10]

Harvard presented John Quincy with few intellectual challenges, and he graduated second in his class in July 1787, often skipping lectures to go fishing and occasionally dancing so late with Cambridge girls that he overslept and missed classes the next morning. He made friends with a few of the most academically advanced members of his class, learned to play the flute, joined the Handel Sodality, and oversaw the progress of his two younger brothers, Charles, a sophomore, and Thomas Boylston, a freshman.

In London, meanwhile, his older sister Nabby had married, and to John Quincy's pleasant surprise, his mother reacted to the absence of small children in her household with newfound warmth and empathy for her adult offspring. "It is not in your power to remedy the evils you complain of," she said in response to her son's irritation with the Harvard faculty. "Whilst the salaries are so small, it cannot be expected that gentlemen of the first abilities will devote their lives to the preceptorship."

Get all the good you can, and beware you do no ill to others. You must be conscious of how great importance it is to youth that they respect their teachers. Therefore whatever tends to lessen them is an injury to the whole society. . . . If you are conscious to yourself that you possess more knowledge upon some subjects than others of your standing, reflect that you have had greater opportunities of seeing the world and obtaining a knowledge of mankind than any of your contemporaries, that you have never wanted a book, but it has been supplied to you; that your whole time has been spent in the company of men of literature and science. My paper will allow me room only to add my blessing to you and your brothers from your ever affectionate A. Adams.[11]

As a principal speaker at his class graduation, John Quincy earned plaudits from alumni as well as classmates; even President Willard conceded in a letter to John Quincy's parents, "I think he bids fair to become a distinguished character."[12]

Although college life had isolated him, news of Shays's Rebellion in Springfield, Massachusetts, permeated every corner of the land and awakened John Quincy to the woes facing American society. "The people are said to be discontented and to complain of taxation, of the salaries of public officers, and of debts public and private," he wrote to his mother. "I suspect that the present form of government will not continue long. . . . The poor complain of its being oppressive. . . . The men of property think the Constitution gives too much liberty to the unprincipled citizen."[13]

The "Constitution," as John Quincy called it, was, in fact, the Articles of Confederation, which the states had signed during the Revolutionary War. The Articles recognized each state as sovereign and independent and left the Continental Congress impotent, with no power to levy taxes— even to pay its troops. Still unpaid at war's end and beset by property taxes, farmers in western Massachusetts had rebelled. A former captain in the war, Daniel Shays, a farmer struggling to keep his property, convinced neighbors that Boston legislators were colluding with judges and lawyers to raise property taxes and foreclose when farmers found it impossible to pay. With that, he exhorted farmers, "Close down the courts!"—and they did. Farmers marched across the state and shut courthouses in Concord,

Worcester, Northampton, Taunton, Great Barrington, and, finally, Cambridge, where John Quincy and other Harvard students watched from the safety of their classroom buildings.

Hailed by farmers across the nation, the shutdowns ended foreclosures in most of Massachusetts. Determined to expand his success and seize control of state government, Shays led a force of five hundred men to Springfield to raid the federal armory. About 1,000 more farmers joined him, but as they approached the arsenal, soldiers unleashed a few artillery blasts that fell short of the approaching farmers but demonstrated the advantages of cannonballs over pitchforks. A militia from Boston then chased the farmers to their homes and captured most of their leaders, although Shays fled to safety in what was then the independent republic of Vermont.

As John Quincy had predicted, fears that Shays's Rebellion would ignite a national uprising spurred Congress to urge revisions in the Articles of Confederation to strengthen federal government powers. On May 25, 1787, delegates from twelve of the thirteen states met in Philadelphia and began writing a new constitution that created a new, more powerful federal government.

In the meantime, John Quincy went to Newburyport, about forty miles northeast of Boston, to study law with the renowned New England attorney Theophilus Parsons, who would later become chief justice of the Massachusetts Supreme Court. One of five Harvard men under Parsons's tutelage, John Quincy enthused at first about "frolicks" with his friends, often serenading as "the bottle went round with unusual rapidity, until a round dozen had disappeared." Nor did women escape his attention, although he rebelled at the popular pastime of so-called kissing games. "'Tis a profanation of one of the most endearing demonstrations of love," he railed in his diary. "A kiss unless warmed by sentiment and enlivened by affection may just as well be given to the air as to the most beautiful or the most accomplished object in the universe."[14] He said he much preferred singing "good, jovial, expressive songs such as we sang at college."[15]

While studying law he began writing poetry, a pastime that quickly became a passion—indeed, one so serious that he considered abandoning his studies and returning to Paris to study literature and become a full-time poet.

"Around her face no wanton Cupids play," he wrote in a poem he called "A Vision"—part of a collection of satirical portraits of nine of his women friends.

> Her tawny skin defies the God of Day.
> Loud was her laugh, undaunted was her look,
> And folly seemed to dictate what she spoke.[16]

He did, of course, study some law, but a prodigious reader like John Quincy consumed so much law so quickly that he filled the rest of his time reading history, including "about fifty pages a day" of Edward Gibbon's six-volume epic *The History of the Decline and Fall of the Roman Empire.* Although his studies of law proved satisfying, ordinary practice—wills, deeds, and bankruptcies—bored him to distraction. "God of heavens!" he complained poetically. "If those are the only terms upon which life can be granted to me, Oh! Take me from this earth before I curse the day of my birth."[17]

After John Quincy's parents learned of their son's growing disenchantment, John Adams felt it was time for him and Abigail to resume their roles as parents, and he wrote to Secretary of State John Jay to end his assignment in Britain. In fact, both Adamses were homesick and missed their boys. They had not seen John Quincy in three years. Four years had passed since John Adams had last seen Charles—then a boy of fourteen—and nine years since he had seen Thomas, who was seven at the time. Charles was now eighteen, Thomas sixteen, and both were in trouble for participating in student riots at Harvard.

On June 17, 1788, John and Abigail Adams landed in Boston. John Adams had not set foot in America for nine years, and Governor John Hancock led Boston—indeed all of America—in welcoming him. Next to George Washington himself, and perhaps Benjamin Franklin, Americans held John Adams in highest esteem. Hancock invited him and Abigail to stay at Hancock House, his lavish mansion on the summit of Beacon Hill overlooking the Common and the rest of Boston. Charles and Thomas rushed over from Harvard to join them, and John Quincy arrived from Newburyport for their first family reunion in nearly a decade.

Offered every public office but the presidency itself—along with many lucrative opportunities in private practice—John Adams made it clear he wanted to serve as the nation's first vice president under George Washington. Accordingly, on January 7, 1789, the Electoral College elected George Washington first President of the United States and John Adams as the nation's first vice president. Three months later, on April 20, 1789, Adams climaxed a weeklong trip from Massachusetts and crossed the bridge onto the northern end of Manhattan Island, where throngs of well-wishers lined the roads to welcome him to New York, the nation's temporary capital. A troop of New York cavalry awaited with Foreign Affairs Secretary John Jay and congressional leaders to escort him southward to the city and his temporary lodgings at Jay's magnificent mansion. The next morning, the Senate's president pro tempore greeted him at Federal Hall and showed him to his chair in the Senate chamber, where he assumed the presidency of that body. A week later, on April 29, Adams witnessed the presidential swearing in and George Washington's first inaugural address.

A year after his father's inauguration, John Quincy passed his bar exams, and on August 9, 1790, he opened a law office in Boston and waited for his family's name and fame to draw a stream of clients to his door.

He waited in vain.

"Very busy with nothing to do," he wrote in his diary. "Long walk, but solitary," he wrote a day later. "Little to do. Reading Cicero."[18]

More than a month later, he found a few clients at the courthouse—all indigent petty criminals who paid him nothing. By mid-November, he had handled fewer than a dozen cases, none of which had yielded a penny, leaving him completely dependent on the £9-per-month allowance that his father had been sending him since his days at Harvard.

"I have a profession without employment," he lamented to his sister Nabby. "The hope of supporting myself [is] probably somewhat distant."[19]

A month later, he wrote to his mother, saying that "there would not be a happier being in the United States . . . could I have just enough business to support my expenses, so as to relieve me from the mortification of being, at my time of life, a burden to my parents."[20]

His father tried to cheer him up: "It is accident commonly which furnishes the first occasions to a young lawyer to spread his reputation."

> I remember it was neither my friends nor patrons among the great and learned: it was Joseph Tirrel the horse jockey who first raised me to fame. . . . Some odd incident, altogether unforeseen and unexpected, will very probably bring you into some popular cause and spread your character with a thousand trumpets at a time. Such a thing may not happen in several years. Meantime, patience, courage.[21]

John Adams tried lifting his son's spirits by giving him power of attorney and control of the family's financial affairs in Braintree and Boston, including management of several income-yielding properties, with a retainer of £25 per quarter. Early in 1791, John Adams and Abigail gave their son another morale booster by inviting him to the national government's new seat in Philadelphia. The visit threw John Quincy back into the midst of the powerful and famous and restored his conviction that he was bound for greatness. He heard debates in Congress, attended Supreme Court proceedings, and dined with such illustrious figures as Elbridge Gerry. He climaxed his visit by joining his parents at dinner with George and Martha Washington at the presidential mansion.

John Quincy returned to Boston with a new sense of excitement. Although his law practice showed no signs of improvement, life in the federal capital had enthralled him, and he decided to force his way into the national political picture. Early in June, he wrote the first of eleven essays he called *Letters of Publicola*, assailing two icons of the American Revolution—Thomas Paine and, of all people, his friend Secretary of State Thomas Jefferson, author of the Declaration of Independence. Paine's pamphlets *Common Sense* and *The Crisis* had roused Americans to fight for independence from

Britain, and to these he had just added another work, *The Rights of Man,* which called for a similar uprising in England to overthrow the monarchy. After Jefferson endorsed it, *The Rights of Man* received widespread distribution in America.

"His intention," John Quincy complained to Boston's *Columbian Centinel,* "appears evidently to be to convince the people of Great Britain that they have neither liberty nor a constitution—that their only possible means to produce these blessings to themselves is to 'topple down headlong' their present government and follow implicitly the example of the French." John Quincy blasted Paine's assumption that the majority of the English people opposed monarchy. "It is somewhat remarkable that, in speaking of the particular right of forming a constitution, Mr. Paine denies to a nation . . . [the] right to establish a government of *hereditary succession.* . . . He supposes the essence of a free government to be the submission of the minority to the will of the majority, [but] in a free government the minority never can be under an obligation to sacrifice their rights to the will of the majority."[22]

John Quincy's attack on Paine caused a furor—in Europe as well as America, coming as it did when the French Revolution was reaching a peak of savagery that sent emotional tremors across the United States. Radicals had seized control of the National Assembly and imprisoned King Louis XVI and his family in their own palace. Two years earlier, most Americans had hailed the French Revolution as an extension of America's own revolution and the spread of democracy to the Old World. Jefferson, the American minister to France at the start of the revolution in July 1789, called it "an illumination of the human mind."[23] In the two years that followed, however, widespread drought combined with national bankruptcy to produce famine, mass unemployment—and mob action. Rioters raged through cities, towns, and villages, looting and burning manors, châteaus, and any other structure that smacked of aristocratic plenty. Although Jefferson dismissed the violence as an unfortunate consequence of social progress, Vice President Adams said the French revolutionaries "make murder itself as indifferent as shooting a plover."[24]

The slaughter appalled President Washington and other American statesmen. Secretary of Treasury Alexander Hamilton condemned radical leaders
of the French Revolution as "assassins reeking with the blood of murdered
fellow citizens."[25]

The American press reflected the divisions in the cabinet. Philadelphia's
Gazette of the United States condemned French atheism, anarchy, and mass
slaughter, while its rival, the *National Gazette*, reminded readers how France
had ensured America's victory over British tyranny in the struggle for liberty
and independence. As groups gathered outside newspaper offices to read the
papers, the French Revolution—and Paine's defense—divided the American
people.

"Perhaps the strongly excited passions of the hour . . . contributed to
the result," John Quincy concluded, but the *Publicola* essays "at once attracted great attention, not less in Europe than in America. They were
reprinted in the papers of New York and Philadelphia . . . and elicited numerous replies. . . . The reputation of *Publicola* spread far beyond the
confines of the United States. No sooner did the papers arrive in England
than they were collected and published in London. . . . Another edition
was . . . published in Glasgow . . . and still a third at Dublin."[26]

As he had hoped, fame thrust John Quincy onto Boston's political stage,
giving him more than enough to do to occupy his time. Although his law
practice did not expand, government officials across the region appointed
him to citizen committees—to improve Boston's police procedures, to recommend redistricting, and to look at so-called blue laws. Braintree asked
him to convert its legal status from a parish to a town, which he promptly
renamed Quincy, after his great-grandfather Colonel John Quincy. He
thrust himself into every major political controversy. After Boston voted to
permit theaters to open and perform plays, the state legislature defied
Bostonians and banned theatrical productions. After police arrested an ac-
tor, "a mob of about two hundred people collected together . . . to pull
down the theater," and John Quincy wrote three newspaper essays that
heaped scorn on the legislative majority and opponents of theater. In con-
trast to his previous stand against anarchy, he called on supporters of the-

ater to commit civil disobedience—urging actors to continue to perform
and audiences to attend. "No obedience is due to an unconstitutional act of
the legislature," he declared—in effect, espousing a concept of nullification
of laws that he would later despise.

John Quincy's essays put his name before Boston's public just as a banking collapse was producing a windfall of legal work from investors trying to
recoup their losses. "The bubble of banking is breaking," he wrote to his
father. "Seven or eight failures have happened within these three days, and
many more are inevitable in the course of the ensuing week. The pernicious
practice of mutual endorsements upon each other's notes has been carried . . . to an extravagant length and is now found to have involved not
only the principals, who have been converting their loans from the bank
into a regular trading stock, but many others who have undertaken to be
their security."[27]

"The late failures in Boston," Abigail beamed as she wrote to her husband after visiting John Quincy, "have thrown some business into the
hands of our son. He is well and grows very fat."[28]

John Quincy Adams grew fatter in the days that followed. By early
1793, events overseas—and their repercussions in America—had intensified the divisions between Americans who supported the French Revolution and its opponents. President George Washington pleaded for national
unity, saying it would be "unwise in the extreme . . . to involve ourselves in
the contests of European nations."[29] When newspapers ignored his pleas,
Washington considered a formal proclamation of neutrality to ensure
American independence from both English and French influence.

In France, Jacobin extremists had seized control of the four-year-old
revolution, overturned the monarchy, sent King Louis XVI to his death on
the guillotine, and discarded the constitution. On February 1, 1793, France
declared war on Britain, Holland, and Spain. Under the Franco-American
alliance of 1778, each nation had pledged to aid the other in the event of an
attack by foreign enemies, and France now demanded that the United States
join her war against Britain. In April, Edmond Genet, the new minister
plenipotentiary to the United States, bypassed normal diplomatic protocol

*French ambassador Edmond Genet arrived in the
United States with secret plans to incite rebellion
against the Washington administration and install a
government that would join France in war against
Britain.* (FROM A NINETEENTH-CENTURY ENGRAVING)

and appealed to the American people to pressure the President and Congress
to join the French war against England.

"In the United States," the French minister cried out, "men still exist
who can say, 'Here a ferocious Englishman slaughtered my father; there
my wife tore her bleeding daughter from the hands of an unbridled Englishman,' and those same men can say, 'Here a brave Frenchman died
fighting for American liberty; here French naval and military power hum-
bled the might of Britain.'"[30]

Secretary of State Jefferson hailed Genet's arrival. "The liberty of the
whole earth depends on the success of the French Revolution," Jefferson
exulted as he urged Washington to support the French. "Nothing should
be spared on our part to attach France to us. Failure to do so would gratify the combination of kings with the spectacle of the only two republics
on earth destroying each other."[31]

Outraged by Jefferson's embrace of French revolutionaries "wading through seas of blood," Treasury Secretary Hamilton argued against American participation, calling it self-destructive. He reminded the President that Britain remained America's most important trading partner, buying the majority of her exports, producing the majority of her imports, and yielding most of the government's revenues through import duties. To war beside France against Britain, Hamilton asserted, was not only economically suicidal but morally indefensible. Riding a wave of popularity in Boston, John Quincy marched into the fray to support the President: "To advise us to engage voluntarily in the war," he declared, "is to aim a dagger at the heart of this country."

> We have a seacoast of twelve hundred miles everywhere open to invasion, and where is the power to protect it? We have a flourishing commerce expanding to every part of the globe, and where will it turn when excluded from every market on earth? We depend upon the returns of that commerce for many necessaries of life, and when those returns shall be cut off, where shall we look for the supply? We are in a great measure destitute of the defensive apparatus of war, and who will provide us with the arms and ammunition that will be indispensable? We feel severely at this moment the burden of our public debt, and where are the funds to support us in the dreadful extremity to which our madness and iniquity would reduce us?[32]

John Quincy's words anticipated those of the President. With the United States all but defenseless, without a navy and only a minuscule army in the West fighting Indians, the President knew he could not risk war with England—or any other nation, for that matter. As John Quincy had noted, the powerful British navy could easily blockade American ports and shut coastal trade, while the British military in Canada could combine with Spanish forces in Florida and Louisiana to sweep across the West and divide it up between them. Washington agreed with Hamilton that France had embarked on an offensive, not a defensive, war and that the Franco-American treaty of 1778 did not apply. He also saw the economic good sense of seeking a rapprochement with England and issued the neutrality proclamation he had been considering.

"It behooves the government of this country," the President told Congress, "to use every means in its power to prevent the citizens . . . from embroiling us with either of these powers [England or France] by endeavoring to maintain a strict neutrality. I therefore require that you will . . . [take] such measures as shall be deemed most likely to effect this desirable purpose . . . without delay."[33]

John Quincy seconded the President, stating that "an impartial and unequivocal neutrality . . . is prescribed to us as a duty."[34]

Genet, however, responded differently, buying boldfaced newspaper advertisements that called on "Friends of France" to ignore Washington's Neutrality Proclamation and enlist in the French service to fight the British. "Does not patriotism call upon us to assist France?" his advertisements asked. "As Sons of Freedom, would it not become our character to lend some assistance to a nation combating to secure their liberty?"[35]

Francophiles across the United States rushed into the streets to protest the President's stance and demand that Congress declare war against Britain. An estimated 5,000 supporters rallied outside Genet's hotel in Philadelphia and set off endless demonstrations that raged through the night into the next day—and the next. Vice President Adams described "the terrorism excited by Genet . . . when 10,000 people in the streets of Philadelphia, day after day, threatened to drag Washington out of his house and effect a revolution in the government or compel it to declare war in favor of the French Revolution and against England." Adams "judged it prudent and necessary to order chests of arms from the war office" to protect his house.[36] Fearing for the safety of his wife and grandchildren, Washington made plans to send them to the safety of Mount Vernon.

Adding to the turmoil was the sudden arrival of the French fleet from the Antilles. Genet ordered gangways lowered and sent French seamen to join Jacobin mobs in the crowded streets. "The town is one continuous scene of riot," the British consul wrote in panic to his foreign minister in London. "The French seamen range the streets by night and by day, armed with cutlasses and commit the most daring outrages. Genet seems ready to raise the tricolor and proclaim himself proconsul. President Washington is unable to enforce any measures in opposition."[37]

As pro-French mobs formed on street corners demanding Washington's head, Genet sent the President an ultimatum "in the name of France" to call Congress into special session to choose between neutrality and war. Genet warned Washington that if he refused to declare war against Britain, Genet would "appeal to the people" to overthrow the government and unite with France. "I have acquired the esteem and the good wishes of all republican Americans by tightening the bonds of fraternity between them and ourselves," Genet ranted. He predicted that Americans would "rally from all sides" to support him and "demonstrate with cries of joy . . . that the democrats of America realize perfectly that their future is ultimately bound with France."[38]

Infuriated by the Frenchman's behavior, John Quincy assailed Genet's "political villainy." In a series of articles, he condemned the Frenchman's activities in America; he labeled as "piracy" and "highway robbery" the attacks on British ships by privateers sponsored by Genet. Writing under the pseudonym "Columbus," John Quincy called Genet "the most implacable and dangerous enemy to the peace and happiness of my country." He called Genet's conduct "obnoxious" and urged the President to demand his recall. "In a country where genuine freedom is enjoyed," John Quincy declared, "it is unquestionably the right of every individual citizen to express without control his sentiments upon public measures and the conduct of public men. . . . The privilege ought not, however . . . to be extended to the conduct of foreign ministers."[39]

John Quincy's articles "attracted much attention in the principal cities of the continent and drew forth many comments," he recalled in his memoirs. "It fell under the eye of Washington, then . . . anxiously considering the very same class of questions in a cabinet almost equally divided in opinion. He seems to have been impressed by the proof of Mr. Adams's powers to such an extent as to mark him out for the public service at an early opportunity."[40]

John Quincy's articles generated national and international comment, with Boston Federalists embracing him—and even naming him the city's official July 4 orator, the highest nonelective honor Bostonians conferred on one of their own each year. With his oratory, John Quincy pleased Federalists and Antifederalists alike by predicting that American liberty would soon inspire oppressed peoples in Europe to mirror the American Revolution.

In the weeks that followed, President Washington reacted fiercely to Edmond Genet's activities, demanding—and obtaining—his recall by the French government. Washington also accepted Jefferson's resignation. To Washington's relief, a new French ambassador, Jean-Antoine-Joseph Fauchet, arrived in Philadelphia at the beginning of 1794—with a warrant for Genet's arrest and a guillotine aboard ship to punish him for his indiscretions as French minister. Genet pleaded with the new secretary of state, Edmund Randolph, not to enforce the warrant, all but sobbing that a former Paris police chief was waiting below deck on Fauchet's ship, sharpening a blade to sever his neck. A former Virginia governor and close friend of Washington, Randolph turned to the President for guidance.

"We ought not to wish his punishment," Washington decided generously, granting the Frenchman political asylum and the protection of the government he had tried to overthrow.[41] Fearing Fauchet's agents would kidnap him, Genet sneaked out of Philadelphia during the night and found his way to a secluded hideaway on a friend's farm in Bristol, Connecticut, where he temporarily disappeared from public view. With Genet's disappearance, the Francophile press in the East ended its provocations, and rioters all but vanished from the streets of eastern cities.

Although John Quincy's articles attacking Genet had impressed President Washington, they apparently did not please John Adams. Worried that his son was focusing less on building his law practice than writing newspaper essays without recompense, John Adams admonished John Quincy and reiterated his ambitions for his son's rise to national leadership and the presidency. "The mediocrity of fortune that you profess ought not to content you. You come into life with advantages which will disgrace

President George Washington appointed John Quincy Adams American minister to Holland and set the young man on the path to a life of public service. (LIBRARY OF CONGRESS)

you if your success is mediocre. And if you do not rise to the head not only of your profession but of your country it will be owing to your own *Laziness, Slovenliness* and *Obstinacy*" (his italics and caps).[42]

John Adams had no sooner posted his letter when news arrived that made him regret having written it, and trembling with excitement, he quickly scratched out a second letter to his son:

President Washington is determined to nominate you to go to Holland as Resident Minister. . . .

The salary is 4500 dollars a year. . . . Your knowledge of Dutch and French, your education in that country, your acquaintance with my old friends there will give you many advantages. . . . It will require all your prudence and all your other virtues as well as all your talents. It will be expected that you come here to see the President and secretary of state before you embark. I shall write you as soon as the nomination is made and advised by the Senate. Be secret. Don't open your mouth to any human being on the subject except your Mother.[43]

Impressed by young Adams's writings, Washington had first considered naming him U.S. District Attorney for New England, but after reviewing the young man's early experiences with his father and Francis Dana in Europe and recognizing his command of French, Dutch, and German as assets possessed by few Americans in government, he decided to send John Quincy to Holland. The assignment would not require critical decisions, but it would put John Quincy in a key listening post in Europe's swirling diplomatic cosmos—a perfect assignment for a young diplomat with John Quincy's credentials.

At first, John Quincy believed that his father had arranged the appointment, and he writhed with anger, disgust, and shame. He soon learned, however, that his appointment "had been as unexpected to him [his father] as to myself and that he had never uttered a word upon which a wish on his part could be presumed that a public office should be conferred upon me." Indeed, the elder Adams knew nothing of Washington's decision until notified by Secretary of State Randolph three days before the Senate confirmation. After reassuring himself that Washington had appointed his son solely on the basis of the young man's qualifications, John Adams let his pride pour onto the pages of a letter to his son, saying that the appointment was "the result of the President's own observations and reflections . . . as proof that sound principles in morals and government are cherished by the executive of the United States and that study, science and literature are recommendations which will not be overlooked."

It will be a serious trust. . . . It ought to make a deep impression. . . . Such trusts are sacred. . . . The law of nations and diplomatic researches should engage his early attention as well as the Dutch language, but especially every thing relative to the interests of the U.S. A few years spent in the present grade will recommend him to advancement to higher stages and larger spheres. The interests, views and motions of the belligerent powers will engage his constant attention and employ all his sagacity. He must consult with the President. . . . He must attend a little to his dress and person. No man alive is more attentive to these things than the President. . . . I shall drop hints from time to time for I have many things to say.[44]

When he had emptied his mind, heart, and soul of advice, Adams concluded,

It is a serious trust that is about to be committed to you. I hope you will reflect upon it with due attention, collect yourself, let no little weakness escape you, and devote yourself to the service of your country. And may the blessing of heaven attend you.

So prays your affectionate father, John Adams.[45]

Her son's appointment moved Abigail as much as it had her husband, and, unable to contain her excitement, she wrote to Martha Washington "acknowledging the honor conferred . . . by the President."

I have the satisfaction to say to you, Madam, perhaps with the fond partiality of a parent, that I do not know in any one instance of his conduct either at home or abroad that he has given me any occasion of regret, and I hope from his prudence, honor, integrity and fidelity that he will never discredit the character so honorably conferred upon him. Painful as the circumstance of a separation from him will be to me, Madam, I derive a satisfaction from the hope of his becoming eminently useful to his country.[46]

John Quincy Adams closed his law office and plunged headlong into the world of diplomacy and government. To his delight, he found himself mixing, as he had in his youth, with some of the world's most celebrated political figures, at one moment engaged in discussions with the President of the United States and the secretary of state; at another, meeting with Treasury Secretary Hamilton or Secretary of War Henry Knox; then sharing tea with such visiting dignitaries as the enigmatic Charles-Maurice de Talleyrand-Perigord, or more simply Talleyrand.

Born an aristocrat, Talleyrand had been a French Catholic bishop before discarding his clerical robes and renouncing the church in favor of secularism and revolution. A member of the revolutionary National Assembly, he went to England as a special emissary of the Jacobins but paid a few too many visits to the lavish London quarters of the Duc d'Orléans, pretender to the French throne. When Talleyrand returned to France, Jacobins accused him of royalist collaboration, and he fled the guillotine for America, having only just arrived when he met John Quincy. Although he fully expected a presidential reception worthy of his aristocratic lineage, Washington refused to see him because reception of exiled aristocrats might be seen as a public rebuff of the French revolutionary government. Talleyrand twisted the President's rejection into a deep hatred of all things American—even the women, whom he described as "adorable at fifteen, faded at twenty-three, old at thirty-five, decrepit at forty or forty-five, losing their shape, their teeth and their hair." He would soon direct his hatred for America toward John Quincy's father.[47]

John Quincy spent the rest of the summer of 1794 studying State Department documents and meeting with Secretary of State Randolph. Randolph told John Quincy to stop in London on his way to The Hague and deliver a trunk load of documents for former chief justice John Jay, the former secretary of state, who was negotiating a new treaty with Britain. Relations between the two nations had soured since they had signed the 1783 peace treaty, whose terms both Britain and the United States had openly violated. American state courts were first to violate them by blocking collection of prerevolution debts by British merchants and payment of compensation to loyalists for confiscation of their properties and estates. The British, in turn, retaliated by refusing to abandon military posts in the Northwest Territory in Ohio, Indiana, and Illinois and, worse, inciting Indian attacks on American settlers in the area. Relations between the two nations deteriorated still more after the outbreak of war between England and France provoked the British navy to seize neutral ships trading with France and the French West Indies. By April 1794, when Washington sent John Jay to England, the British had seized more than 250 American ships and impressed hundreds of American sailors into the British navy.

Unnerved by the prospect of being alone and all but friendless in Holland for three years, John Quincy asked his brother Thomas Boylston—the youngest of the three Adams boys—to come to Europe with him as an aide. Thomas had graduated from Harvard, studied law, and passed his bar exams in Philadelphia, where he had planned to open a law office. Their mother Abigail was delighted with John Quincy's offer to his younger brother. "I have always wished that your brother might have an opportunity of going abroad," she wrote to John Quincy, "and as you are inclined to have him accompany you, I think . . . you may be mutually beneficial to each other, and it will not be so solitary to you. I will not take my own personal feelings into the question. Whatever may be for the benefit of my children I acquiesce to." Abigail began to cry as she pleaded, "Let me hear from you by every . . . "She then crossed out the word "every" and wrote "post"—"Let me hear from you by the post."

Shaken by the prospect of losing her oldest and youngest sons, she added, "I have a request to make of you and your brother. If there is a miniature painter . . . sit for your likenesses . . . and give them to Mr. Anthony to set with a lock of each of your hairs to be put on the back together with your names. . . . You must spare time for it if possible."[48]

John Quincy attended to every detail but the portraits as he prepared to leave for Europe. His father sent him one last message of advice. "The post at the Hague," he enthused to his son, "is an important diplomatic station which may afford many opportunities of acquiring political information and of penetrating the designs of many cabinets in Europe."

In three or four years you may be promoted to the rank of minister plenipotentiary—possibly in less time if you discover to the President talents and principles for so high a trust. . . . I would not advise you to fix any unalterable resolutions except in favor of virtue and integrity and unchangeable love to your country. . . . Endeavor to obtain correspondences with able men in the southern and middle states as well as the northern ones and these will inform and advise you. If my life should be spared, I hope to be one of them and will give you my best opinions and advice as circumstances occur. I wish you a pleasant voyage and much honor, satisfaction and success in your mission. I am with constant affection, your friend and father, John Adams.[49]

On September 17, 1794, twenty-seven-year-old John Quincy Adams, an independent man at last, departed for Europe. His father sent him and Thomas a farewell note:

I once more wish you a prosperous voyage and a happy life. Remember your characters as men of business as well as men of virtue, and always depend on the affection and friendship of your father.[50]

Strengthened by his father's blessing, John Quincy sailed off to help guide his nation's destiny as one of the first ministers of its embryonic foreign service, but the storms of war blackened the seas ahead and seemed to bode ill for his mission to keep America free of foreign intrigues and war.

CHAPTER 5

$\mathcal{N}$ever Was a
Father More Satisfied

The entire world seemed aboil as John Quincy Adams's ship bounded into the dark Atlantic toward Europe. As he and his brother saw their native land slip over the horizon, war and revolution engulfed the world. Behind them in America, rebel torches had set skies aglow in western Pennsylvania to protest a federal tax on whiskey. Congress had imposed it without the consent of the states—much as Parliament had imposed the stamp tax without the consent of the colonies thirty years earlier in 1765. Adding to the turmoil, Indian tribes had swept across Ohio, Indiana, and Illinois, attacking white settlements. Although Britain had ceded the territory to the United States after the Revolutionary War, British troops had remained and fostered the Indian attacks to harass the new American government and provoke its collapse.

In Europe, meanwhile, the revolutionary zeal of Maximilian Robespierre's Jacobins had metamorphosed into insanity, with Robespierre striding into the Convention, or national assembly, and demanding the arrest and execution of every member. By then, the number of widows

and orphans created by the guillotine had reached staggering proportions; they and tens of thousands of ordinary citizens who had gone into
hiding to escape the blade suddenly emerged en masse and marched to
the Convention doors roaring, "À bas Robespierre!" ("Down with Robespierre!"). Facing the same fate on the guillotine whether or not they continued to shy before Robespierre's schizophrenic screams, a handful of
Convention delegates summoned the courage to demand his arrest and
that of each of his terrorist confederates. To the surprise of all, the rest of
the Convention stood and shouted their agreement. Puzzled soldiers in
the Convention hall looked at each other, then sided with the delegates
and led the psychotic Norman lawyer away in chains. The following day,
July 28, 1794, troops loyal to the Convention carted Robespierre, his
brother, and twenty of his political allies to the guillotine for execution.
The guillotine claimed the heads of seventy more Robespierre confederates the following day. Although the French people celebrated by mas-
sacring hundreds more Jacobins across the nation, the slaughter did not
end the famine that gripped the nation, and the new revolutionary government that took over from Robespierre—a five-man Directory that
included Corsican general Napoléon Bonaparte—proclaimed an end to
private property.

"The earth belongs to no one; its fruits belong to every one," declared
François Noël Babeuf. "There is but one sun, one air for all to breath. Let
us end the disgusting distinctions between rich and poor . . . masters and
servants, governor and governed."[1] As the poor rose in rebellion and
joined equally deprived soldiers in rioting, Napoléon rallied them to his
banner, assuaging their anger and hunger with promises of rich pastures
across French borders: "You have no shoes, uniforms, shirts and almost no
bread," he called out to his followers.

> Our stores are empty while those of our enemies are overflowing. I will
> lead you into the most fertile plains in the world. Rich provinces and
> great cities will be in your power. There you will find honor, glory and
> wealth. It is up to you to conquer. *Marchons!*[2]

At Napoléon's command, French revolutionary armies poured into neighboring Dutch, Austrian, German, and Italian territories, pillaging farmlands, villages, and towns. Royal armies seemed helpless.

"The war has not been very favorable to the glory of sovereigns," John Quincy said, observing the obvious.[3]

Thomas Adams wrote to his mother to calm her fears. "Holland will negotiate the most favorable terms with the French that they can, but it scarce admits a doubt that the French will be able to impose what terms they please. It will not be a pleasant thing to reside in that country at this period, but . . . we may chance to escape molestation."[4]

Meanwhile, the French navy warred with Britain on the high seas and provoked the British to attack and seize ships they suspected of trading with their enemy—neutrals as well as belligerents. Apart from preventing arms and ammunition from reaching France, the British intended to halt the flow of foodstuffs and starve the French into submission. With each American ship the British seized, they impressed dozens of English-speaking seamen into the Royal Navy, and without a navy of its own to protect her merchant fleet, the United States could not retaliate.

A month before John Quincy Adams left for Europe, President Washington acted decisively to end the turmoil on American soil. He ordered Major General "Mad" Anthony Wayne to attack Indians in the West, and on August 20, Wayne's legion of 1,000 marksmen crushed the Indian force and sent surviving warriors reeling westward. Buoyed by Wayne's victory, President Washington ordered Treasury Secretary Alexander Hamilton to assemble a fighting force to attack the whiskey rebels outside Pittsburgh. On September 19, with John Quincy two days out to sea, nearly 13,000 troops from four states converged on Carlisle and Bedford, Pennsylvania, and at 10 a.m. on September 30, Washington took field command of the army—the first and last American President to do so. Only at the last minute did he cede command when aides warned him he was too important to the nation to risk injury or death in battle.

At Washington's side was Hamilton, who had first served Washington as a twenty-two-year-old captain seventeen years earlier during the

Revolutionary War, which also began as a protest against taxes. Now, as secretary of the Treasury, Hamilton had imposed—and Washington had endorsed—a tax that provoked a similar rebellion, which the two old comrades in arms were determined to crush. The irony was not lost on either man.

By early December, an elated vice president wrote to his son, "Our army under Wayne has beaten the Indians and the militia have subdued the insurgents, a miserable though numerous rabble." Abigail Adams was equally enthusiastic: "The insurgency is suppressed in Pennsylvania . . . [and] General Wayne's victory over the savages has had a happy effect upon our tawny neighbors. . . . The aspect of our country is peace and plenty. The view is delightful and the more so when contrasted with the desolation and carnage which overspread a great proportion of the civilized world."[5]

Both parents enthused over their son's career. "Your rising reputation at the bar," John Adams wrote to his son, "your admired writings upon occasional subjects of great importance, and your political influence among the younger gentlemen of Boston sometimes make me regret your promotion and the loss of your society to me." He signed it, "With a tender affection as well as great esteem, I am, my dear son, your affectionate father John Adams." Abigail ended her letter with the hope that "you will not omit any opportunity of writing to her whose happiness is so intimately blended with your prosperity and who at all times is your ever affectionate Mother Abigail Adams."[6]

Although John Quincy's ship developed leaks "like a water spout," he and his brother landed safely in Dover on October 14, less than a month after leaving Massachusetts. As their coach from shipside reached London Bridge, however, "we heard a rattling . . . a sound as of a trunk falling from the carriage. My brother immediately alighted and found the trunk of dispatches under the carriage. . . . Our driver assured us that the trunks could not have fallen unless the straps had been cut away." The incident left John Quincy shaken:

John Quincy Adams, at twenty-nine, sailed to Europe to assume the post his father had once held as American minister to Holland. (AFTER A PORTRAIT BY JOHN SINGLETON COPLEY; NATIONAL PARKS SERVICE, ADAMS NATIONAL HISTORICAL PARK)

Entrusted with dispatches of the highest importance . . . to negotiations between the two countries, with papers particularly committed to my care *because* they were highly confidential by the President of the United States . . . with what face could I have presented myself to the minister for whom they were intended? . . . The story would be resounded from one end of the United States to the other.[7]

His memoirs go on interminably, as he relived the incident and postulated how "the straps were cut by an invisible hand."[8] Adams was immensely relieved to deliver the trunk to John Jay's quarters the next morning, along with papers for Thomas Pinckney, the American minister plenipotentiary in Britain.

Far from being in "a situation of small trust and confidence," as he had feared when he accepted his assignment in Holland, John Quincy Adams spent the next three days helping to determine the fate of his nation with Chief Justice John Jay and U.S. ambassador to England Thomas Pinckney, former governor of South Carolina. Together they put the finishing touches on a treaty that would set the course of Anglo-American relations—and, indeed, much of the Western world—for the foreseeable future.

Jay had arrived in London four months earlier, on June 6, and obtained the British government's agreement to exclude noncontraband goods from the ban on American trade with France and the French West Indies. He had also won three other major concessions: withdrawal of British troops behind the Canadian border from the Northwest Territory, limited resumption of American trade with the British East and West Indies, and establishment of a most-favored-nation relationship between the two nations, with preferential tariffs for each. Both sides agreed to set up a joint commission and accept binding arbitration to settle British and American financial claims against each other. The treaty made no mention of two issues that had long provoked American anger toward Britain: impressment of American sailors into the British navy and failure to compensate southern planters for thousands of slaves the British had carried away during the Revolutionary War. The slave issue lay behind the fanatical southern support for France and the willingness—indeed, eagerness—of southerners to join France in war against Britain.

Although Jay had hoped to win concessions on both issues, he recognized that Britain had little incentive to yield on either. Aside from her economic and military power, Britain had scored an important naval victory over the French fleet that left British warships in full command of the Atlantic Ocean, with no need to cede privileges to weaker nations.

"As a treaty of commerce," John Quincy concluded, "we shall never obtain anything more favorable. . . . It is much below the standard which I think would be advantageous to the country, but with some alterations which are marked down . . . it is preferable to a war. The commerce with their West India Islands . . . will be of great importance."[9]

John Quincy left with his brother for Holland on October 29, arriving in The Hague two days later and settling into their official quarters. He had effectively established himself as American minister by January 19, 1795, when General Charles Pichegru, commander of the French Army of the North, marched into the Dutch capital with a contingent of 2,000 to 3,000 soldiers. Their arrival caused so little disruption that John Quincy's brother Thomas went to theater the following evening with the American consul general, Sylvanus Bourne. A day later, John Quincy went with Thomas and Bourne to the French authorities, who told them "they received the visit of the *citoyen ministre* of a free people, the friend of the *peuple français* with much pleasure. That they considered it *tout à fait une visite fraternelle.*"*

> The substance of the business was that I demanded safety and protection to all American persons and property in this country, and they told me . . . that all property would be respected, as well as persons and opinions. . . . They spoke of the President, whom, like all Europeans, they called General Washington . . . that he was a great man and they had veneration for his character.[10]

General Pichegru had served with French forces in the American Revolution and was true to his word, doing nothing to interfere with John Quincy's activities or those of other Americans in Holland. Despite the presence of French troops, The Hague proved to be exactly what Secretary of State Edmund Randolph and President Washington had anticipated—a listening post in the heart of Europe, and for John Quincy Adams, it proved the perfect first post in the diplomatic service. His academic training combined with his knowledge of languages and an extraordinary memory to accumulate names, descriptions, and thinking of dozens of

---

*"Altogether a fraternal visit."

diplomats from everywhere in Europe, along with invaluable military and political intelligence from warring parties and other sectors of the continent. "Dined with the French generals Pichegru, Elbel, Sauviac," the pages of his journal disclose, "and a Colonel . . .

" . . . the Dutch general Constant and a colonel Comte d'Autremont . . .

" . . . the minister of Poland Midleton . . .

" . . . the Prussian secretary Baron Bielefeld . . .

" . . . the Russian minister . . .

"The French made use of balloons during the last campaign in discovering the positions of their adverse armies . . . Pichegru and the other generals assured us on the strongest terms that it was of no service at all. . . . 'Oh! yes,' said Sauviac, 'the effect was infallible in the gazettes.'"[11]

John Quincy spent as many as six hours a day writing reports, which included twenty-seven letters to the secretary of state from November 1794 to August 1795 and ten long, explicit letters to his father, the vice president. He emerged as one of Europe's most skilled diplomats and America's finest intelligence gleaner. He prophesied that while Britain and France wore each other down in war, America would grow and prosper. "At the present moment, if our neutrality is preserved," he predicted, "ten more years will place the United States among the most powerful and opulent nations on earth."[12]

John Quincy's reports elated his father. "Never was a father more satisfied or gratified," Vice President John Adams wrote to John Quincy in the spring of 1795, "than I have been with the kind attention of my sons."

> Since they went abroad, I have no language to express to you the pleasure I have received from the satisfaction you have given the President and secretary of state, as well as from the clear, comprehensive, and masterly accounts in your letters to me of the public affairs of nations in Europe, whose situation and politics it most concerns us to know. Go on, my son, and by a diligent exertion of your genius and abilities, continue to deserve well of your father but especially of your country.[13]

In addition to visits, dinners, and other social events with diplomats and French officers, John Quincy continued his studies, reading histories of every European state while adding Spanish to the three other languages he was able to read and speak. "The voice of all Europe," he discovered, had hailed President George Washington's Neutrality Proclamation. Although it had not attracted much attention initially, it quickly established a new principle of international law as well as American constitutional law. Although rules abounded governing relations between warring nations, the world had ignored the rights of neutrals until George Washington raised the issue.

"The nations that have been grappling together with the purpose of mutual destruction," John Quincy wrote, "are feeble, exhausted, and almost starving. Those that have had the wisdom to maintain neutrality have reasons more than ever to applaud their policy, and some of them may thank the United States for the example from which it was pursued."[14]

As the end of his first year in the diplomatic service approached, John Quincy was quite content with his new career. Although he called Holland "insignificant" in comparison to diplomatic posts in Paris and London, he told his father that it was "adequate to my talents . . . without being tedious or painful . . . and leaves me leisure to pursue a course of studies that may be recommended by its amusement or utility. Indeed, Sir, it is a situation in itself much preferable to that of . . . a lawyer's office for business which . . . is scarcely sufficient to give bread and procures more curses than thanks."[15]

To his surprise, John Quincy's next set of State Department orders emanated from a new secretary of state—Timothy Pickering of Massachusetts, whom Washington had named to replace John Randolph. Randolph had resigned following charges he had accepted bribes from the French government. For John Quincy Adams, the appointment was not unpleasant. Born in Salem, Pickering was a Harvard graduate and lawyer, a staunch Federalist who had served with distinction in the Revolutionary War and as postmaster general before becoming secretary of war early in 1795.

Pickering asked John Quincy to travel to London in the absence of American minister Thomas Pinckney to execute the formal exchange of signed copies of the Jay Treaty with the British government. Pinckney had gone to Spain to negotiate a treaty giving Americans navigation rights on the Mississippi River.

When the terms of the Jay Treaty became known in America in March 1795, Washington loyalists hailed Jay for averting another brutal war with England and forcing Britain to deal with the United States for the first time as an equal and independent sovereign state. But as Washington and Jay both knew it would, the treaty provoked a storm of controversy over what it did not accomplish—especially among advocates for states' rights, Francophiles, and Anglophobes, all of whom attacked the treaty as pro-British. Washington loyalists in the Senate, however, outnumbered opponents, and the Senate ratified the treaty on June 24—ironically, just as Jay himself slipped away from the fray over foreign affairs by winning election as governor of New York.

By then, the savagery of the French Revolution had eroded popular support for the French in America, while the Jay Treaty with Britain was producing economic benefits. In the West, Britain's troop pullback into Canada had ended the flow of arms to hostile Indians. Without British military support, the Indians ceded most of Ohio, Indiana, Illinois, and Michigan to the United States, ending Indian forays in the West and opening the vast Ohio and Mississippi river valleys to American settlement. Meanwhile, Thomas Pinckney won Spain's agreement to free Mississippi River navigation for Americans and to allow them to deposit goods in New Orleans for export overseas. Elated by the prospects of a western economic boom, Americans quickly forgot their objections to the Jay Treaty.

Although John Quincy had set out for England on October 20 to exchange copies of the signed treaties, ill winds and a variety of dockside misunderstandings prevented his reaching London until November 11, by which time Pinckney's secretary had completed the transaction. All that remained was the ceremonial presentation of the document to the king. Early in December, British undersecretary of foreign affairs George Hammond, a cunning and vicious anti-American whom John Quincy knew from the 1783 Paris peace talks, summoned Adams to his office. Although Hammond had been England's first minister to the United States in 1791 and had married a Philadelphian, his efforts to undermine the American government seemed to know no bounds. He lost no time trying to trap John Quincy in an indiscretion by asking if he had heard of the President's "intending to resign" in the wake of the Genet affair.

"No!" John Quincy replied simply and sharply.

"What sort of a soul does this man suppose I have?" John Quincy confided to his diary that night. "He talked of Virginians, the southern people, the Democrats, but I let him know that I consider them all in no other light than as Americans." He asked whether Pinckney had worked out an agreement with Spain, then hammered John Quincy with rumors of a political revolt against George Washington. John Quincy deftly parried Hammond's thrusts.

"All governments have their opposition who find fault with everything," John Quincy said nonchalantly. "Who has better reason to know that than you in this country?" he smiled condescendingly. "But in America, you know, opposition speaks in a louder voice than anywhere else. Everything comes out; we have not lurking dissatisfaction that works in secret and is not seen, nothing that rankles at the heart while the face wears a smile so that a very trifling opposition makes a great show."[16]

"Hammond is a man of intrigue," John Quincy reported in his diary. "His question whether Mr. Pinckney has signed the treaty in Spain, implies at least that he knows there was a treaty to sign. . . . If I stay here anytime, he will learn to be not quite so impertinent."[17] Adams surmised that Hammond was either intercepting his mail or having him followed. He determined to be more discreet in what he did, said, and wrote.

In fact, Hammond's intelligence was better than John Quincy's—and even better than that of Vice President John Adams. On January 5, a month after Hammond had met with John Quincy, John Adams wrote to Abigail, "I have this day heard news that is of some importance. It must be kept a secret wholly to yourself. One of the ministry told me that the

President was solemnly determined to serve no longer than the end of his present period. . . . You know the consequence of this to me and to yourself. Either we must enter into ardors more trying than any ever yet experienced or retire to Quincy, farmers for life. I am . . . determined not to serve under Jefferson. . . . I will not be frightened out of the public service nor will I be disgraced in it."[18]

Far from expressing joy at her husband's thinking, Abigail quoted a warning from Charles Churchill's epic poem *Gotham*:

> You know what is before you: "the whips and scorpions, the thorns without roses, the dangers, anxieties and weight of empire"—and can you acquire influence sufficient as the poet further describes: "to still the voice of discord in the land"?[19]

The day after meeting with Hammond, John Quincy presented his credentials to King George III before addressing him with prepared remarks: "Sir. To testify to your majesty the sincerity of the United States of America in their negotiations, their President has directed me . . . " and he went on to give the king a copy of the Jay Treaty along with a letter from President Washington.

"To give you my answer, Sir," the king responded with a typically noncommittal royal reply, "I am very happy to have the assurances of their sincerity, for without that, you know, there would be no such things as dealings among men."[20]

In France, however, the Directory responded angrily to the Jay Treaty, insisting it was a violation of "the alliance which binds the two peoples." The French recalled their ambassador, and when the American government retaliated by recalling ambassador James Monroe, the French ordered seizure of all American ships sailing into French waters, with confiscation of all cargoes and imprisonment of American seamen for ransom.

While waiting for Pinckney's return to London, John Quincy went to hear debates at the House of Commons and visited Joshua Johnson, the wealthy Maryland merchant who lived near the Tower of London in a lavish brick mansion, where he also served as American consul. Staffed by eleven servants, Johnson's home was a center of opulence and hospitality for visiting diplomats and other dignitaries. John Quincy had first met Johnson in 1781 as a fourteen-year-old, when he and his father were in Nantes, awaiting passage to America after John Adams's first diplomatic assignment in Paris. Johnson's three oldest daughters—barely more than infants when John Quincy first met them—had blossomed into attractive young ladies. Burdened with four other, younger girls and a young son, the Johnsons were eager to marry off their three oldest, and they welcomed the son of America's vice president with great warmth. They invited him to their oldest daughter's birthday ball, where John Quincy "danced till 3 in the morning" and found "Mr. Johnson's daughters pretty and agreeable. The oldest performs admirably on the pianoforte; the second, Louisa, sings; the third plays the harp."[21]

Evidently enchanted by the three girls, he spent part of almost every succeeding day or evening in January with the Johnsons, playing cards, walking in the park, and accompanying them to theater, concerts, and balls. Although the Johnsons expected he would marry their oldest daughter, John Quincy surprised the entire family on February 2, 1796, by telling twenty-year-old Louisa Catherine, the Johnsons' second daughter, that he intended to marry her.

Louisa was beautiful, cultured, and fluent in French, the language of diplomats. Musically talented, elegant in dress, bearing, and manners, she was quiet and respectful in the presence of gentlemen and a lively conversationalist when appropriate. And she was comfortable among the rich and powerful. For John Quincy, a rising star in the diplomatic world, Louisa Catherine Johnson, the English-born daughter of an American diplomat, seemed a perfect match.

In his letters home, John Quincy only hinted of a liaison at first, without identifying Louisa. Fearing her son's intended was English and would destroy his prospects for political success in America, Abigail fretted, "I would hope for the love I bear my country, that the siren is at least *half-blood*."[22] With memories of Bunker's Hill and the Boston occupation

*Twenty-year-old Louisa Catherine Johnson, the
English-born daughter of the American consul
in London, caught John Quincy Adams's eye, and
he proposed marriage to her in February 1796.*
(PORTRAIT BY EDWARD SAVAGE, NATIONAL PARKS
SERVICE, ADAMS NATIONAL HISTORICAL PARK)

swirling in her head, Abigail still despised the British. John Quincy's father was more philosophical than his wife, however. "Alas! Poor John!" he
remarked to Abigail. "If the young man really loves her, I will not thwart
him. . . . Ambition and love live together well. . . . A man may be mad
with both at once. . . . His father and his mother too know what it is. . . .
Witness Caesar and Anthony with Cleopatra and many others."[23]

A letter from John Quincy eventually calmed both their fears:

Your apprehensions as to the tastes and sentiments of my friend [were]
perfectly natural, and all your observations on the subject were received
by me with gratitude, as I know them to proceed from serious concern

and the purest parental affection. . . . But she has goodness of heart and gentleness of disposition as well as spirit and character and with those qualities, I shall venture upon the chances of success and hope you will find her . . . such a daughter as you would wish for your son.[24]

Moved by his letter, Abigail answered contritely, "I consider her already as my daughter." She went on to ask for a miniature portrait and lock of her future daughter-in-law's hair.[25] John Adams also sent his blessing, telling his son, "You are now of age to judge for yourself; and whether you return [to England] and choose her or whether you choose elsewhere, your deliberate choice will be mine."[26]

Although Louisa had wanted to marry immediately, John Quincy refused, insisting he could not consider marriage until he was financially secure. His salary, he insisted, was not enough to afford proper lodgings for a minister and his wife, let alone a wife used to luxuries. His plan was to finish his three-year assignment in Holland and, in 1797, return to Massachusetts, reestablish his law practice, and then marry. A month after John Quincy had proposed, he spent one last "evening of delight and of regret, and I took my leave of the [Johnson] family with sensations unusually painful."[27]

"On my return from England," he wrote in his diary, "I determined to resume a life of applications to business and study,"[28] and, indeed, he reveled in the calm and relaxation of intense, solitary study. "To improve in the Dutch language, I have usually translated a page every day. . . . My progress in Italian is slow. . . . The language is enchanting. . . . To keep alive my Latin, I have begun to translate a page of Tacitus every day . . . into French."[29]

His official duties seldom required more than a few hours a day. He wrote to the *Leyden Gazette*, for example, protesting an article asserting that "disgust at the ingratitude of the American people had induced General Washington to retire from his eminent station." John Quincy asked the editor to "have the goodness to correct . . . an imputation both injurious to the President and people of the United States."

The reasons assigned by the President himself for declining to be viewed as a candidate for the approaching election are his time of life, his strong inclinations towards a retired life, and the peaceable, calm and prosperous state of affairs in that country. . . . The imputation of disgust to General Washington and of ingratitude to the Americans is merely the calumny of English spirits beholding the felicity of the Americans.[30]

As summer neared its end, John Quincy learned that George Washington had promoted him from minister to minister plenipotentiary, with a new assignment in Lisbon, Portugal, to begin in the spring of 1797. His salary would double to $9,000 a year and allow him an additional $4,500 a year for expenses—enough to marry Louisa and take her with him to his new post. The promotion was not only a reward for his good work and steadfast loyalty to the President's policies; it was the President's way of publicly demonstrating his confidence in John Quincy's diplomatic skills. Although reluctant to postpone his return to America by another three years, John Quincy agreed to take the post after his brother Thomas promised to go as well.

"I am still delighted with your facts, your opinions, and your principles," Vice President John Adams wrote to his son. "You need not be anxious about the succession to the presidency. . . . No man who has been mentioned or thought of, but has a just value of your merits. Even if your father should be the person, he will not so far affect a disinterest as to injure you. If Jefferson, Henry, Jay, Hamilton or Pinckney should be elected, your honor and promotion will be in no hazard."[31]

On September 19, 1796, the *American Daily Advertiser* published President Washington's Farewell Address stating emphatically that he would not serve after his second term in office. He also warned Americans of the dangers of divisive political parties at home and urged them to unite in a "fraternal union." In foreign affairs, he urged keeping the United States a perennially neutral nation, out of foreign wars and with no long-term ties to any foreign nations.

In the vicious election campaign that followed, Federalists supported Vice President John Adams, who pledged to continue Washington's policy of rapprochement with Britain within the context of neutrality in foreign conflicts. Adams's chief opponent was former secretary of state Thomas Jefferson, who called himself a Democrat-Republican, supported the French Revolution, and sought closer ties to France, regardless of the effects on trade with England.

French minister Pierre August Adet tried to influence the election with pamphlets urging Americans to vote for Jefferson but only succeeded in provoking widespread revulsion against France and eroding the influence of Francophiles in America. Federalists demonized Adet and warned that a Jefferson presidency would be "fatal to our independence, now that the interference of a foreign nation in our affairs is no longer disguised."[32] The *Connecticut Courant* warned that the French minister was trying to "wean us from the government and administrators of our own choice and make us willing to be governed by such as France shall think best for us—beginning with Jefferson."[33] Even Republicans were offended by Adet's meddling, with one of them railing that Adet had destroyed Jefferson's chances for election and "irretrievably diminished the good will felt for his government and the people of France."[34]

In the end, John Adams eked out a victory over Thomas Jefferson by three Electoral College votes, by rule relegating Jefferson to the vice presidency.

In the days before the election, Abigail Adams had repeatedly warned her son not to demand any special consideration if his father won, and John Quincy had responded accordingly: "I hope my ever dear and honored mother . . . that upon the contingency of my father's being placed in the first magistracy, I shall never give him any trouble by solicitation for office of any kind."

> Your late letters have repeated so many times that I shall in that case have nothing to expect that I am afraid you have imagined it possible that I might form expectations from such an event. I had hoped that *my mother*

President John Adams, America's second President,
ignored charges of nepotism and, on the advice of
George Washington, retained his son John Quincy
Adams in America's foreign diplomatic corps.
(LIBRARY OF CONGRESS)

knew me better; that she did me the justice to believe that I have not been
so totally regardless or forgetful of the principles which my education has
instilled, nor so totally destitute of a personal sense of delicacy as to be
susceptible of a wish in that direction.[35]

Deeply touched by her son's letter, Abigail Adams sent it on to her husband, who shared it with Washington. The President had, in fact, worried
that John Adams's revulsion at nepotism might lead him to dismiss his son
from the diplomatic corps, and, indeed, Adams had planned to do just that.
After Washington read John Quincy's letter, he told Adams, "The sentiments do honor to the head and heart of the writer, and if my wishes would
be of any avail, they should go to you in the *strong hope* [his italics] that you
will not withhold merited promotion for Mr. John [Quincy] Adams because he is your son."

For without intending to compliment the father or the mother . . . I give it as my decided opinion that Mr. Adams is the most valuable public character we have abroad, and that he will prove himself to be the ablest of all our diplomatic corps. . . . The public, more and more as he is known, are appreciating his talents and worth, and his country would sustain a loss if these are checked by over delicacy on your part.[36]

"Go to Lisbon," the President-elect wrote to reassure his son, "and send me as good intelligence from all parts of Europe as you have done."[37]

After John Quincy told Louisa of his new appointment—and the enormous increase in his salary—they saw no reason to postpone their marriage. He and Thomas packed up their things and shipped everything to Lisbon before sailing to London for the wedding. To their consternation, however, unexpected letters arrived from the secretary of state and from John Quincy's father, the new President, directing him not to proceed to Lisbon but to wait for a commission to the Prussian court in Berlin. Although Berlin was a far more important post than Lisbon, neither John Quincy nor Louisa (nor Thomas, for that matter) was pleased about foregoing Portugal's sunny climes for the long, grey, dismal winters of northern Europe. And John Quincy was livid about having spent $2,500 to ship most of his and Thomas's clothes, furniture, and books—especially his books—to Lisbon.

John Quincy Adams married Louisa Catherine Johnson in an Anglican service in London on July 26, 1797, with his brother and her parents and sisters attending. Two weeks earlier, John Quincy had turned thirty; his bride was twenty-two; and in the course of three idyllic months honeymooning in the English countryside, they wrote to his "Dear and Honored Parents" to share their joy: "I have now the happiness of presenting you another daughter," John Quincy wrote, "worthy as I fully believe of adding one to the number of those who endear that relation to you. The day before yesterday united us for life. My recommendation of her to your kindness and affection I know will be unnecessary."

Louisa Catherine appended her own appeal for the Adamses' parental support:

> The day before yesterday, by uniting me to your beloved son, has given me a claim to your parental affection, a claim I already feel will inspire me with veneration to pursue the path of rectitude and render me as deserving of your esteem and tenderness. . . . To be respected . . . and to meet the approbation of my husband and family is the greatest wish of my heart. Stimulated by these motives . . . will prove a sufficient incitement never to sully the title of subscribing myself your Dutiful Daughter.[38]

The joys of their honeymoon suddenly vanished, however, when they returned to London. They knew, of course, that they faced three years of northern European winters in Berlin and enormous difficulties recovering John Quincy's possessions in Lisbon. What they did not—could not—expect was an angry mob at the front door of the Johnson mansion in London, screaming for John Quincy to pay thousands of pounds in overdue bills.

CHAPTER 6

A Free, Independent, and Powerful Nation

When John Quincy and his bride crossed London Bridge to the Johnson family mansion after their honeymoon, they expected relatives, friends, and other well-wishers to greet them. Instead, they found a mob of angry, twisted faces, screaming for "money! my money!" During John Quincy and his new wife's absence, Louisa's father's business had collapsed. A cargo-filled ship had sunk in mid-ocean, and one of his partners absconded with company funds. Bankrupt and facing debtors' prison if he remained in England, he fled to America with his wife and children, leaving behind the angry creditors who now blocked John Quincy and Louisa's access to her parents' home.

With no other recourse, Joshua Johnson's creditors demanded that John Quincy cover his father-in-law's debts. The press accused Louisa and her father of having lured the unsuspecting American into marrying a penniless woman to bilk him of his money. "It is forty-three years since I became a wife," Louisa would recall years later, "and yet the rankling sore is not healed which then broke upon my heart of hearts."[1]

Her father's bankruptcy erased the £500 dowry he had pledged to John Quincy and, indeed, gave John Quincy the legal right to recant his marriage vows, but he stood by his bride even as she sank into despondency under the weight of humiliation. As he tried to comfort her, John Quincy faced serious difficulties of his own. Having arranged to transfer his belongings from Lisbon to Berlin, he now learned that the Senate had postponed voting on his appointment to the Prussian court. Although it had unanimously approved his appointment to Lisbon by President Washington, it balked at approving his appointment by President Adams after newspapers assailed the President for nepotism.

Noting that Washington had refused to select even the most distant relatives for office, Boston's *Independent Chronicle* called John Quincy "the American Prince of Wales"—sent abroad "to prosecute his studies." The newspaper charged that, as the first appointment of his father's administration, "this young man, from an obscure practitioner of the law, has been mounted on the political ladder with an uncommon celerity. Young John Adams's negotiations have terminated in a marriage with an English lady. . . . It is a happy circumstance that he has made no other treaty."[2] And *Aurora* editor Benjamin Franklin Bache, Benjamin Franklin's grandson and John Quincy's former schoolmate, demanded that President John Adams resign "before it is too late to retrieve our deranged affairs."[3]

Abigail was furious at what she called "misrepresentations" and "billingsgate" (vulgar abuse). John Quincy reacted with equal rage. "My old schoolfellow Bache," he snapped, "has become too thoroughbred a democrat to suffer any regard for ancient friendship or any sense of generosity for an *absent* enemy to suspend his scurrility."[4]

Despite Abigail's protests, Bache's "billingsgate" had its desired effect on the Senate, which postponed consideration of John Quincy's Berlin appointment three times before acceding to the President's wishes. John Quincy Adams, his wife Louisa, and his brother Thomas set sail for Hamburg, on October 18, 1797, elated by the prospects of a new adventure. As they put to sea, Louisa added to their collective joy by announcing that she was pregnant.

On November 7, the Adamses reached Berlin's gates, only to be "questioned by a dapper young lieutenant who did not know—until one of his private soldiers explained to him—who the United States of America were."[5]

By the time they reached Berlin, King Frederick William II had died, and John Quincy had to send to Philadelphia for new papers designating him minister plenipotentiary to the new court of King Frederick William III. The papers arrived just before Christmas—as did all the furniture, baggage, and books from Lisbon. With all their personal possessions in hand, John Quincy, Louisa, and Thomas were, at last, able to move from their hotel into a house of their own. A few days later, John Quincy presented his papers at court, where the new king, his three highest ministers, and other dignitaries received him warmly after he demonstrated his fluency in both French and German. Royal society embraced John Quincy and Louisa as an American prince and princess. The pair attended royal banquets and balls, and John Quincy spent three days as a guest of honor at "the grand annual reviews of the troops"—a spectacle of color, parades, and precision marching by tens of thousands of soldiers over hundreds of acres. Always gathering intelligence to relay to the secretary of state, he noted, "There were five regiments of cavalry of twelve hundred men each and ten regiments of infantry of two thousand men each. The troops are in admirable condition and exhibit a very fine appearance."[6]

With an elegant house—and expense account—John Quincy and Louisa opened their doors to European society and looked forward to a festive Christmas, when tragedy struck. Louisa miscarried—not once, but twice in succession over the next six months. "For ten days," he wrote to his father, "I could scarcely leave her bedside for a moment."[7]

Her miscarriages left her so pale that the queen urged her to use rouge on her cheeks and gave her a box, which John Quincy insisted she must return. Only actresses and "fallen women" wore makeup in New England, and when John Quincy saw his wife wearing rouge as they were to leave for the ball one evening, he told her that "unless I allowed him to wash my face, he would not go." Louisa said, "He took a towel, drew me on his knee, and all my beauty was washed away."[8]

Although John Quincy kissed her later and put the incident behind him, Louisa never forgot it. Decades later, the wound still festered, as she recalled her husband's response. Louisa's pallor, however, continued to provoke "teasing about my pale face" at court. Months after the first incident, she again applied a touch of rouge and "walked boldly forward to meet Mr. Adams. As soon as he saw me, he requested me to wash it off, while I with some temper refused," and John Quincy left without her. Louisa went on her own to dine with friends, and when John Quincy met her at the end of the evening, "we returned home as good friends as ever."[9] John Quincy never explained his uncharacteristically hurtful behavior.

Between Louisa's illnesses, John Quincy attempted to negotiate extending a treaty of amity and commerce with Prussia for another ten years. Benjamin Franklin had negotiated the original treaty, but by the time John Quincy Adams appeared in Berlin, the status of the United States had changed. Now a trading nation of consequence and all but out of debt, the United States had become a valuable trading partner, and the Prussians eagerly renewed their ties—on John Quincy's birthday, July 11, 1799.

The treaty renewal, however, came at just the wrong time for both countries. The French Directory's foreign minister, Talleyrand, had just proclaimed what he called France's "natural right" to give law to the world and recover the colonial empire of the 1750s that France had lost to Britain in the Seven Years War. French troops swept across the Rhineland, Switzerland, Italy, Venice, Dalmatia, and the Ionian Islands, and French warships wreaked havoc on Anglo-American trade in the Caribbean and on the Atlantic. By the time John Adams assumed the presidency, the French had seized 340 American ships—more than half the American merchant fleet, with cargoes valued at more than $55 million. Hundreds of American seamen languished in prison chains in Brest, Bordeaux, and the French West Indies. Insurance rates on American cargoes soared and threatened to price American exports out of world markets. After France rejected Charles Pinckney as America's new ambassador, President Adams and the Federalist-controlled Senate threatened war.

"France has already gone to war with us," the President bellowed. "She is at war with us, but we are not at war with her."[10]

The Republican majority in the House of Representatives, however, demanded that Adams send a mission to France to try to heal the rupture— much as Washington had sent John Jay to Britain three years earlier, in 1794, to heal relations with that nation. In the fall of 1797, Adams sent Republican Elbridge Gerry of Massachusetts and Federalists John Marshall of Virginia and Charles Cotesworth Pinckney of South Carolina, a cousin of Charles Pinckney. When they arrived in France, three intermediaries told the Americans that the Directory expected the same fealty and remunerations as "the ancient kings of France" and that to begin negotiations they would have to pay a tribute of $250,000 in cash to Talleyrand and arrange a loan to the French government of $12.8 million.[11]

"No!" Pinckney shouted. "Not even six pence! We are unable to defend our commerce on the seas, but we will defend our shores."[12] In April 1798, Marshall and Pinckney abandoned their mission. "There is not the least hope of an accommodation with this government," Pinckney declared.[13] Talleyrand insisted the three American envoys had "twisted the meaning of honest conversations."[14]

By then, John Quincy had been sending a stream of vital intelligence reports to both his father and the secretary of state, gleaned in part through clever banter with the French minister to the Prussian court—"the citizen Caillard, whom I had formerly known as secretary of the French legation in St. Petersburg."[15]

"The fleet from Toulon," he wrote in one report to the secretary of state, "is said to have arrived in Corsica. . . . Its destination is Alexandria in Egypt. . . . The Danish chargé d'affaires told me that . . . by his last accounts from Copenhagen, they were expecting the arrival of the Russian fleet. . . . He said that . . . they were substantially in a state of war with France."[16] And in another report, he warned the secretary of state that a group of French agents masquerading as the "*friends of liberty . . .* threatens the United States with a speedy revolution."[17] When William Vans Murray, who replaced John Quincy in The Hague, complained that foreign agents had deciphered his coded letters to the secretary of state, John Quincy warned that "your private letters to the secretary of state cannot escape the inspection of persons not entitled to them. . . . Everything leaks out, either through treachery or ungovernable curiosity or misplaced confidence."[18]

Outraged by French government conduct toward his envoys, President Adams asked Congress for funds to strengthen American defenses, arm merchant ships, build a navy, and prepare for war. When Republicans insisted on proof of French government demands for bribes, the President sent them the dispatches he had received from Pinckney, Marshall, and Gerry, describing their encounters with the men who had solicited bribes but identifying them as only "X," "Y," and "Z." When Republicans scoffed at the allegations, John Quincy's intelligence work exposed the three mystery men as the shady Swiss financier Jean Conrad Hottinger; another Swiss-born banker from Hamburg, Monsieur Bellamy; and Lucien Hauteval.

"Z, or Hauteval," John Quincy wrote, "I knew very well when long before the establishment of the French Republic he called himself Monsieur le Comte d'Hauteval."

> I was present at the performance of mass after the head of Louis XVI was cut off, at which the said Hauteval thundered out the '*Domine salvum fac regem*' with as much devotion and enthusiasm as if he had been ready to suffer martyrdom for the cause. I know not how many millions of livres he assured us he had lost by the revolt of the blacks in St. Domingo. He had been a member of the colonial assembly . . . been obliged to flee the island. . . . The next I heard of him was in Paris in 1796 when and where he . . . had been trying to get appointed Minister of France to the United States.[19]

As Federalists had hoped, the XYZ dispatches—and John Quincy's revelations of their identities—muffled Francophile voices in Congress and across America. Even Abigail Adams put aside her Anglophobia and recognized that "the olive branch tendered to our Gallic allies . . . has been rejected with scorn. . . . Public opinion is changing here very fast, and the people begin to see who have been their firm unshaken friends, steady to their interests, and defenders of their rights and liberties."[20]

Abigail was prescient. The XYZ dispatches provoked a frenzy of war fever and violent anti-French demonstrations. Mobs attacked the home of John Quincy's schoolmate, the fanatically pro-French *Aurora* editor Benjamin Franklin Bache, and across the nation, town after town formed militia companies to serve the nation. More than 1,000 young men in Philadelphia marched to the President's house and volunteered to fight the French. President Adams came out to address them, dressed incongruously in full-dress military uniform complete with sword—and a scabbard that was too long for his stature and scraped the ground. Abigail greeted another group wearing a flowerlike device radiating bows of black ribbon that Federalists immediately converted into a black cockade to symbolize their opposition to the tricolor cockade of the French Revolution.

"Every black cockade will be another Declaration of Independence," wrote the editor of Boston's *Columbian Centinel*. Within days, Abigail's black cockade had sprouted on the hats of the President, his cabinet members, and every "good American" man, woman, and child across the land.

"I will never send another minister to France," President Adams proclaimed to Congress at the end of June 1798, "without assurances that he will be received, respected and honored as the representative of a great, free, powerful, and independent nation."[21]

Federalists and Republicans alike held their collective breath as they awaited the President's request for a declaration of war against America's former ally. Instead, he asked Congress to create a Department of the Navy and authorize acquisition of twelve ships with up to twenty guns each. He asked for an embargo on all trade with France, and once Congress supported his requests, he ordered the navy to seize French privateers and other raiders in or near American waters. Congress authorized the President to call 80,000 state militiamen to active duty, and the President appointed George Washington commander in chief. The aging Washington immediately named Alexander Hamilton inspector general and second in command.

"I am happy . . . to express my warm and cordial participation in the joy which all true Americans have felt . . . by your acceptance of the command of her armies," John Quincy wrote to the former President.

> However much to be regretted is the occasion which has again summoned you from your beloved retirement, there is every reason to hope that the spirit of firmness and dignity which your example has so powerfully contributed to inspire and maintain will either obviate the necessity of another struggle for our independence or once more carry us victoriously and gloriously through it.[22]

To the President's delight, construction and refitting of American warships proceeded faster than expected, and by the end of October, the navy had launched three frigates, armed more than 1,000 merchant ships, and cleared American coastal waters of French marauders. With offshore shipping protected from French assault, the President ordered the U.S. Navy to "sweep the West India seas" of French ships. Although the French had captured more than eight hundred American vessels by then, in fewer than four months after the embryonic U.S. Navy went to sea, it had captured eighty-four French ships. American squadrons gained control of Caribbean waters, and on February 9, 1799, Captain Thomas Truxton's *Constellation* scored the first major victory in the quasi-war, engaging and capturing the French navy's big frigate *Insurgente* off the island of Nevis.

America's naval success stunned Talleyrand and the Directory. France was already suffering from the embargo that had closed American markets to important French exports, such as wines, brandies, silks, linen, and porcelain, while British ships prevented French ships from carrying sugar and other essentials from the French Antilles back to France. French fortunes were declining dramatically on other fronts as well. Napoléon and his forces had invaded Egypt, and on August 1, 1798, a week after French troops marched into Cairo, Admiral Horatio Nelson's British fleet surprised and annihilated the French fleet of 55 warships and 280 transports at Aboukir Bay, near Alexandria. The French army was trapped in Egypt.

"The present situation of France," John Quincy reported to his father, "has produced a great and important change in her conduct toward us. It is no longer an overbearing minister of external relations [Talleyrand] who keeps three ministers waiting five months without reception . . . attempting to dupe and swindle them by his pimping spies. . . . No longer a self-imagined conqueror . . . prescribing tribute as the preliminaries to hearing claims for justice."[23] John Quincy told his father that the French government now seemed determined "to effect a reconciliation with the United States"—and with good reason: plague had killed half the French army in Egypt, and Napoléon had abandoned the rest of his troops and secretly sailed away in the dead of night for France with a handful of trusted aides. Within a year, invading English forces would force the ill-fated French expeditionary force in Egypt to lay down its arms and surrender. In the meantime, France suffered a similar humiliation in Ireland when a British fleet trapped and captured nine French warships and transport vessels carrying a French invasion army into Donegal Bay.

As the aura of French invincibility began to dissipate, Russia organized alliances to halt French expansion in Europe. An Anglo-Russian army landed in Holland, while another Russian force joined the Austrians and pushed French forces out of the Bavarian and Italian Alps, Switzerland, and the Rhineland. In Tuscany, Italian patriots rebelled and sent French forces fleeing northward, while slaves in what is now Haiti staged a massive rebellion, butchering more than 10,000 French troops, 3,000 French civilians, and the army's commander in chief, Napoléon's brother-in-law. In France proper, royalists staged a massive counterrevolution in the western and central provinces. Besieged from all directions and stripped of revenues from foreign plunder, France faced economic collapse unless Talleyrand could restore the flow of supplies and foodstuffs from her former ally, the United States.

Under pressure from the rest of the Directory, Talleyrand ordered American seamen and other Americans released from prison, reopened French ports to American ships, and ordered an end to French attacks on American ships. He issued a formal invitation to peace talks that conspicuously included President Adams's own words to Congress, pledging that "whatever plenipotentiary the government of the United States might send to France to put an end to the existing differences between the two countries would be undoubtedly received with the respect due to the representative of a free, independent, and powerful nation."[24]

Sensing a sharp increase in official European respect for the United States, John Quincy urged his father to accept Talleyrand's invitation, and his father sent a new group of peace commissioners to Paris.

With the massive retreat of French troops, central Europe grew safe for travel, and after Louisa had recovered from still another miscarriage, she and John Quincy left Berlin in mid-July for a three-month vacation in the Silesian countryside, with stops in Toplitz and Dresden along the way. John Quincy sent his brother Thomas an astonishing forty-three pages of beautifully written letters, which Thomas forwarded to a Philadelphia literary weekly, *Port Folio,* for publication. They later appeared in London as an elegant 387-page book titled *Letters from Silesia,* by "His Excellency John Quincy Adams." Translated into French, they also appeared in Paris to great acclaim. Although John Quincy's literary ambitions centered on poetry, he suddenly emerged as a renowned author of magnificent prose.

When the Adamses returned to Berlin, they learned to their astonishment that Napoléon had returned from Egypt and landed at Saint-Raphaël on the south coast of France near present-day Cannes, setting off joyful street demonstrations in Paris. He marched into that city a week later to the cheers of tens of thousands, and the French army, its spirits revived by his return, forced the Anglo-Russian forces to withdraw. A month later, Napoléon masterminded a coup d'état that left him in sole control of the French government. He retained Talleyrand as foreign minister, ordering him to negotiate an immediate peace with the United States and restore trade relations. On September 30, 1800, the French and American governments signed a new treaty of peace and amity that respected American rights—and independence—under the Neutrality Proclamation that George Washington had issued seven years earlier.

New England Federalists, however, were furious, having already geared up their shipbuilding facilities to build the new navy. War had generated wealth for New Englanders for nearly a century of perennial Anglo-French conflicts. When Secretary of State Pickering, already at odds with the President over other issues, added his voice to the cry for war, President Adams dismissed him for insubordination, and Pickering returned to New England harboring a bitterness for John Adams that would affect the entire Adams family for years to come—especially John Quincy. John Adams named Virginia's John Marshall to replace Pickering as secretary of state.

With little left to do on the diplomatic front in Berlin, John Quincy Adams and Louisa spent much of the winter dining and dancing at royal dinners and balls. John Quincy used his spare moments to plunge into translations of German literature, including the epic poem *Oberon*, a medieval legend about a fairy king, and the fables of Christian Gellert.* Free of any tension-producing diplomatic obligations, the Adamses thrived in the relaxed gaiety of the winter social season, and when Louisa found herself pregnant again, she actually blossomed for a change—eating heartily at holiday dinners and often dancing into the morning hours at royal balls. For the first time ever, she joined her husband on his vigorous, five-mile walks each day. As she approached term, the king banned all traffic in the street in front of the Adams home to ensure quiet, and the queen sent a servant to wait on Louisa.

Until Louisa's pregnancy, John Quincy had seldom attended religious services, but in the winter of 1801, he added daily Bible reading to his routine after the sudden death of a young army officer at an otherwise joyful,

---

*By 1899, John Quincy Adams had gained recognition as "father of German studies in America," and as late as 1940, the Adams translation of *Oberon* continued to appear and draw praise for its "unusually scholarly and literary merit, remarkable for its . . . genuine artistry."

turn-of-the-century New Year's party on December 31, 1799. The young man fell to the floor in mid-sentence, without a final cry or gasp.

> It was at first supposed he had only fainted. A surgeon and physician were called in and every expedient possible was used to bring him to life, in vain. I came away . . . to prevent the story from coming too abruptly to my wife . . . and when the fact that the youth was certainly dead had become unquestionable, the scene that ensued was dreadful—faintings, hysteric fits, convulsions, and raving madness marked the shock of this calamitous accident. . . . I passed the period between the two centuries in communion with my own soul and in prostration to the being who directs the universe, with thanksgiving for his numerous blessings in the past times.[25]

John Quincy feared the young man's death was an omen of worse things to come, and a few days later he learned that his nation's revered leader, George Washington, had died two weeks earlier, on December 14, 1799. For once, it was Louisa who had to calm and comfort her husband when the news arrived.

In the days that followed, John Quincy discovered and studied the sermons of John Tillotson, archbishop of Canterbury from 1691 to 1694 and advocate of simpler, more comprehensible terms that eschewed obscure metaphors. A contemporary of John Locke, he called for reconciliation between Christian faiths and emphasized morality. John Quincy embraced Tillotson's thesis, reading and rereading the ten volumes of Tillotson's sermons for the rest of his life. As he began to embrace religion, however, he had no idea that American Federalists, infuriated by federal property taxes, had split ranks and allowed Thomas Jefferson's Democrat-Republicans to strip his father of the American presidency.

With his former secretary of state, Boston's Timothy Pickering, calling for secession, New England Federalists had turned against the President. "The five States of New-England," Pickering ranted, "can have nothing to fear . . . [from] instituting a new . . . nation of New-England, and leav[ing] the rest of the Continent to pursue their own imbecile and dis-jointed plans, until they have . . . acquired magnanimity and wisdom suf-ficient to join a confederation that may rescue them from destruction."[26]

After counting the Electoral College votes in 1800, Vice President Thomas Jefferson and former New York senator Aaron Burr Jr. had each won seventy-three votes, while John Adams had garnered only sixty-five. Ironically, Adams would have easily won reelection if Hamilton and Pick-ering had not divided the Federalists, shunting sixty-four Federalist votes to Pinckney. It was a politically fatal defeat for the President and suicide for the Federalist Party, which would never again field a viable candidate for national leadership.

The tie vote in the Electoral College sent the decision to the House of Representatives, which elected Jefferson President on the thirty-sixth ballot, on February 17, and relegated Burr to political obscurity as vice president. In two of his last acts in office, President John Adams named Secretary of State John Marshall as chief justice of the Supreme Court, and to prevent possible dismissal and humiliation of his son when the Republicans took control of the Department of State, he recalled John Quincy from Berlin, ending his seemingly unobstructed rise to national leadership.

When he learned of his father's defeat, John Quincy wrote to console him, adding, "I hope and confidently believe that you will be prepared to bear this event with calmness and composure, if not with indifference; that you will not suffer it to prey on your mind or affect your health."

> In your retirement you will have not only the consolation . . . that you have discharged all the duties of a virtuous citizen, but the genuine plea-sure of reflecting that by the wisdom and firmness of your administration you left . . . [the] country in safe and honorable peace. . . . In resisting . . . the violence of France, you saved the honor of the American name from disgrace. . . . By sending the late mission you restored an honorable peace to the nation, without tribute, without bribes, without violating any pre-vious engagements. . . . You have, therefore, given the most decisive proof that . . . you were the man not of any party but of the whole nation.[27]

On March 4, Thomas Jefferson took the oath of office as America's third President at the first inauguration to be held in the new, permanent federal capital of Washington City, as it was called at first. In his inaugural address, the new President appealed for an end to the bitter conflict between Anglophiles and Francophiles and between Federalists and Republicans. "Every difference of opinion is not a difference of principle," Jefferson asserted. "We have called by different names brethren of the same principle. We are all republicans; we are all federalists."[28]

In the written transcript of his address that he sent to Congress, he purposely left the words "republicans" and "federalists" uncapitalized. The election campaign, however, had left John Adams too bitter to attend the inauguration, and he never heard Jefferson's speech. In any case, few Federalists believed Thomas Jefferson could halt the secessionist fever infecting the nation. The death of Washington in 1799 had left the young republic without a strong leader to unite vastly different, conflicting regional interests across the continent, and Congress had become a battleground for those interests instead of a center of collegial mediation, compromise, and unification.

On April 12, 1801, after four miscarriages, Louisa Adams gave birth to John Quincy's first child. "I have this day to offer my humble and devout thanks to almighty God for the birth of a son at half-past three o'clock in the afternoon," he prayed as he wrote in his diary.[29] Three weeks later, the infant was baptized George Washington Adams, and John Quincy prayed for "the favor of almighty God that he may live and never prove unworthy of [the name]."[30] By then, John Quincy had received his letter of recall, and the following day he presented it to his friend King Frederick, then went to say farewell to Louisa's friend the queen. "In less than half an hour, all was over."[31]

On June 17, Louisa and John Quincy Adams sailed from Hamburg, Germany, with their infant son, and after an uneventful Atlantic crossing, they disembarked in Philadelphia, where brother Thomas Boylston Adams awaited with the shocking news that their middle brother, twenty-nine-year-old Charles, had died of alcoholism. Several days later, Louisa and

John Quincy separated for the first time since their marriage, with John traveling northward for a reunion with his parents and relatives, while Louisa took the baby to Washington, where her parents had settled after fleeing London. All but penniless when they arrived, they had turned for help to their son-in-law's family, and John Adams had not only loaned them money but appointed Joshua Johnson superintendent of the Treasury Stamp Office, drawing enormous political flak for his generosity. By the time Louisa arrived, however, her father had died, and the rest of the family was living in the home of one of her married sisters.

After a joyful reunion with his family, John Quincy suddenly found himself without prospects for a job in the public sector. Republicans controlled government, and his mother and father could only suggest his "applying yourself solely to your own private affairs" by reestablishing a law practice.[32]

John Quincy bought a house in Boston, then traveled to Washington for the first time to escort Louisa and baby George back to Massachusetts. While in the capital, he dined with Thomas Jefferson, his friend from his adolescence in Paris and now third President of the United States. When he took office, Jefferson promptly fired most of his predecessor's appointees, including Joshua Johnson. Jefferson apologized, saying he had not known that Johnson was John Quincy's father-in-law.

After meeting with the President, John Quincy took Louisa to Mount Vernon to visit Martha Washington and show her the baby boy who had joined legions of newborn American boys bearing her husband's name.

The Adamses arrived in Massachusetts in late November in time for Louisa's formal induction into the huge Adams clan at her first Thanksgiving in America. After settling in their home in Boston, John Quincy set up his embryonic law practice and soon found it as boring as he had on his first try a decade earlier. Boston, however, reeked of politics, and the scent quickly lured him from his office—to the firehouse, for example, to become a volunteer fireman and to the influential congregation of the Old Brick Meeting House, where he purchased a pew. He also joined organizations that generated speaking opportunities before audiences of prominent Bostonians.

In April 1802, he won election to the state senate on the Federalist ticket and started two years of what he called "the novitiate of my legislative labors." He spent most of his time tilting at political windmills—as he would the rest of his life. In one sortie, he tried unsuccessfully to strip the legislature of its control over the judiciary; in another he tried just as unsuccessfully to block legislators from using public funds to underwrite a new bank "whose shares were reserved to . . . members of the legislature."[33] About his futile political battles, he wrote,

> I was not able either to effect much good or to prevent much evil. I attempted some reforms and aspired to check some abuses, I regret to say, with little success. I [lacked] experience, and I discovered the danger of opposing and exposing corruption. . . . The mammon of unrighteousness was too strongly befriended.[34]

Because Federalists often shared the same beds of corruption with opposition Republicans, they soon found John Quincy's campaigns against corruption as much a threat to their own political health as it was for their political foes. "A politician in this country must be a man of a party," he lamented. "I would fain be the man of my whole country." Then, with a malicious grin, he added, "I have strong temptation and have great provocation to plunge into political controversy."[35]

At the time, each state legislature elected two of its own members to the U.S. Senate. To remove John Quincy from its midst without alienating powerful Adams family supporters in Boston, the Massachusetts legislature pretended to honor John Quincy by electing him to the U.S. Senate and sending him off to Washington in the hope that it would not hear from him again for at least six years. John Quincy, however, was about to shock the Massachusetts legislature and the nation's entire political establishment with what became a courageous, lifelong crusade against injustice.

CHAPTER 7

A Profile in Courage

On July 4, 1803, Louisa Catherine Adams gave birth to her second child, John Adams II, named for his illustrious grandfather. Two months later, John Quincy sold their house in Boston, and the family started for the nation's new capital in Washington. The move did not go smoothly. After carting their trunks to New London, Connecticut, they boarded the packet to New York, only to have two-year-old George Washington Adams behave like a two-year-old and throw his shoes overboard, then scamper away giggling with a bundle of keys to the family trunks, which promptly followed the little boy's shoes into the sea.

When they sailed into Newark, New Jersey, the inns were full—indeed overflowing—with hysterical New Yorkers fleeing a yellow fever epidemic. The Adamses huddled in a room at a tavern until Thomas Adams, still practicing law in Philadelphia, learned of their plight and sent a carriage to bring them to Philadelphia and then to Washington.

The city of Washington remained, at best, a developing outpost of civilization, its streets mostly mud tracks that often disappeared from view into fetid swamps. In fact, the city was a gigantic marsh, perforated by islands of reclaimed land topped with shabby boardinghouses, inns, taverns, stables, and, occasionally, government buildings—most of them still under construction. There was no church, hospital, museum, or park. Snakes slithered in and out of low-lying houses; a heavy rain turned muddy streets into raging torrents, and rats competed with pigs for footing and food on the few slime-coated islets of high ground. Clouds of insects surged through the air; disease was rampant; influenza reached epidemic proportions every winter. Clots of shacks—largely slave quarters—added to the horror. As John Quincy's grandson Henry would put it years later after visiting his grandmother Louisa in Washington for the first time, "Slavery . . . was a nightmare, a horror, a crime, the sum of all wickedness. . . . Slave states were dirty, unkempt, poverty-stricken, ignorant, vicious!"

The two wings of the Washington Capitol stood all but isolated on a hill above the city's mire, connected by a long, unpainted wooden shed and devoid of the domed central structure that would one day tie them together. According to one New England visitor, Pennsylvania Avenue was a mile of "rough road, bordered here and there by Congressional boarding-houses, with veritable swamps between" that led from the Capitol to the President's house, which stood "in the midst of rough, unornamented grounds. Then another stretch of comparative wilderness till you came to Georgetown."[1]

"We want nothing here," the witty Senator Gouverneur Morris liked to tell visitors, "nothing but houses, cellars, kitchens, well-informed men, amiable women, and other little trifles of the kind, to make our city perfect."[2]

British minister Anthony Merry lacked Morris's sense of humor:

> I cannot describe . . . the difficulty and expense which I have to encounter in fixing myself in a habitation. By dint of money I have just secured two small houses on the common which is meant to become in time the city of Washington. They are mere shells of homes, with bare walls, and without fixtures of any kind, even without pump or well. . . . Provisions of any kind, especially vegetables, are frequently hardly to be obtained at any price. So miserable is our situation.[3]

A French diplomat was no kinder in his appraisal: "My God!" he lamented. "What have I done to be condemned to reside in such a city?"[4]

Washington had only about seven hundred houses, of which one-third were brick and the rest wood. Paid only $6 a day in the House and $7 in the Senate, members of Congress often had to live as bachelors in squalid, cheaply built boardinghouses—usually, if they could, with friends from the same state or political party. Affluent government officials avoided the city as much as possible, preferring to live with their families in more substantial homes in nearby Georgetown, where Louisa Adams's brother-in-law Walter Hellen, a wealthy—and generous—tobacco merchant and speculator, owned an enormous mansion. Hellen, who had married Louisa's older sister Nancy, had housed his mother-in-law and her offspring after Joshua Johnson's death, and he now invited John Quincy Adams, Louisa, and their two children to fill a nest of unused rooms in his spacious home, even giving John Quincy a quiet corner of his own for reading.

Senate life put no constraints on the family at first. It sat for less than three hours on weekdays—from noon until 2 or 3 p.m., and John Quincy enjoyed the forty-five-minute walk—about two and a half miles—to and from the Capitol, always getting home for the family's 4 p.m. dinner. "At eleven this morning," John Quincy wrote in his diary on his first day in the Senate, "I took my seat . . . after delivering my credentials . . . and being sworn to support the Constitution of the United States. . . . There was little business done, and the Senate adjourned soon after twelve."[5]

When the Senate adjourned early enough, he often stopped to hear debates in the House of Representatives before walking home. With no churches in Washington, John Quincy made do with the two nondenominational services in the Capitol and at the Treasury—the first on Sunday morning, the second in the afternoon. Already well known by the city's leading figures, John Quincy and Louisa were instant favorites on the social scene, attending dinners and balls at the President's House, as the future White House was then called. When Louisa was not with him, John Quincy often retired to a quiet corner with Secretary of State James Madison to play chess. The two had not liked each other when they first met, but their deep interest in history drew them closer, and their encounters over the chessboard cemented their friendship. Unlike other southern political leaders, Madison had gone north to Princeton for his higher education and shared much of the same academic background as John Quincy.

The easy Senate routine allowed John Quincy to enjoy life at home as he had seldom done before, drawing closer to Louisa, who grew so robust she learned to ride and joined her husband on horseback excursions. The short Senate days left him ample time to resume his voracious reading and to read to his sons. Occasionally, he simply "passed the evening idly with George . . . or with the ladies."[6] During his first days in Washington, his time on the Senate floor produced nothing but bonhomie with his thirty-three colleagues, including the other senator from Massachusetts, former secretary of war and secretary of state Timothy Pickering.

As envisaged at the Constitutional Convention, the Senate was "to consist of the most distinguished characters, distinguished for their rank in life and their weight of property, and bearing as strong a likeness to the British House of Lords as possible."[7] For this reason the framers of the Constitution gave state legislatures, rather than the people, the power to elect senators.

It was not long, however, before John Quincy found himself disagreeing with most of his colleagues—Federalist as well as Republican. Several weeks after he first took his seat, the Senate considered the Louisiana Purchase. Comprising an area of about 1 million square miles, Louisiana was the largest territory any nation had ever acquired peacefully from another in recorded history—larger than Great Britain, France, Germany, Spain, and Portugal combined. The United States had agreed to pay about $15 million—or about four cents an acre, compared with the average price of $2 an acre for which the U.S. government then sold federal lands to settlers. The acquisition would offer prospects of untold wealth to hundreds of thousands of Americans waiting to claim lands in the western wilderness.

Until his military setbacks in Egypt, western Europe, and Santo Domingo, Napoléon had intended sending 20,000 French troops to organize new French settlements in Louisiana, but a blast of Arctic air late

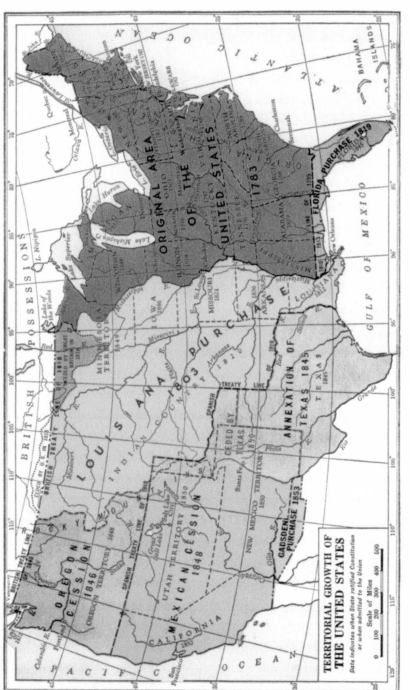

Senator John Quincy Adams championed Senate approval of the Louisiana Purchase, an area of about 1 million square miles that offered prospects of untold wealth to hundreds of thousands of Americans waiting to claim lands in the West.

in 1801 froze the fleet of troop transports in thick ice that prevented its departure. Frustrated by his incredible streak of misfortune, Napoléon exploded in uncontrollable rage:

"Damn sugar," he shouted at his god. "Damn coffee, damn colonies. . . . I shall cede Louisiana to the United States."

Although New England Federalists called the Louisiana Purchase too costly for the nation, their opposition actually stemmed from regional political, social, and economic issues. Virginia had emerged from the Revolutionary War as the largest, most powerful state in the Union, with the most territory, the most people, and the richest economy. With Thomas Jefferson as President and Madison likely to succeed him, Virginia had drained New England of much of its political power and influence; many New Englanders feared that the new states emerging from the Louisiana Purchase would ally themselves with Virginia and leave New England little more than an impotent commercial backwater. Adding Louisiana to the nation would extend slavery across the entire West, end all hopes of abolishing slavery in America, and allow western settlers to use slave labor to create vast new farms that would undersell and bankrupt small New England farms. The Mississippi River valley to New Orleans would become the primary artery for American international trade and destroy New England's banking and shipping industries.

Boston's *Columbian Centinel* led New England opposition, calling the Louisiana Territory "a great waste, a wilderness unpeopled with any beings except wolves and wandering Indians. . . . We are to give money of which we have too little for land of which we already have too much." But a euphoric Tennessean wrote to President Jefferson, "You have secured to us the free navigation of the Mississippi. You have procured an immense fertile country: and all those blessings are obtained without war and bloodshed."[8]

Initially, Jefferson was equally elated, saying the Louisiana Purchase had ensured "the tranquility, security and prosperity of all the Western country" and had permanently united East and West. But the President's enthusiasm had limits. A strict constructionist, he knew the Constitution did not grant the government authority to buy foreign territory, let alone govern it, and that the Louisiana Purchase required a constitutional amendment. Federalists immediately grasped at the President's reservations as a mechanism for rejecting the purchase. The President's reservations appalled expansionists, who warned that the acquisition would be null and void if the Americans did not sign it within six months.

"Be persuaded," American minister to France Robert Livingston warned Jefferson from Paris, "that France is sick of the bargain, that Spain is much dissatisfied, and that the slightest pretext will lose you the treaty."[9]

With the Louisiana Purchase facing rejection, John Quincy Adams, alone among Federalists to favor the acquisition, acted to save it. As he told his parents, he believed deeply that the United States was

> destined by God and nature to be coextensive with the North American continent . . . and become the most populous and powerful people ever combined under one social compact . . . speaking one language, professing one general system of religious and political principles, and accustomed to one general tenor of social usages and customs.[10]

To ensure what others called the nation's "manifest destiny," he studied the Louisiana Purchase agreement, then moved for the addition of a simple phrase: "with the assent of the French government." John Quincy argued that the phrase converted the document from an unconstitutional purchase agreement into a formal—and constitutionally sanctioned—treaty. Whether or not his assertion had any legal or constitutional justification, he was so eloquent a lawyer that he convinced the Senate it did. Despite fierce opposition from Federalists, the Senate approved his motion and ended the furor (and Jefferson's misgivings) over whether the government could acquire Louisiana.*

A Republican newspaper predicted that "the Hon. John Quincy Adams will certainly be denounced and excommunicated by his party,"[11] and,

---

*To ensure the validity of the purchase, John Quincy later proposed a constitutional amendment, but Congress deemed it unnecessary.

*President Thomas Jefferson found Senator John
Quincy Adams a valuable ally in consummating the
Louisiana Purchase, but an implacable foe in efforts
to pack the Supreme Court.* (LIBRARY OF CONGRESS)

indeed, the denunciations came like cannon shots. "Like a kite without a
tail," one Boston Federalist leader snapped at John Quincy. "He will pitch
on one side and the other, as the popular currents may happen to strike."
A Federalist newspaper charged John Quincy with "political patricide" for
supporting President Jefferson, who had unseated John Quincy's father
from the presidency. But *Aurora* editor Benjamin Franklin Bache, the
avowed political enemy of the Adamses, called John Quincy's political
courage "gratifying, coming from a high New England Federalist."[12]

John Quincy was quite prepared for the attacks, writing in his diary
that he had fully expected "the *danger* of adhering to my own principles.

> The country is so totally given up to the spirit of party that not to follow
> blindfold one or the other is an inexpiable offense. . . . Between both, I

see the impossibility of pursuing the dictates of my own conscience without sacrificing every prospect not merely of advancement, but even of retaining that character and reputation I have enjoyed. Yet my choice is made, and, if I cannot hope to give satisfaction to my country, I am at least determined to have the approbation of my own reflections.[13]

Federalist Timothy Pickering, the other Massachusetts senator, responded to the Louisiana Purchase by stepping up efforts to unite New England states with New York—and perhaps Nova Scotia—in a Northern Confederacy that would secede from the Union under the aegis of the British Empire. "I gave the first warning to Mr. Jefferson," John Quincy asserted, "to be upon his guard against the intrigues of the British government through the governor of Nova Scotia with the disaffected party in New England."[14]

John Quincy's father also learned of the Pickering conspiracy. "Mr. P[ickering]," John Adams wrote to his former political opponent Thomas Jefferson,

carried with him from his friends in Boston a project of a division by the Potomac, the Delaware, or the Hudson, i.e., as far as they could succeed, and communicated it to Gen. Hamilton. There can be little doubt . . . that there is a party in New England . . . who wish to urge the nation to war with France and to shelter themselves and their commerce under the wings of the British navy. I have long opposed these people in all such projects . . . and the consequence will soon be, if it is not already, that I and my sons and all my friends will be hated throughout New England.[15]

John Quincy compounded Federalist outrage by attending with Louisa President Jefferson's private family dinners at the presidential mansion—and then joining seventy congressional Republicans at a dinner the President hosted with his cabinet to celebrate the Louisiana Purchase. "Scarcely any of the Federalist members were there," John Quincy noted. "The dinner was bad and the toasts too numerous."[16]

But just as Jefferson thought he had lured John Quincy into the Republican fold, the New Englander proved him wrong by voting with Federalists against giving the President power to tax the people of Louisiana and appoint territorial officials. John Quincy argued that both bills violated the Constitution by depriving the people of Louisiana of their right to self-determination, and he introduced three resolutions—"which produced a storm as violent as I expected":

> *Resolved*, That the people of the United States have never . . . delegated to this Senate the power of imposing taxes upon the inhabitants of Louisiana without their consent.
>
> *Resolved*, That by concurring in any act of legislation for imposing taxes upon the inhabitants of Louisiana without their consent, the Senate would assume a power unwarranted by the Constitution and dangerous to the liberties of the United States.
>
> *Resolved*, That the power of originating bills for raising revenues being exclusively vested in the House of Representatives, these resolutions be carried to them by the secretary of the Senate.

"After a debate of about three hours," John Quincy shook his head sadly, "the resolutions were rejected."[17]

Despite his defeats on the Senate floor, John Quincy remained a consummate constitutional scholar and applied to become, and was sworn in as, an attorney and counselor in the U.S. Supreme Court. He made a point of spending an hour or two a day listening to court proceedings, and, a week after his swearing in, on February 16, 1804, it was his turn to stand and argue his first case—and lose.

Notwithstanding his status as a constitutional lawyer, John Quincy continued outraging both Republicans and Federalists at every turn. He even opposed an inoffensive resolution for senators to wear black crepe arm bands for a month to memorialize the deaths of three patriots, including his father's cousin Samuel Adams, a signer of the Declaration of Independence.

"I asked for the constitutional authority of the Senate to enjoin upon its members this act," Adams wrote in his diary. Told it was not binding upon its members, "I then objected against it as improper in itself, tending to unsuitable discussions of character and to an employment of the Senate's time in debates altogether foreign to the subjects which properly belong to them. This led to a debate of three hours." Adams lost not only the debate but the goodwill of most of his Senate colleagues, who now viewed him as an unconscionable turncoat and chronic malcontent.

"The agency of party is so organized in our country," he groaned, "that the undertaking to pursue a course altogether independent of it as a public man is perhaps impracticable. However this may be, I do not regret having made the attempt and, whether in public or private life, it is my unalterable determination to abide by the principles which have always been my guides.[18]

John Quincy even aroused the ire of his chess mate, Secretary of State Madison, by opposing a new treaty with Britain fixing the boundary between Canada and the United States from the Great Lakes to the Pacific Ocean. Left open by the 1783 treaty of peace ending the Revolutionary War, the line, by convention, had run along the Forty-ninth Parallel. Madison's treaty would have dropped it southward and ceded Britain a strip of land about 150 miles wide, including Lake of the Woods in northern Minnesota and Puget Sound in northwestern Washington. Adams roared his opposition and cowed the Senate into rejecting the treaty, leaving the lands in the so-called Adams Strip in the United States.

Despite the friction John Quincy's unpredictably independent voting engendered, Senate membership was too small, the number of committees too large, and John Quincy Adams's knowledge of the law and the foreign world too vast to ostracize him. He soon found himself on more than a dozen committees, conducting himself on each with total disregard to party. On one he revised the articles of war, on another he helped acquire books for the Library of Congress, and on a third he helped revise Senate rules. His work on one committee included writing legislation for the Louisiana Territory and laws for the District of Columbia; on still another,

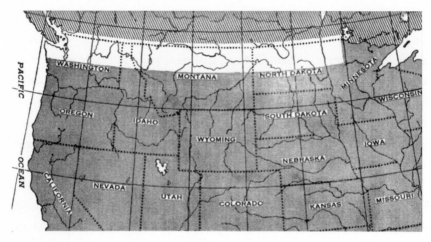

John Quincy Adams ensured the inclusion of the 150-mile-wide "Adams Strip" on the American side of the Canadian-American border.

he proposed building a network of roads across the Appalachian Mountains to connect Atlantic coast ports with the Ohio River valley—a scheme originally proposed by George Washington when the states were still a confederation.

> *Resolved*, That the secretary of the treasury be directed to prepare . . . a plan for . . . opening roads, for removing obstructions and making canals . . . which, as objects of public improvement, may require and deserve the aid of government.[19]

Washington's—and Adams's—scheme would have allowed western crops, pelts, furs, and ores to travel directly to Atlantic sea-lanes to Europe instead of following the circuitous route down the Mississippi River and across the Gulf of Mexico.

Deemed by most senators to be an unconstitutional federal intrusion in state prerogatives, Adams's proposal for domestic improvements went down to defeat without even a word of debate. "I have already seen enough," he responded, "to ascertain that no amendments of my proposing will obtain in the Senate as now filled."[20] He believed Senator Pickering and other Federalists "hate me rather more than they love any principle."[21]

John Quincy proved far more popular at the President's House than he did in the Senate. His language skills and overseas travels as a diplomat combined with his erudition to make him a favorite among diplomats who dined with Jefferson. And whenever ladies attended such functions, Louisa attracted as much attention as her husband or more, being as fluent in French as he but far more extroverted.

Despite her son's status in Washington, Abigail Adams was far less able than her husband to accept him as other than her little boy. "You must not let the mind wear so much upon the body," she warned her thirty-seven-year-old senator-son as Christmas approached in 1804. "You eat too little and study too much."[22] And fully two years later, as he approached his thirty-ninth birthday, she cautioned,

> I hope you never appear in the Senate with a beard two days old or otherwise make what is called a shabby appearance. Seriously, I think a man's usefulness in society depends much upon his personal appearance. I do not wish a senator to dress like a beau, but I want him to conform so far to the fashion as not to incur the character of singularity nor give the occasion to the world to ask what kind of mother he had.[23]

Over the winter, the Adamses learned of the failure of a London bank where John Quincy had placed a sizable portion of his father's European accounts, and to prevent his parents from sustaining any losses, John Quincy filled "the chasm created by this circumstance."[24] To compensate for his loss, he looked for ways to cut his own spending and decided that moving the family back and forth between Washington and Quincy twice a year had become a luxury he could no longer afford. In a bitter confrontation with Louisa, he told her she and the boys would have to stay put the year around—either in Washington or Quincy; her choice. When the Senate adjourned in the spring of 1804, John Quincy was ready to leave for his parents' home in Quincy, and after an angry exchange with her husband, Louisa chose to stay with the boys in Georgetown at the comfortable home of her sister and brother-in-law. If they were to be separated half the year during each of the six remaining years of his Senate term, she told John Quincy she "preferred passing the summer months with my family to living alone in Quincy through five dreary winters."

When John Quincy accused her of disloyalty, she snapped back, "I do not think, my beloved friend, you do me justice. I prefer a separation from you rather than separation from them. I don't think my affection for you admitted of doubt." To add to his guilt after he had left, she wrote to him that three-year-old George "is very angry with you. He says you are very naughty to go away and leave him. . . . John calls everybody Papa he sees. Poor little fellow was too young when you left us to remember you."

Without his father, however, George, at three, became ungovernable, chasing the chickens and ducks unmercifully whenever he was left to himself. And Louisa grew miserable without her husband. "Life is not worth living on such terms," she admitted. She was wretched in Washington and realized that without him, "I must be wretched everywhere."[25]

Their separation left him equally distressed. He missed his children and longed for the comfort of Louisa by his side at night. True to form, he turned to poetry to effect a reconciliation, sending her some playful eroticism from John Donne's *To His Mistress Going to Bed* (1669):

Your gown going off, such beauteous state reveals.
Licence my roving hands.
Full nakedness! All joys are due to thee.
As souls unbodied, bodies uncloth'd must be
To taste whole joys.[26]

John Quincy promised to dip into capital if necessary to end their separation and prevent their ever again being apart. Before he returned to Washington, Harvard's overseers invited him to stand for the college presidency, but he was too intent on rejoining his wife and children and declined in favor of returning to Washington. He arrived in time for the presidential election.

On July 11, 1804, while John Quincy was still in Massachusetts copying Donne's erotic verses for Louisa, Senate president Aaron Burr Jr., the vice president, shot and killed former Treasury secretary Alexander Hamilton in a duel. Fifteen years in the making, their enmity had reached a climax earlier in the year during the New York gubernatorial election campaign, when Burr called for "a union at the northward" between New York and the New England states to thwart the assumption of power by Jefferson, Madison, and Virginia's political dynasty. Fearing civil war, Hamilton all but ensured Burr's defeat in the gubernatorial election by calling the vice president "a dangerous man who ought not to be trusted with the reins of government."[27] Jefferson had already rejected Burr as a potential running mate in 1804, and Burr's defeat in the gubernatorial race effectively ended his political career. As Hamilton's barbs struck, the editor of the *American Citizen* added to their sting by calling Burr the "most mean and despicable bastard in the universe . . . so degraded as to permit even General Hamilton to slander him with impunity."[28] Burr sued the editor, then challenged Hamilton to the fatal confrontation.

After the duel, outraged Hamilton supporters posted handbills bearing the words "Hang Burr!" on walls across New York City. A grand jury indicted Burr for murder, but he fled to a hideaway on a Georgia plantation. When the Senate reconvened on November 5, however, John Quincy joined other members in a collective gasp as Burr stepped through the door and strode down the aisle to his accustomed chair as president of the Senate.

"The coroner's inquest," John Quincy wrote in disbelief, "found a verdict of willful murder by Aaron Burr, vice president of the United States. The grand jury . . . found a bill against him for murder. Under all these circumstances Mr. Burr appears and takes his seat as president of the Senate of the United States."[29]

John Quincy grew even more annoyed when the Senate voted to go into executive session—and promptly left the Capitol to go to the horse races. And they repeated the exercise for the next ten days. "The consideration of executive business," John Quincy fumed, was "merely for the sake of having on the *printed* journals an *appearance* of doing business though there was really none to do. This vote passed. . . . Mine was the only voice heard against it."[30]

Earlier in the year, an effort by President Jefferson to alter the Federalist bias of the Supreme Court came to fruition when he coaxed his political allies in the House of Representatives to impeach Associate Justice Samuel Chase. A signer of the Declaration of Independence and appointee of President Washington, Chase had, at times, displayed outrageous political bias in his rulings, but he crossed a particularly dangerous political line by attacking the adoption of universal white manhood suffrage in his native state of Maryland. Until then, only property owners had been able to vote. Chase argued that the "constitution will sink into a mobocracy, the worst of all possible government," and he cited as "a mighty mischief" the doctrine "that all men in a state of society are entitled to enjoy equal liberty and equal rights."[31]

Calling his words an improper political address in a judicial proceeding, the House of Representatives charged him with sedition and treason—both of them "high crimes and misdemeanors" and a basis for impeachment under the Constitution and removal from office. With John Quincy howling his objections, Chase went on trial before the Senate the following February. In one of the most important trials in American history, the House of Representatives threatened to convert the American republic into an autocracy by criminalizing political dissent. Although John Quincy did not like Chase, he argued that the constitutional phrase "high crimes and misdemeanors" referred to indictable criminal acts—not political statements— and he convinced the Senate to support him. On March 1, 1805, after the Senate had voted, Vice President Burr announced, "There not being a constitutional majority who answer 'guilty' to any one charge, it becomes my duty to declare that Samuel Chase is acquitted upon all the articles of impeachment brought against him by the House of Representatives."[32] In what was then the most significant defense of the First Amendment ever mounted, John Quincy had prevented the American President and the House of Representatives from criminalizing free speech.

"This was a party prosecution," John Quincy reflected afterwards, "and has issued in the . . . total disappointment of those by whom it was brought forward."

> It has exhibited the Senate of the United States fulfilling the most important purpose of its institution, by putting a check upon the impetuous violence of the House of Representatives. It has proved that a sense of justice is yet strong enough to overpower the furies of faction. . . . The attack on Mr. Chase was a systematic attempt upon the independence and powers of the Judicial Department and, at the same time, an attempt to prostrate the authority of the National Government before those of the individual states.[33]

Just before the Chase trial, the Electoral College had announced the results of the presidential elections, with Thomas Jefferson the overwhelming victor over South Carolina Federalist Charles Cotesworth Pinckney, winning 162–14. With Aaron Burr out of the picture, former New York governor George Clinton, an ardent Republican, easily won the vice presidency. Republicans gained control of both houses of Congress. With their own seats secure until 1809, John Quincy and one-third of his colleagues had not faced reelection, but he now stood alone in the Senate, shunned by Federalists and Republicans alike because he invariably put preservation of the union and the nation's independence from foreign influence ahead of party interests.

The day after the Chase trial, Vice President Burr announced his retirement from the Senate, and with his resignation, the Eighth Congress adjourned. The following day saw the President return to the Capitol for his second inauguration, and, perhaps chastened by his setback in the Chase case, he "delivered an inaugural address in so low a voice that," according to John Quincy, "not half of it was heard by any part of the crowded auditory."[34]

After the inauguration, John Quincy's sons contracted chicken pox, but the Adamses nonetheless managed to go to Quincy for the summer, where they took up residence in what now seemed the somewhat crude old farmhouse in which John Quincy had been born.

It stood at a distance from, but on the same land as, the newer, more luxurious retirement "mansion" where John and Abigail had installed themselves and where John Quincy spent evenings discussing politics with his father. After renovating the old house into a comfortable summer retreat, John Quincy took up gardening as a new hobby that allowed him to spend more time in the fresh air.

Early in June, Harvard named John Quincy professor of oratory and rhetoric, a chair created by a bequest in 1771 from Nicholas Boylston, a first cousin of John Quincy's grandmother. John Quincy worked out terms that would allow him to lecture when the Senate was out of session, with payment of $348 per quarter. Although he would not begin until the following year, in June 1806, he snapped up copies of Cicero's *Orations*, Thomas Leland's *Demosthenes*, and works by Aristotle to prepare his first lectures.

During the next session of Congress, John Quincy dined frequently at the President's House with Jefferson and Secretary of State Madison, and after an uneventful winter session, he returned to Massachusetts to prepare his Harvard lectures and open his Boston law office. Too far along with another pregnancy, Louisa again remained with her family in Washington and, in early July, lost another child. John Quincy wrote to her, repeating his thanks to God "for having preserved you to me through the dangers of that heavy trial both of body and mind which it has called you to endure."[35]

In 1806, the endless Anglo-French conflict spilled into the Atlantic again. The British reversed course and seized American ships, confiscated cargoes, and impressed hundreds of seamen. Early in 1807, John Quincy proposed—and the Senate passed—three resolutions, two of which assailed British actions as "unprovoked aggression" and "a violation of neutral rights." The third resolution authorized the President to embargo all U.S. exports. Jefferson, Madison, and John Quincy believed that ending the flow of essential American goods to both England and France would force

John Adams built this lavish "mansion" as a retirement home for himself and his wife, Abigail. See illustration no. 2, page 10, to view the entire Adams family farm. (PAINTING BY G. FRANKENSTEIN, 1849; NATIONAL PARKS SERVICE, ADAMS NATIONAL HISTORICAL PARK)

those countries to end their war with each other and their depredations on American ships. The embargo would not prevent imports from entering American ports, but ships carrying such goods would have to leave port empty, and few shipowners could afford such one-way trade. John Quincy was the only Federalist in either house of Congress to vote for the embargo, which he believed was a middle ground between a suicidal naval war with Britain and passive acquiescence to British rule over international sea-lanes.

Political isolation in Congress only intensified his loneliness. After the Christmas holidays, Louisa had remained in Boston with John II to be near George's boarding school and see him on Sundays. Though surrounded by in-laws, John Quincy longed for his wife and children. At the end of a particularly cold winter day in Washington, he wrote to Louisa before going to bed, "I will not say I can neither live with you nor without you; but in this cold weather I should be very glad to live with you."[36]

Increasingly obsessed by thoughts of his wife, he spent his lonely evenings writing poems, dedicating *A Winter's Day* "To Louisa":

> Friend of My Bosom! would'st thou know
> How, far from thee, the days I spend.[37]

In another poem, he pleaded with Louisa to

> Fling the last fig leaf to the wind
> And snatch me to thy arms![38]

She replied playfully, calling his words "the sauciest lines I ever perused" and asking whether he would like her to publish them.[39]

When Congress adjourned in the spring of 1807, John Quincy returned to Massachusetts to find Louisa pregnant again, and in mid-August, she gave birth to their third son, Charles Francis Adams, whom John Quincy named for his dead brother Charles and for Francis Dana, the diplomat John Quincy had served as an adolescent in Russia.

As Boston Federalists demanded reconciliation with Britain, the British stepped up their outrages against American vessels on the high seas, with the worst occurring on June 22, 1807, when the British frigate *Leopard* hailed the USS *Chesapeake* just outside the three-mile territorial limit off Virginia's Norfolk Roads. As the American ship slowed, the British commander demanded permission to search the *Chesapeake* for four men he claimed were British deserters. When the American commander refused, the *Leopard* fired without warning, killing three Americans and wounding eighteen. The British boarded and, stepping over the dead and wounded on the deck, seized four men they claimed were British deserters. They hung one of the men from the yardarm and impressed the three others. The attack convinced President Jefferson and John Quincy that, short of war, the only effective way to prevent British attacks was to withdraw American ships from the oceans, impose the congressionally sanctioned embargo, and try to undermine the British economy.

When Britain refused to pay reparations for the *Leopard* attack, Congress converted John Quincy's resolution into the Non-Importation Act, which effectively ended all American foreign trade in December 1807. Although aimed at punishing Britain, the act punished Americans more. Within weeks, the embargo had shut New England's shipbuilding industry, its shipping trade, and its fishing fleet. With export outlets closed, farmers—north and south—found their produce a glut on the market. By spring, a wave of bankruptcies had shut businesses and farms across New England and New York—quite the opposite of what Jefferson, Madison, and John Quincy had expected. All three believed the United States could survive as a self-sufficient economy, abandoning imports in favor of home manufactures and mitigating the effects of the embargo while the U.S. government built a larger navy and armed her cargo ships. The huge farm surpluses overwhelmed the internal economy, however, and plunged the nation into economic catastrophe.

Although most of the nation blamed Jefferson for the country's economic plight, Federalists and, it seemed, all of Boston blamed John Quincy Adams. "I would not sit at the same table with that renegade," declared one Federalist.[40]

"Most completely was I deserted by my friends in Boston and in the state legislature," John Quincy admitted. "I can never be sufficiently grateful to Providence that my father and my mother did not join this general desertion."[41]

In January 1808, he added to Federalist anger by attending the Republican caucus in Congress to witness the nomination of his good friend from across the chessboard, Secretary of State Madison, to succeed President Jefferson. In the balloting for vice president, John Quincy received one vote, which effectively ended his ties to the Federalist Party. John Quincy, however, now viewed Federalists as the party of secession, disunion, subservience to Britain, and the end of American independence. "To resist this," he declared, "I was ready, if necessary, to sacrifice everything I have in life, and even life itself."[42]

In May 1808, Massachusetts Federalists met in Boston, their "principal object," according to Republican governor James Sullivan, being "the

political and even the personal destruction of John Quincy Adams."[43]
Then and there—nine months prior to the expiration of John Quincy's
term—the Federalists elected his successor, then passed resolutions in-
structing their senators—Pickering and Adams—to vote to repeal the
embargo. On June 8, 1808, John Quincy "immediately resigned what remained of my Senate term."

> They had passed resolutions in the nature of instructions . . . which I dis-
> approved. I chose neither to act in conformity with those resolutions nor
> to represent constituents who had no confidence in me. . . . [They] re-
> quired me to aid them in promoting measures tending to dissolve the
> union and to sacrifice the independence of the nation. I was no represen-
> tative for *them*.[44]

As usual in times of distress, John Quincy turned to his father for advice and consolation. "Your situation you think critical," the former President counseled his son.

> You are supported by no party; you have too honest a heart, too indepen-
> dent a mind, and too brilliant talents to be sincerely and confidentially
> trusted by any man who is under the dominion of party maxims or party
> feelings. . . . In the next Congress . . . you will be numbered among the
> dead, like . . . the brightest geniuses of the country. . . . Return to your
> professorship, but above all to your office as a lawyer. Devote yourself to
> your profession and to the education of your children.[45]

His father had made it clear: John Quincy Adams's career in public
service had come to an end, his dream—and the dream of his parents—
to ascend to national leadership shattered.

CHAPTER 8

Diplomatic Exile

Although Republicans urged John Quincy to run as their 1808 senatorial and even gubernatorial candidate, he was too disgusted with public service and chose to return to private life. At their request, however, he continued feeding his views on foreign relations to Republican leaders in Congress. Though a private citizen, he remained, after all, one of the nation's leading foreign affairs analysts, and his first advice went to his friend President Jefferson. With New England secessionists threatening armed insurrection, he advised the President to narrow the scope of the embargo to France and England; the President heeded John Quincy's advice, and the renewal of trade with noncombatant nations immediately improved the nation's economy.

Although Boston Federalists shunned him professionally and socially, enough Republicans found their way to John Quincy's law office to set him on the path to prosperity. Indeed, his legal and oratorical skills even earned him several cases before the U.S. Supreme Court—some of historic importance.

Early in March 1809, Boston land speculator John Peck retained John Quincy for what grew into a landmark case in contract law and, indeed, one of the most important cases in Supreme Court history. For $3,000, Peck had sold Robert Fletcher 15,000 acres that Peck had obtained in a state grant from the 30-million-acre Yazoo land tract in Georgia. As it turned out, land speculators like Peck had bribed Georgia legislators—en masse—to make the grants. After the press exposed the scandal, a new legislature cancelled all Yazoo land sales, including Peck's sale to Fletcher. Fletcher sued to get his money back, but John Quincy argued that the legislature's cancellation of Fletcher's agreement to buy Peck's land violated Article I of the Constitution, which prohibits states from "impairing the obligation of contracts." The Supreme Court stunned the nation by sustaining John Quincy's argument, ignoring the justice of Fletcher's claim in favor of the letter of the Constitution declaring the inviolability of contracts and reasserting the constitutional prohibition against state interference in the rights of Americans to acquire property. John Quincy's father had put it bluntly in an earlier pronouncement on the French Revolution: "Property must be secured or liberty cannot exist."[1] Now John Quincy had elicited a Supreme Court decision banning state interference in the rights of Americans to life, liberty, and property. Hailed by Americans across the nation, the decision raised John Quincy to the top of his profession.

On March 8, 1804, three days after James Madison had taken his oath as fourth President of the United States, Madison asked John Quincy to be American minister plenipotentiary to Russia and asked for an immediate reply. John Quincy accepted—without consulting his wife and engendering a furious response from her when he returned to Boston. He tried to explain his rash decision—as much to himself as to her:

> My personal motives for staying at home are of the strongest kind: the age of my parents and the infancy of my children both urge to the same result. My connection with the college is another strong tie which I break with great reluctance. . . . To oppose all this I have the duty of a citizen to obey the call of his country . . . by the regular constitutional authority . . . the vague hope of rendering to my country some important service; finally, the desire to justify the confidence reposed by Mr. Madison in me . . . by devot-

ing all my powers to . . . the welfare of the union. These are my motives—
and I implore the blessing of Almighty God upon this my undertaking.[2]

John Quincy's explanation was an elaborate rationalization. As he himself admitted later, Federalists despised him so much they had pledged to
prevent his ever again entering public service. It was James Madison's
friendship and generosity that reopened the door just enough for Adams
to slip back into government. "I was proscribed in my native state for voting for the embargo and resenting British impressment and commercial
depredations," he wrote to a friend years later. "Mr. Madison sent me for
eight years to honorable diplomatic exile in Europe."[3]

In his last lecture at Harvard, he issued a stirring encomium for his implacable embrace of neutrality: "Let us rejoice," he cried out against Federalist Anglophiles, "that the maintenance of our national rights against
Great Britain has been committed to men of firmer minds."

> If our nominal independence of France rested upon no other foundation
> of power than the navy of England, the consequence would be that we
> should again be under the domination of England. Her argument would
> be that in all reason we ought to contribute our share to support the ex-
> pense of protecting us and we should soon be called upon for our contri-
> bution of men as well as money.[4]

Federalist attacks on John Quincy did not influence his students, who
crowded about him after his lecture, many with tears in their eyes, invent-
ing questions to keep him in their midst. "I called the students *my unfail-
ing friends*," he wrote to his brother a few days after his ship had put to sea
on the way to Russia. He had asked his brother to have his two dozen Harvard lectures bound and published, and they later appeared in two volumes, *Lectures on Rhetoric and Oratory*.[5] He said his compliment to the
students "was justly their due. For they had withstood a most ingenious
and laborious attempt to ruin me in their estimation."

Youth is generous, and although the majority of the students were made to believe that I was a sort of devil incarnate in politics . . . yet they never could be persuaded to believe . . . and they have all confirmed me in the belief that the safest guide for human conduct is integrity. I have inflexibly followed my own sense of duty. . . . I have lost many friends and have made many enemies . . . but the students at college are . . . the only steady friends that I have had. They have been willing still to be considered as my friends at a time when neither my name nor my character was in fashionable repute.[6]

John Quincy's decision to go to Russia without a word of warning, let alone discussion, devastated Louisa—left her angry, distraught, heartbroken. The boys were hysterical. The meager State Department budget—and the lack of an English-language school in St. Petersburg—would mean leaving nine-year-old George and six-year-old John II behind in Quincy. With John Adams too old and Abigail ill too often to cope with two growing boys, John Quincy boarded them with John Quincy's aunt and uncle. He put brother Thomas in charge of their education.

Fearful they would die before ever again seeing their son, John and Abigail Adams were too distraught even to come to shipside to say goodbye. "This separation from a dear son," sixty-four-year-old Abigail wrote to one of her grandchildren, "at the advanced age both of your grandfather and me was like taking a last leave of him and was felt by us both with the heaviest anguish."[7]

Although former Federalist friends stayed away, a crowd of Republicans cheered at dockside as the champion of union and independence boarded his ship with his wife and baby on August 5, 1809. Church bells rang out in Boston and Charlestown as the ship left the quay and sailed into the bay, and all the ships in the harbor sounded a salute—including the legendary *Chesapeake*. As darkness fell and he lost sight of his native land, John Quincy Adams retreated to a quiet corner of the ship with his God and penned,

Oh, grant that while this feeble hand portrays
The fleeting image of my earthly days,
Still the firm purpose of this heart may be
Good to mankind and gratitude to Thee![8]

John Quincy and Louisa were not without friends aboard ship. Louisa's younger sister Catherine had come as a companion to help mind Charles Francis, and William "Billy" Smith, Nabby's son, had come as John Quincy's secretary. Four young Harvard graduates each paid their own way to sit at the feet of and assist John Quincy—much as he had assisted Francis Dana when he was a youngster. Two were studying law with him in his Boston office and planned studying international law with him in Russia. A third was the son of Maryland senator Samuel Smith, brother of the new secretary of state, Robert Smith, while the fourth, Alexander H. Everett, planned making a career in the diplomatic service.

Despite the presence of friends and companions, John Quincy and Louisa missed their boys dreadfully, and John Quincy took to writing all but daily "Letters to My Children," describing his and their mother's adventures. He also tried to impart—as his father had imparted to him—his deep sense of obligation to his country for the liberties he enjoyed and his passion for public service. "Take it, then, as a general principle to be observed as one of the directing impulses of life," he wrote to his boys, "that you must have some one great purpose of existence . . . to make your talents and your knowledge most beneficial to your country and most *useful to mankind*."[9]

John Quincy lightened the tone of some letters, noting in one that he had passed a night on the Grand Bank of Newfoundland "catching cod, of which in the interval of a six-hour calm, we have caught upwards of sixty." He then posed a conundrum that he left unanswered, asking for the "links . . . in the association of ideas" between "cod fishing on the Grand Bank and the history of the United States."[10]

After a pleasant Atlantic crossing, they approached a line of storms as they neared the Danish coast and put into port, where John Quincy "had the mortification to find there upwards of four hundred of my countrymen, the masters and crews of the greater part of thirty-six American vessels, belonging with their cargoes to citizens of the United States captured and detained by privateers under Danish colors, and arrested for many months."[11] Without diplomatic credentials to show the Danish government, John Quincy had no authority to lodge a formal protest, but he displayed "a memorial" that he drew up, addressed "to the President of the United States," hoping to intimidate Danish officials into releasing the Americans. He thrust it under the nose of every official he could find, before admitting in his report to the secretary of state, "My good offices may probably be of no avail to them."[12]

On October 13, 1809, eighty days after they had left Boston, John Quincy's ship reached Kronstadt, on Kotlin Island in the Gulf of Finland opposite St. Petersburg. A Russian admiral greeted them and sailed John Quincy and his entourage across to the Russian capital—only days before the Arctic winds surged in from the North Pole and wrapped the gulf— and all Russia—in an impenetrable deep freeze for the winter.

The map and political fortunes of Europe had changed radically in the eight years since John Quincy Adams had last set foot in the Old World. Napoléon had seemed on the run in 1801, having suffered humiliating defeats by a powerful English fleet in Egypt and raging mobs of hungry slaves in Haiti. After selling Louisiana and abandoning his territorial ambitions in the New World, he turned to consolidating his power at home—first, by restoring troop morale, then by ensuring the superiority of their arms and artillery, and finally, by setting them loose to assault the fragile defenses of Europe's tiny, divided nations. By the time John Quincy returned to Europe, Napoléon's armies ruled—directly or by proxy—the lands stretching from the North Sea to the Mediterranean and from the Straits of Gibraltar to Russia's western borders. Napoléon's boot had trampled over Portugal, Spain, Italy, Naples, the Vatican, Switzerland, western Austria, the Netherlands, Belgium, the German states, Prussia, and Poland. Although French troops had stopped short of Vienna, they encamped so near that Austrian

Emperor Napoléon I brought the Pope from Rome to crown him and his wife, Josephine, emperor and empress. (RÉUNION DES MUSÉES NATIONAUX)

officials feared shifting a leaf of official paper without a nod of approval by a French officer.

Determined to outdo even Charlemagne, Napoléon ordered a religiously based coronation that would exceed in grandeur the coronation ceremonies of all previous French kings. Charlemagne at least had traveled to Rome to force the Pope to crown him; Napoléon abducted Pope Pius VII and brought him to Paris for the coronation. Like Charlemagne, Napoléon took a crown from the Pope, placed it on his own head, and anointed himself "Emperor for Life." He then took a second crown and put it on the head of his wife, Josephine.[13]

By the time John Quincy arrived in St. Petersburg, Britain stood alone with her powerful navy as the only western deterrent to French territorial ambitions. With French troops massed along the channel coast for an invasion of Britain, British warships attacked and sank any and all ships bound to or from continental Europe in an effort to starve Napoléon's Grande Empire. British attacks had destroyed almost as many neutral Russian ships on the Baltic and North Seas as they had American ships on the Atlantic. Both Russia and the United States saw establishment of diplomatic relations as a possible way of solving their common problems with England. President Madison, therefore, purposely flattered the Russians by appointing the son of a former American President as U.S. minister plenipotentiary. His gesture did not go unnoticed.

Besides the United States, only Napoléon's France and the Kingdom of Sweden had ministers plenipotentiary at the czar's court, while ten other nations maintained diplomatic ties through ordinary ministers. The Russian chancellor, or prime minister, therefore invited John Quincy to a private audience the day after his arrival and to be guest of honor at an elaborate banquet for the diplomatic corps. A week later, the czar summoned John Quincy to the breathtakingly beautiful Imperial Palace where, to John Quincy's enormous surprise and relief, the Russian ruler awaited him in his private office—alone. When John Quincy entered, Czar Alexander I—about ten years younger than the American—stepped forward, hand outstretched to greet Adams, saying, "Je suis très content de vous recevoir"—"I'm very happy to see you here."[14] John Quincy reported that the czar took him by the arm—an astonishing gesture of familiarity in a world where divinely appointed royals never touched commoners.

Alexander I had acceded to the throne after a band of noblemen assassinated his father, the harsh despot Paul I. Unlike his father, Alexander had studied under a liberal Swiss educator, and after becoming czar, he granted amnesty to political prisoners and repealed many of his father's harshest laws and edicts. Foreign wars, however, erupted along Russia's borders, and Alexander found himself in a vise, first joining Britain in the war against

Napoléon and, when the French army defeated Russian forces at the Battle of Friedland in 1806, agreeing to join the French coalition against Britain. Russia was still a nominal French ally when John Quincy arrived in St. Petersburg in 1810, although Alexander refused to restrict overseas trade to the French sphere of influence as Napoléon had demanded. Like the United States, Russia championed freedom of the seas as a basic tenet of international law.

John Quincy, of course, spoke French as well as or better than the czar. He also understood enough Russian to allow the czar to digress into occasional anecdotes in his native tongue. At their first meeting, the czar walked John Quincy to a window overlooking the Neva River, then confided that he considered the American foreign policy of neutrality to be "wise and just" and that "they may rely on me not to do anything to withdraw them from it."[15] John Quincy was ready with a reply:

> The political duty of the United States towards the powers of Europe is to forbear interference in their dissensions. . . . The United States, by all the means in their power, consistent with their peace and their separation from the political system of Europe, will contribute to the support of the liberal principles to which your majesty has expressed so strong and so just an attachment.[16]

John Quincy's first meeting with the czar quickly grew into an unprecedented relationship between a monarch and a commoner, with the czar inviting John Quincy to join him in morning walks on the quay along the Neva. The two men discussed international news, and the czar continually peppered John Quincy with questions about life in America. Nor was the friendship limited to the two men, although Louisa's friendship with the czarina had started somewhat differently.

"I went with a fluttered pulse," Louisa recalled, "dressed in a hoop with a silver tissue skirt with a train, a heavy crimson velvet robe with a very long train . . . white satin shoes, gloves, fan, etc. and over all this luggage my fur cloak . . . and thus accoutered I appeared before the gentlemen of our party who could not refrain from laughter at my appearance." A countess greeted her, escorted her to the reception room where the empress was to enter, and instructed her "that I must stand unmoved until her Imperial Majesty walked up to me; that when she came up I must affect to kiss her hand which her Majesty would not permit and that I must take my glove off so as to be ready and take care in raising my head not to touch her majesty."[17]

It was two-year-old Charles Francis Adams, however, who inadvertently shattered imperial protocol, catching the Russian royal couple by surprise and winning their hearts. When John Quincy and Louisa brought him to the palace for his first visit, the childless czar and czarina fell to their hands and knees with joy, laughing at the antics of the little American boy, whom they subsequently invited regularly to attend balls and banquets for children at the Imperial Palace.

Clearly favorites of the czar and his court, the Adamses became the centerpieces of social events in the Russian capital. Invited to every diplomatic function, large and small, John Quincy sent more intelligence about European affairs to the State Department than any other U.S. minister in Europe. With easy access to the czar, John Quincy persuaded the Russian leader to intervene with the Danish government to free American ships and their seamen. The czar then ordered the release of American ships held for ransom by local satraps in Russian ports and opened Russian waters to free trade with the United States. Within weeks, American ships were sailing in and out of Russian ports, developing profitable new trade routes for both the United States and Russia.

As in Berlin, most of John Quincy's work in Russia was to listen to other diplomats and gather intelligence for the State Department. Trapped by Russia's bitterly cold winter, the diplomatic community warmed itself with free-flowing vodka and champagne at lavish banquets and balls that routinely lasted until 3 or 4 a.m. and left most participants drunk, talkative, and exhausted.

"I went in a chariot and four," John Quincy wrote to his brother Thomas to describe the Russian chancellor's hospitality, "attended by two footmen and driven by a coachman on the carriage box and a postilion . . . on the right-side horse of the leading pair." Upon his entering the chancellor's palace, a row of twenty footmen stood "like so many statues" on either side of a broad marble staircase. A dinner of innumerable courses of fish, poultry, and meats climaxed with multiple desserts of fruits and ice creams, accompanied by a choice of liquors and frozen champagne. "The attention of the servants to the guests at the table is so vigilant," John Quincy told Thomas, "that you scarcely have occasion to ask for anything. The instant you have emptied your plate or that you lay down your knife and fork or spoon, your plate is taken away and a clean one is given you in its stead." He said the footmen "see your need for fresh bread as soon as you do yourself. . . . Everything moves like a piece of clockwork."[18]

Louisa was equally astonished, calling the chancellor's banquet "like a fairy tale," with the emperor's table "served on solid gold. That of the corps diplomatique with silver. The chancellor was said to have 300 servants of different grades, 150 at least wearing magnificent liveries according to their grades."[19]

The evenings of luxury, however, contrasted sharply with the Adamses' own living conditions. With a salary of only $9,000 a year and another $9,000 in annual living expenses, John Quincy could hardly compete with the French ambassador's expense allowance of $350,000 a year or even the Dutch minister's modest $17,500-a-year allowance.* It took months, but John Quincy finally found an affordable house to rent for about $2,100 a year, but he had to spend nearly $6,000 on furnishings. "The firewood," he explained, "is, luckily, included as a part of the rent," as were salaries for

---

*John Quincy's annual salary was second only to that of the President of the United States, who was paid $25,000 a year. The vice president and cabinet officers were paid only $5,000 a year each; the chief justice of the Supreme Court, $4,000; and associate justices, $3,500 each.

more than a dozen servants—a steward, a cook and two assistant cooks, a servant to tend the fires, a coachman and postilion, two footmen, a porter, valet, lady's maid, housemaid, and laundry maid. "The porter, the cook, and one of the footmen are married," John Quincy complained in a letter to his mother,

> and their wives live in the house. The steward has two children, and the washerwoman a daughter, all of whom are kept in the house. I have baker's, milkman's, butcher's, greengrocer's, poulterer's, fishmonger's and grocer's bills to pay monthly, besides tea, coffee, sugar, wax and tallow candles. On all these articles of consumption, the cook and steward first make their profits on the purchase and next make free pillage of the articles themselves. The steward takes the same liberty with my wines.[20]

One evening, John Quincy stepped into his cellar and found 373 bottles missing—272 of them "the choicest and most costly wines I had."[21]

Their expenses left the Adamses unable to reciprocate the many invitations they received from the czar and members of the diplomatic corps, but no one seemed to care. The Adamses—John Quincy, Louisa, and her attractive younger sister Catherine—all spoke French beautifully and made up in social skills what they lacked in their ability to entertain. John Quincy did such a good job explaining the Puritan American ethos to the czar that the Russian ruler gave his staff instructions to exempt the Adamses from the many dress requirements, including the costly and elaborate wigs worn by men and women and the exorbitantly expensive, bejeweled gowns of noble ladies—a different one each night through the season.

After the Adamses arrived at an Imperial Palace ball with Louisa's sister Catherine—"Kitty," as her family called her—the thirty-two-year-old czar made the twenty-four-year-old the target of amorous advances. Day after day, he appeared magically at one turning or another as the two American ladies took their daily walks. Louisa recalled that, at a ball at the French embassy, "he sought [Kitty] out himself to dance, and she, not knowing the etiquette, began laughing and talking to him as she would have done to an American partner . . . and produced a buzz of astonishment"—especially as he danced into the dinner hour and forced hungry guests to delay their meal until he took a seat.

Her dance floor tryst with Czar Alexander provoked a spate of invitations for Kitty and her family to attend theater presentations, receptions, and other events that the czar attended. Each invitation included instructions for the Adamses to use the czar's private entrance. Soon, his attentions broadened, with the czar appearing wherever Kitty and her sister happened to be—in the park, at the museum, at the concert hall or theater . . . anywhere and everywhere. Although unnerved by the frequency of their encounters, Louisa dared not interfere with the czar's attentions. Although he acted like a smitten schoolboy, he was nonetheless a schoolboy with absolute power over the life and death of every living being in the land.

As the Adamses continued dining and dancing in St. Petersburg, Abigail Adams had taken her son's complaints about his low wage and high living costs straight to the President. Even the President hesitated tangling with Abigail Adams, and in September 1810, when Supreme Court Associate Justice William Cushing died, Madison submitted John Quincy's name to the Senate, which immediately approved the appointment. Born and raised in Massachusetts and educated at Harvard, Cushing had been the first justice appointed to the Supreme Court by President George Washington twenty-one years earlier.

To the astonishment of all, John Quincy turned down the appointment, using as his excuse the pregnancy of his wife and the impossibility, given her history of miscarriages, of her traveling without endangering her own life and that of her unborn child. His refusal devastated his parents, with his mother saying the Supreme Court appointment would have ensured "the preservation of your family from ruin." John Adams feared his son's refusal would provoke "national disgust and resentment."[22] As he had when his son had resigned from the Senate, John Adams again predicted an end to John Quincy's career in public service and to his hopes for assuming national leadership.

CHAPTER 9

Restoring Peace to the World

John Quincy and Louisa Adams were enjoying life in Russia too much to leave, and he still hated the thought of devoting his entire life to the law. As he told his brother Thomas, "I am conscious of too little law even for practice at the bar, still less should I feel myself qualified for the bench of the Supreme Court of the United States."

> I am also and always shall be too much of a political partisan to be a judge. . . . If the servile drudgery of caucuses, the savage buffeting of elections, the filth and venom of newspaper and pulpit calumny, and the dastardly desertion of . . . friends . . . are to be my lot as it has been in time past, I shall with the blessing of God live through it again as I have done before.[1]

After John Quincy turned down the Supreme Court nomination, two of his law students decided to return home to America, freeing the Adamses of two responsibilities. On July 11, John Quincy celebrated his forty-fourth birthday; two weeks later, he and Louisa celebrated their fourteenth wedding anniversary; and two weeks after that, on August 11, Louisa gave birth to a baby girl.

"My child!" Louisa cried joyfully "A daughter! The first I was ever blessed with. . . . My sister went and announced her birth to her father and he soon came in to bless and kiss the babe."[2]

The birth of a girl enthralled John Quincy as much as it did Louisa. "I think this will convince you," he wrote playfully to his mother, "that the climate of St. Petersburg is *not* too cold to produce an American."

In an Anglican service on September 11, "my little babe was christened," Louisa wrote, "and she was named after *me* by her father's special desire contrary to my wish." Although the czar offered to be the little girl's godfather, John Quincy declined discreetly for a myriad of religious, political, and logistical reasons.

In the ecstasy of watching her baby grow, Louisa wrote, "O she grows lovely. Such a pair of eyes!! I fear I love her too well."[3]

The renewed joys of fatherhood combined with watching the mysterious mother-daughter bond to make John Quincy long for his sons. "My dear boys are never out of my thoughts," he wrote to his brother Thomas. "Your account of George's rapid improvement in learning to read was a banquet to my soul. There are so many things that I want them to learn that I can scarcely wait with proper patience for the time when they ought to be taught them."[4]

The birth of his daughter seemed to him "the proper time" to change the tone of his daily letters to his children. "I want to write to my son George upon subjects of serious import," he said, "but I . . . find my ideas so undigested and confused." His heart wanted to tell his eleven-year-old that he loved him, but his Puritan mind could only express that love as his father had—with guidance: "I advise you, my son, in whatever you read and most of all in reading the Bible to remember that it is for the purpose of making you wiser and more virtuous."

I have myself for many years made it a practice to read through the Bible once every year . . . that it may contribute to my advancement in wisdom and virtue. . . . You must soon come to the age when you must govern yourself. . . . You know some of your duties and . . . it is in the Bible that you must learn them and from the Bible how to practice them. Those duties are to God, your fellow creatures and you yourself.[5]

Writing to his son made John Quincy regret having rejected the Supreme Court appointment. His rash decision would mean remaining in Europe, apart from his boys, indefinitely. He wrote to his parents declaring, "I can no longer reconcile either to my feelings or to my sense of duty their absence from me. I must go to them or they must come to me."[6]

In the spring of 1811, Secretary of State Robert Smith resigned. From the first, he had proved himself incompetent and all too cozy with the British ambassador, who promised an end to the British blockade of American ports if President James Madison ended the embargo on British trade. After Madison responded accordingly, the British government repudiated their minister and recalled him from the United States, leaving an embarrassed President puzzling whether to reimpose the embargo and risk plunging the nation into another recession.

President Madison dismissed Smith and appointed James Monroe secretary of state. Experienced in foreign affairs, Monroe had represented the nation in both Britain and France and, next to John Quincy, was the nation's foremost European affairs expert. The appointment, however, outraged New England's Federalists, who accused Madison of perpetuating the "Virginia dynasty" by giving Monroe an office that had become the stepladder to the presidency. Federalist newspapers called Madison and Monroe James I and James II. The British were even less pleased. Monroe was as outspoken a Francophile as his mentor Jefferson, and the British responded to his appointment by attacking an American ship within sight of New York and impressing a seaman. Under orders to protect American ships, the frigate *President* countered by attacking the British ship *Little Belt*, killing nine and wounding twenty-three. When the new British minister demanded an explanation, Monroe replied angrily that American ships had as much right to *recover* impressed seamen as British ships had to impress them in the first place. He then renewed American demands that Britain cease depredations on American shipping and respect the rights of neutral ships carrying noncontraband.

When the British refused, Congress declared British impressment and ship seizures an affront to the nation's rights and honor. On April 1, 1812, Madison went to Congress and requested a sixty-day reinstatement of the embargo on British trade; ten days later, Congress authorized him to prepare for war and call up 100,000 militiamen for six months' service.

War fever was infecting Europe as well. After Russia refused to cease trading with Britain, Napoléon ordered French troops to the Russian border. Fearful of an imminent invasion, foreign diplomats sent their wives and daughters home from St. Petersburg, leaving Louisa Adams and her sister Kitty as the only foreign ladies in the diplomatic corps—and Kitty as the only target for the czar's amorous glances. In mid-January 1812, however, the Adamses—and the czar—noticed a decided change in Kitty's demeanor. She was pregnant—not by the czar, but by John Quincy's nephew Billy Smith, Nabby's son. John Quincy was irate, and after he had a "very solemn conversation" with his nephew, Smith married Kitty Johnson in a private ceremony at the Adams house in early February.

Tragedy marred their marriage from the start, however, and seemed to envelop the rest of the family. Kitty's baby was stillborn. Then the two newlyweds learned that Billy's mother, John Quincy's older sister Nabby, was dying from cancer, and as Billy and Kitty prepared to leave for America, the Adamses' one-year-old, Louisa Catherine, came down with dysentery. A common disease in St. Petersburg, it gripped the baby in convulsions, fever, and dehydration for two months—then claimed her life.

"At twenty-five minutes past one this morning," John Quincy sobbed over his diary on September 15, "expired my daughter Louisa Catherine, as lovely an infant as ever breathed the air of heaven."[7] Louisa was out of the room when the baby died, but having nursed her daughter for nearly two months, she had spent her last emotions and, according to John Quincy, "received the shock with fortitude and resignation." Two days later, he and his nephew accompanied the baby's diminutive coffin to the graveyard of the Anglican church, where John Quincy "saw her deposited in her last earthly mansion." Louisa had caught a bad cold and was too sick to accompany her husband, who returned home in a state of near collapse. He tried to make sense of his loss, to explain the inexplicable:

> Perhaps an affectionate parent praying only for the happy existence of his child could wish no better for it than that it might be transported to the abodes of blessedness before it has lived to endure the pangs and sorrows inseparable from existence in the body. As life is the gift of God . . . it is our duty to be grateful for it. . . . We ought perhaps be no less grateful for the death of a tenderly loved child than for its life. . . . Had it pleased God to prolong the life of my darling infant, to what miseries, distress and sufferings might she not have been referred? . . . In the bosom of her Father and her God, she has no more suffering to endure.[8]

By spring of 1812, the American embargo had combined with Napoléon's embargo to cripple British foreign trade and domestic industrial production. Factories and mills shut down, unemployment rose, and food prices soared. British exports dropped by one-third, and employers and workers united in demanding that Parliament restore good relations with the United States by ending depredations against American ships. On June 23, Parliament agreed. The Americans had at last won their long-running conflict with Britain's parliament.

But the victory came too late.

It took a month or more for messages to cross the Atlantic, and unaware of Parliament's decision, President Madison asked Congress to declare war on Britain, citing impressment, the blockade of American ports, seizure of American ships, and incitement of Indians on the frontier as his reasons. On June 4, after three days of debate, the House agreed; the Senate followed suit two weeks later. Not knowing that the British had sued for peace, American troops charged into Canada along three fronts in northern New York: at the Saint Lawrence River, at Niagara in western New York, and farther west at the Detroit River.

Just as American troops were invading Canada, war erupted in Europe when Napoléon ordered his 450,000-man Grande Armée into Russia. With Britain's fleet in control of the Baltic Sea, Russian forces blocked the paths to St. Petersburg, funneling French troops westward onto the Russian steppes. Within weeks, the French had overrun Minsk and reached Smolensk—almost without firing a shot. After a fierce battle at Borodino, Russian troops retreated to Moscow, and after the civilian population had fled, the soldiers set the city afire, leaving nothing but smoldering ashes for the French army to plunder when it marched in on September 14.

Only an occasional echo of battlefield explosions reached St. Petersburg, but the war nonetheless brought diplomatic activity to a halt and left John Quincy with almost nothing to do. Even the czar had left—to be with his generals at the front. John Quincy managed to score a last-minute diplomatic triumph, however, by coaxing the czar to give America's Robert Fulton "the privilege for the term of fifteen years" to build and sail steamboats between St. Petersburg and Kronstadt and along navigable Russian rivers whenever the war permitted.[9]

Without food or other resources in Moscow for the approaching winter, the French had to retreat. On October 19, however, swarms of mounted Cossacks thwarted the French about-face with fierce hit-and-run attacks. Darting in and out of snow gusts like ghosts, the Cossacks slaughtered French troops at will and left every farm and village along the way in ashes, without a grain of wheat, stick of wood, or shred of canvas to nourish, warm, or shelter a Frenchman. The "scorched earth" strategy left the French nothing to harvest but cold, hunger, and death. With surviving French troops in full flight, Napoléon abandoned them on December 3 and fled to Paris. Only about 20,000 of his half million troops survived their long retreat. John Quincy described the disaster to his mother:

> Of the immense host with which he [Napoléon] invaded Russia, nine-tenths at least are prisoners or food for worms. They have been surrendering by ten thousands at a time, and at this moment there are at least one hundred and fifty thousand of them in the power of Emperor Alexander.

From Moscow to Prussia, eight hundred miles of road have been strewed with French artillery, baggage wagons, ammunition chests, dead and dying men . . . pursued by three large regular armies of a most embittered and exasperated enemy and by an almost numberless militia of peasants, stung by the destruction of their harvests and cottages. . . . It has become a sort of by-word among the common people here that the two Russian generals who have conquered Napoléon and all his marshals are General Famine and General Frost.[10]

The slaughter of the French army convinced John Quincy more than ever of the wisdom of America's policy "not to involve ourselves in the inextricable labyrinth of European politics and revolutions. The final issue . . . is not yet completely ascertained, but there is no longer a doubt that it must be disastrous in the highest degree to France."[11]

Although they lacked the magnitude of the French invasion of Russia, American incursions into Canada in 1812 proved just as futile. In the West, the British forced 2,200 American troops to surrender without firing a shot in Detroit, ceding control of Lake Erie and the entire Michigan Territory to the British. To the east, some six hundred American troops in western New York crossed into Canada and seized the heights above the Niagara River, only to face a devastating counterattack by 1,000 crack British troops, who forced the American commander to send for help. New York militiamen, however, refused to cross into Canada, saying their terms of service required them to defend only New York State and no other states or foreign territories. As the British savaged the little American legion, survivors fled back into New York.

Farther to the east, just north of Lake Champlain, the largest of the three American forces faced similar humiliation when another group of New York militiamen refused to cross into foreign territory to the north.

Out at sea, America's little navy—twelve fast and highly maneuverable ships—had better results. The forty-four-gun frigate *Constitution* demolished Britain's thirty-eight-gun *Guerrière* off the coast of Nova Scotia in only thirty minutes, killing seventy-nine British sailors and losing only fourteen of her own. Other American ships humiliated Britain's navy off the coasts of Virginia and Brazil. Captain Stephen Decatur's *United States* captured a thirty-eight-gun British frigate near the Madeira Islands off the African coast and brought her all the way back across the Atlantic Ocean to New London, Connecticut, as a prize of war. Complementing the tiny American navy were five hundred privateers, which captured about 1,300 British cargo ships valued at $39 million and forced the British navy to plug America's outlets to the sea with an impenetrable blockade of gunboats along the Atlantic coast and the mouth of the Mississippi River.

Although the navy's exploits lifted American morale, they did little to turn the tide of war, and less than three months after the American army had fired its first shots, Secretary of State Monroe instructed the American minister in London to approach the British foreign office with an offer of peace. The proposal simply repeated America's prewar demands, however, and Britain rejected it.

As word of American defeats reached St. Petersburg, John Quincy Adams's friend the czar offered to mediate the Anglo-American dispute. John Quincy's influence had left the czar an admirer of all things American, although he remained allied to Britain in the war against France. With the U.S. Navy bottled up and British forces in Canada poised to invade, President Madison jumped at the czar's offer, hailing John Quincy as a master diplomat. The President's peace envoys had no sooner sailed off to St. Petersburg, however, when a British frigate renewed the fighting with another attack on the ill-fated USS *Chesapeake,* killing 146 American seamen before capturing the ship and sailing it to Nova Scotia as a prize. With the British sensing victory in the war near at hand, London abruptly rejected the czar's offer to mediate, leaving America's peace envoys bobbing across the Atlantic on a useless voyage.

The humiliation of the *Chesapeake* set Americans aroar with anger at what they now called "Madison's War." New Englanders demanded Madison's resignation, and settlers in the West took matters into their own hands, pouring into army camps to avenge defeats by the British. General

Henry Dearborn, who had failed in his first invasion of Canada at Niagara, now had a corps of ardent patriots to replace the recalcitrant New York militiamen who had refused to fight outside state borders. They sailed across Lake Ontario and swept into York (now Toronto), the capital of Upper Canada (now Ontario), burning the city's public buildings, including the Assembly houses and governor's mansion.

After the raid, the Americans trekked westward around Lake Ontario to Niagara and joined 2,500 troops under Colonel Winfield Scott in capturing Fort Niagara, Fort Erie, and Buffalo's Black Rock Navy Yard, where they freed five American warships. To these ships, Secretary of the Navy William Jones added six new warships, giving Captain Oliver Hazard Perry a lake fleet of ten ships—four more than the British squadron. On September 10, 1813, Perry engaged the British at Put-in-Bay for three hours. The battle left Perry's ship in splinters and killed or wounded 80 percent of his men, but inflicted even more damage on the enemy. The British retreated, ceding control of Lake Erie to the Americans. Perry emerged from the wreckage and sent his famous message: "We have met the enemy, and they are ours."[12]

Perry's victory allowed General William Henry Harrison's troops in the west to rout a combined force of British and Indian warriors on the banks of the Thames River, killing Shawnee chief Tecumseh and giving Harrison control of the Illinois, Indiana, and other northwestern territories. When news of the American victories reached London, the British prime minister reversed his previous stance and sent Secretary of State Monroe an offer to begin direct negotiations for peace at a neutral site in Ghent, Belgium. President Madison named John Quincy to lead the negotiations, promising, as a reward for success, promotion to the highest post in the foreign service as minister plenipotentiary to Great Britain. Rather than risk having Louisa and seven-year-old Charles Francis travel through areas where fighting might still be taking place, John Quincy left St. Petersburg alone on April 28, 1814, relieved at distancing himself from the scene of his daughter's death.

By the time John Quincy had crossed out of Russia, the Russian, Prussian, and other armies allied against Napoléon had captured Paris and forced the French army to surrender. Napoléon abdicated and accepted exile on the tiny isle of Elbe, in the Mediterranean Sea off the Italian west coast. Louis XVIII, the dead Louis XVI's younger brother, acceded to the French throne, freeing 14,000 British troops to sail for North America for a massive land and sea attack against the United States. Even as British and American peace negotiators were preparing to meet in Europe, British ships began shelling U.S. coastal cities, allowing British troops to seize Fort Niagara and take control of Lake Champlain. Coastal raids devastated the entrance to the Connecticut River, Buzzard's Bay in Massachusetts, and Alexandria, Virginia, just across the Potomac River from Washington City. The United States seemed helpless to respond. The government was bankrupt and the President impotent, with no command of his armed forces, no credit with Congress, and little influence over or respect from the American people. Everything he said or did only alienated more of his countrymen. He coaxed Congress into reimposing the Embargo Act—and almost starved the people of Nantucket Island. The embargo so devastated the New York and New England economies that state leaders again threatened secession to negotiate a separate peace with England. Northern merchants openly defied the President and federal law by trading at will with the enemy across the Canadian border—and with British vessels that sailed unimpeded in and out of New England ports.

Recognizing the Embargo Act as a failure and a personal humiliation, Madison asked Congress to end the charade and repeal it. Congress erupted into cheers and overwhelmingly agreed. Congressmen stopped cheering in early August, however, and fled for their lives when a British fleet sailed into Chesapeake Bay. Some 4,000 British troops landed and set up camps along the Patuxent River near Benedict, Maryland, about forty miles southeast of Washington and sixty miles south of Baltimore. Within days they were on the banks of Indian Creek outside Washington at Bladensburg. As the British forded the stream, the shrill scream of rockets pierced American skies for the first time in history, sending bolts of fire into the midst of defending militiamen. To the terror-stricken Americans, the heavens had unleashed the stars.* Their front line broke and fled in panic. With bugler re-treats piercing the air, 2,000 Americans sprinted away, tripping over and trampling each other to escape the advancing British, never firing a shot at the enemy.

A few hours later, British troops entered Washington and began an all-night spree of destruction, burning all public buildings to punish the American government for having burned the public buildings in York. The British spared most private property in the city, although they set fire to four homes whose owners repeatedly shot at passing redcoats. They also spared the Patent Office, as it contained models of inventions and records, which the British commander deemed private property that might well belong to British as well as American patent holders.

A storm the following morning brought bursts of heavy winds that sent flames flying erratically in all directions and forced the British to withdraw to their boats on the Patuxent River.

As British troops burned Washington, British government negotiators sat down with their American counterparts in Ghent to negotiate an end to the war—unaware, of course, of the flames consuming Washington. Join-ing John Quincy was Kentucky congressman and Speaker of the House Henry Clay, who, like John Quincy, was a fierce champion of manifest des-tiny. Virginia-born and self-educated, Clay believed in what he called the "American System," with Americans settling the entire continent and the federal government underwriting a network of roads, canals, and bridges for a comprehensive transportation system. He also favored erecting a tariff

---

*The British first used rockets against France in 1805 and again in 1807 and 1813. Their first use in America came at the Battle of Bladensburg. Invented in China in the early thirteenth century, they were largely used for setting fire to ships in close-range naval warfare until British ordinance officer William Congreve (1772–1822) added such improvements as sheet-iron casings and elongated tail sticks that con-verted them into incendiary bombs. The Congreve rocket carried seven pounds of incendiary materials as far as 3,000 yards.

wall to protect American manufacturers from foreign competition in domestic markets. He arrived in Ghent unprepared to yield to British pretensions to governance over the seas.

Also a champion of westward expansion was former Pennsylvania senator Albert Gallatin. Born and educated in Geneva, Switzerland, he and John Quincy had become good friends in the Senate, and Gallatin went on to become U.S. secretary of the Treasury under Jefferson for eight years. Delaware senator James Bayard, a Federalist, and career diplomat Jonathan Russell, the new American minister to Sweden, made up the rest of the delegation.

Although President Madison had purposely appointed members from all sections of the nation, they presented a united front at the negotiating table behind John Quincy, who was the most experienced diplomat in the group and America's reigning authority on European affairs. And despite their cultural and regional differences, they meshed together magnificently, sharing a rented house, whose servants provided for their needs as efficiently as the staff of a hotel. Although John Quincy took umbrage at Clay's all-night card parties, they found so much in common politically that they became good friends.

"There is on all sides a perfect good humor and understanding," John Quincy wrote to Louisa in one of his weekly letters to her. "We dine all together at four and sit usually at table until six. We then disperse to our several amusements and avocations. Mine is a solitary walk of two or three hours—solitary because I find none of the other gentlemen disposed to join me at that hour. They frequent the coffee houses, reading rooms and the billiard tables. We are not troublesome to each other."[13]

Both sides began negotiations from positions of strength and weakness. In North America, British coastal raids had pushed the Americans behind their borders, and the superior British army threatened to invade at a time when the American government was bankrupt, unable to pay or rearm its troops. Clearly, the Americans wanted—and needed—peace. Britain, however, was just as eager for peace. Her forces had just fought a brutal war in Europe, but with Napoléon alive in Elbe, the British government realized he might return to France and fire up his troops again. Britain also faced possible conflict with Russia, which, like the United States, was demanding freedom of the seas but, unlike the United States, had the ocean-going fire power to attack British ships. In short, Britain did not want to drain its resources in another long war in the American wilderness where it knew from experience it could never score a decisive victory.

The Americans sat down with demands for an end to impressment, which John Quincy termed nothing less than slavery, but before the talks even got under way, the end of the war in Europe left Britain with no need to expand its navy, and it voluntarily ended the practice. John Quincy's other demands included an end to British blockades as well as British depredations on the high seas and recognition of freedom of the seas for neutral ships. John Quincy also demanded compensation for British depredations on American ships during the long Anglo-French war. British negotiators not only rejected his demands but countered with demands of their own, including a southward revision of the Canadian boundary with the United States by about 150 miles. The British also demanded that the United States cede most of Maine to Canada and agree to demilitarization of the Great Lakes and establishment of a huge Indian-controlled buffer zone across present-day Wisconsin, Illinois, Michigan, Indiana, and Ohio. The British also wanted to end American fishing rights off the Canadian Atlantic coast unless Americans granted Britain an equivalent privilege, such as navigation rights on the Mississippi River. John Quincy rejected all the British demands, and as negotiations dragged on, each side backed away or increased its demands, according to news from American battlefields, with British negotiators stiffening after the burning of Washington.

In America itself, the press and public had unleashed a torrent of abuse on President Madison after the British burned the federal capital, but Secretary of State Monroe emerged as a hero, and the President appointed him acting secretary of war. Monroe mobilized the nation, calling in militia from other states, ordering and distributing supplies, and setting up an

Secretary of State James Monroe named John Quincy Adams American minister to Russia, then lead peace commissioner at talks in Ghent, Belgium, to end the War of 1812 with Britain. (LIBRARY OF CONGRESS)

intelligence system and teams of riders to transmit intelligence to his head-quarters. He acted to protect other parts of the country as well, sending a message to General Andrew Jackson in Mobile, Alabama, to take 1,000 troops to defend New Orleans against attack. He promised Jackson 10,000 additional men, then sent express messages to the governors of Tennessee and Kentucky to send militiamen and volunteers to New Orleans. Ignoring the Constitution, Monroe essentially seized the reins of government from the President and Congress, intimidating private banks and municipal corporations into lending him more than $5 million on his own signature to pay and arm more troops.

By September 12, the troops that had burned Washington sailed out of the Patuxent River and up the Chesapeake Bay toward Baltimore, landing about fourteen miles from the city. As British warships came within firing distance of Fort McHenry, troops on shore fought their way to the foot of the fort. The ships opened fire on the fort the next day, September 13, and continued the bombardment through the night. On a nearby ship, attorney Francis Scott Key watched "the rockets' red glare, the bombs bursting in air," and, to his amazement, "by dawn's early light . . . our flag was still there," fluttering in tatters over the fort and inspiring his poem "Defense of Fort McHenry." A newspaper published it a few days later and renamed it "The Star-Spangled Banner."

On September 14, the British abandoned their fruitless assault on Fort McHenry, withdrew their troops, and sailed out of Chesapeake Bay for Jamaica in the British West Indies. Their flight weakened the British negotiating position in Ghent, where John Quincy rejected the British demand for an Indian buffer zone. The United States, he argued, would not cede territorial rights to "savages, whose known rule of warfare is the indiscriminate torture and butchery of women, children, and prisoners."[14]

After a month of talks with no progress, John Quincy grew frustrated. "It appears to me to be the policy of the British government," he wrote to Louisa in St. Petersburg, "to keep the American war as an object to continue or close, according to the events which may occur in Europe or America. If so they will neither make peace, nor break off the negotiation, and the circumstances may be such as to detain us here the whole winter."[15] The British, he said in a subsequent letter, "have withdrawn just so much of their inadmissible demands as would avoid the immediate rupture of the negotiation. They have varied their terms . . . abandoned the claims which they had declared indispensable preliminaries, only to bring them forward again whenever the circumstances of the war might encourage them to insolence and . . . are now delaying their reply to our last note . . . only to receive accounts of success from America . . . to dictate new terms to us."[16]

As both sides realized they had reached an impasse, negotiators fixed on a solution that would relieve them of having to solve any problems. They would simply end the war and relegate all demands of both sides to an arbitration commission to be set up at a later date.

In the end, the Treaty of Ghent represented a stinging defeat for both sides, each of which accepted nothing more than a return to the status quo ante bellum after a costly two-year war. Nevertheless, John Quincy was jubilant at having ended the bloodletting.

"My DEAR AND HONORED MOTHER," John Quincy exulted on Christmas Eve of 1814.

> A treaty of peace between the United States and Great Britain has this day been signed by the British and American plenipotentiaries at this place. . . . You know doubtless that heretofore the President intended in case of peace to send me to England.
>
> If the treaty should be ratified, I am uncertain whether he will still retain the same intention or not. I have requested to be recalled from the mission to Russia. I shall proceed from this place in a few days to Paris, to be there in readiness to receive the President's orders, and I shall write immediately to my wife requesting her to come and join me there. If we go to England, I beg you to send my sons George and John there to me. . . . If any other person should be sent to England, I intend to return as soon as possible to America and shall hope before midsummer to see once more my beloved parents.[17]

The Treaty of Ghent called for release of all prisoners and restoration of all conquered territories except for West Florida, which now fell under American sovereignty. Negotiators did not include a word about the Great Lakes or disputed boundaries along the northern frontier with Canada—or about the issues that President Madison had deemed vital enough for the United States to declare war: ship seizures and impressment. On paper at least, the war had been a waste, leaving 1,877 Americans dead and 4,000

Agreement at Ghent. Admiral Lord Gambier, Britain's chief negotiator, holds the treaty ending the Anglo-American War of 1812 and shakes hands with John Quincy Adams, America's chief negotiator. Albert Gallatin stands to Adams's immediate left, while Henry Clay is seated on the right at the rear. (FROM THE SIGNING OF THE TREATY OF GHENT, CHRISTMAS EVE, 1814, A PAINTING BY SIR AMÈDÉE FORESTIER, 1914; SMITHSONIAN AMERICAN ART MUSEUM, GIFT OF THE SULGRAVE INSTITUTION OF THE UNITED STATES AND GREAT BRITAIN)

wounded and costing millions of dollars in war matériel. It had cost tens of millions of dollars in lost domestic and foreign trade and provoked the collapse of the economy—and the United States had failed to achieve any of the goals for which it went to war. The only triumph at Ghent—for either side—was an end to war and establishment of peace between the two nations—or so they hoped.

At the signing, John Quincy declared to the delegates of both countries, "I hope it will be the last treaty of peace between Great Britain and the United States."[18] At a farewell banquet, Adams stood to toast "His majesty the king of England," after which an orchestra played "God Save the King";

then Lord Gambier, the chief British delegate, rose to toast "the United States of North America," and the orchestra played "Hail, Columbia," which was then the American national anthem.

"I consider the day on which I signed it [the Treaty of Ghent] as the happiest of my life," John Quincy wrote to Louisa, "because it was the day on which I had my share in restoring peace to the world."[19]

On December 24, 1814, as John Quincy and the other negotiators signed the Treaty of Ghent, a fleet of fifty British ships with 7,500 battle-hardened veterans approached the Louisiana shore and glided into Lake Borgne—a large bay on the southeastern coast of Louisiana near New Orleans. Landing forty miles east of the city, a British advance guard marched to within seven miles of the city where, to their shock, General Andrew Jackson awaited in ambush with more than 2,000 frontiersmen. The Americans opened fire and sent the British reeling back to their main force. Jackson then pulled back to a point five miles from the city and deployed 5,000 men in a dry canal that blocked the only route into the city. Compared with the trim-cut uniforms of advancing British troops, the Americans were a largely unwashed, unshaven mixture of militiamen, frontiersmen, woodsmen, hunters, and farmers—to a man, fiercely independent, loyal Jacksonians. Wild, willful, reckless, and often drunk, they were like Jackson himself: fighting cocks who gave no ground in battle.

After a spectacular but indecisive artillery battle on January 1, the British pulled back and waited a week to attack again. As the redcoats advanced in traditional linear style of European warfare, the Americans pressed against the forward wall of the canal and poised their long hunting rifles on the rim. A sudden explosion of high-pitched music startled soldiers on both sides as the British line moved forward. Jackson had ordered a band to sound out "Yankee Doodle," then thundered a command to his troops: "Give it to 'em, boys. . . . Let's finish it up today!"[20] Tennessee and Kentucky woodsmen—all of them crack marksmen in the center of the big ditch—opened fire. The British troops stepped forward mechanically, suicidally pressing onward into the sprays of rifle fire, toppling one by one, each atop the other, then by the dozens. The bodies piled higher and higher until the "horror before them was too great to be withstood: and they turned away, dropping their weapons and running to the rear."[21] After only thirty minutes, the battle was over; the British commanding general and two other generals lay dead, along with more than 2,000 British troops. Jackson's men suffered thirteen dead, thirty-nine wounded, and nineteen missing in action. British survivors limped back to their ships and, on January 27, sailed away from what proved to be the last battle of the war and the last hostile incursion by British troops on American soil.

A few days later, Secretary of State Monroe called members of Congress into the Patent Office building in Washington, the only public building the British had spared from flames. They unleashed a chorus of sustained cheers when he delivered the news of Jackson's victory. Federalists, Republicans, hawks, and doves alike slapped each other on the back, exchanged handshakes, and adjourned to soak in the news with appropriate drinks. What they did not know, however, was the utter uselessness of Jackson's victory. It had not changed the course of the war at all. Two weeks earlier, John Quincy Adams and his American negotiators had signed a treaty ending the war, but like the negotiations when the war began, news of the settlement did not arrive until weeks later, when a British sloop sailed into New York Harbor flying a flag of truce. The war the United States could have won without firing the first shot had ended before they had fired the last.

Nonetheless, Americans—almost unanimously—deluded themselves into calling the war a glorious triumph over the world's most powerful nation—a "second war of independence." The national delusion resulted from a series of coincidences—the United States had scored the victory at New Orleans just before news of peace arrived, and in the public mind, the chronology of the victory made it seem decisive in forcing the British to sue for peace and end depredations on American shipping. In fact, it was the defeat of Napoléon that allowed Britain to harbor her warships and ended her need to impress seamen and seize ships carrying contraband.

On January 7, 1815, John Quincy's colleagues on the American peace commission left Ghent, with John Quincy, Henry Clay, and Albert Gallatin having grown especially close—socially as well as politically. One evening, when the three returned to their hotel after negotiations, the often hot-tempered Clay remarked that one of the British negotiators was "a man of much irritation."

John Quincy corrected his colleague's grammar:

"Irritability is the word, Mr. Clay," said John Quincy. "Irritability." And then fixing him with an earnest look and a tone of voice midway between seriousness and jest, he added, "Like somebody else I know."

> Clay laughed and said, "Aye we do all know him—and none better than yourself."
>
> And Mr. Gallatin, fixing me exactly as I had done Mr. Clay, said emphatically, "That is your best friend." "Agreed," said I, "but one."
>
> And there was . . . truth in the joking on all sides. . . . I can scarcely express to you how much both he [Clay] and Mr. Gallatin have risen in my esteem since we have been here, living together.[22]

Two weeks later, having put his papers in order and received word of his promotion to the London embassy, John Quincy set out for Paris to await Louisa and his seven-year-old son Charles Francis. His wife had left St. Petersburg on January 26, but as each day passed with no word of their whereabouts, John Quincy regretted not having gone to St. Petersburg to accompany them. Reports soon reached Paris of pillaging by renegade soldiers and savage attacks on travelers along Louisa's route from Russia.

CHAPTER 10

Stepladder to the Presidency

As the War of 1812 faded from national memory, Americans began to enjoy the greatest peacetime prosperity they had ever experienced in the more than thirty-two years since Yorktown. Secretary of State James Monroe had taken advantage of General William Henry Harrison's victories in the West to negotiate purchase of Indian lands east of the Mississippi, making the western territory between the Appalachian Mountains and Mississippi River safe for American migration. Secure from attack by British troops and Indians, tens of thousands of Americans streamed westward to carve out farms from virgin plains, harvest furs and pelts from superabundant wildlife, cull timber from vast forests, and chisel ores from rich mountainsides. The land rush added six states and scores of villages and towns to the United States. It generated wealth for almost every free white man in the nation and engendered the greatest social and economic revolution in history. Never before had a sovereign state in the modern world transferred so much land to ordinary citizens, or "commoners." The millions of acres of land they claimed lifted them into the category of "property owners"—the landed gentry—with rights to vote, serve in public office, and govern their communities, states, and nation. To facilitate economic recovery, Congress reestablished a central bank—the Second Bank of the United States—to issue federal currency and serve as a depository for government funds.

As foreign trade resumed with its attendant prosperity, Americans hailed "Old Hickory"—Andrew Jackson—for his victory at New Orleans, Secretary of War and of State James Monroe for his military strategy, and John Quincy Adams for his successful peace negotiations.

On February 12, 1815, Louisa Catherine Adams left St. Petersburg with young Charles Francis to rejoin her husband in Paris, where, he had written, "I shall be impatiently waiting for you."[1] Like her husband, she was eager to cast off the pall that confined her with memories of their dead infant daughter. She left St. Petersburg "without a sign, except that which was wafted to the tomb of my lovely babe."[2] In accordance with John Quincy's instructions, she set out in a large carriage temporarily set on runners to negotiate the snows until they reached roadbeds that permitted normal travel on wheels. Charles Francis and a French nurse rode with her, while two manservants followed in a second carriage on runners, and the two vehicles traveled uneventfully across the Russian snows into Latvia. After an innkeeper warned that "last night a dreadful murder had been committed on the very road I was about to take," they immediately got lost. She and her son endured a terrifying evening "jolted over hills, through swamps, and holes and into valleys into which no carriage had surely ever passed before, and my whole heart was filled with unspeakable terrors for the safety of my child."[3] A local farmer led them back safely to the road toward Konigsberg, Prussia.

Many more frights followed—a broken wheel and a night at an inn that Louisa described as "little more than a hovel," with a "dirty, ugly, and ill-natured" innkeeper and "surly, ill-looking men" as clients.[4] The worst horrors of war confronted them as they crossed a battlefield covered with "an immense quantity of bones." Adding to their terror was the refusal of her two manservants to continue past Frankfurt. Napoléon had escaped from Elbe and was leading a growing army to Paris to reclaim his crown. The two men feared being drafted into his army if they entered France.

Louisa decided to gamble that the confusion created by Napoléon's return would leave government officials uncertain whether to close any borders, and she ordered her driver to speed to the French frontier. After crossing safely into France, her Russian carriage reached the outskirts of Épernay in the heart of Champagne, where a company of French troops, on their way from the Russian campaign to join the emperor, stopped and surrounded them, shouting, "They are Russians! Tear them out of the carriage! . . . Kill them!" Fortunately, a general rode up and examined Louisa's papers, then "called out that I was an American lady going to meet her husband in Paris. At which the soldiers shouted, '*Vive les Américains*' and desired that I should cry '*Vive Napoléon*,' which I did waving my handkerchief. They repeated their first cry, adding, '*Ils sont nos amis*' [They are our friends] and a number of soldiers were ordered to march before the horses."

> My poor boy seemed to be absolutely petrified and sat by my side like a marble statue. . . . The general warned that my situation was a very precarious one; the army was totally undisciplined; that I must appear perfectly easy and unconcerned. . . . In this way we journeyed, the soldiers presenting their bayonets at us with loud and brutal threats every half hour. The road lined each side for miles with intoxicated men, ripe for every species of villainy, shouting and vociferating "*À bas Louis dix-huit! Vive Napoléon!* [Down with Louis XVIII! Long live Napoléon!]" till the whole welkin [firmament] rang with the screech, worse than the midnight owls' most dire alarm to the startled ear.[5]

After two more days of travel and one night at an inn, where "soldiers were crowding into the house all night, drinking, and making the most inappropriate noises," Louisa and Charles Francis reached Paris unharmed on the morning of March 20, forty days after they had left St. Petersburg. At 11 a.m., she and her seven-year-old and his French nurse entered the Hotel du Nord on the rue de Richelieu and reunited with John Quincy Adams for the first time in eleven months. That evening, as John Quincy held "my best friend" in his arms, huge crowds surged through the Paris streets cheering the arrival of Napoléon I and his army of tens of thousands in the capital and at the gates of the Tuileries Palace near the Adamses' hotel.

Napoléon had left Elbe on March 1 with seven hundred armed followers and sailed to the Gulf of Juan, between Cannes and Antibes. He led his men northward, planning to cross the Maritime Alps to Grenoble, but a regiment of troops intercepted them. Instead of attacking, however, they rallied around him, then led his way northward across the mountains, with the number of his followers swelling at each village, town, and city. The people of Grenoble turned out to cheer his return. Lyon followed suit. Marshal Michel Ney, the commander of the French army who had promised Louis XVIII to present his majesty with Napoléon in an iron cage, delivered his sword to Napoléon, welcomed him back to France, and turned over command of his regiments. On the night of March 20, Napoléon, surrounded, it seemed, by the entire French population, marched into Paris and seized power—and the palace—from the king, who had fled with his court.

With Paris in a state of riotous flux, John Quincy packed up his family and prepared to travel to his new assignment in England. Before leaving they drove out to La Grange, east of Paris, to say farewell to the Lafayettes, then headed for the channel port of Le Havre, where thousands of royalists milled about in panic seeking passage to England. Just after the boat carrying John Quincy and his family passed out of French waters, authorities imposed martial law and prevented all other boats from leaving port.

The Adamses arrived in London on May 25 and went to the American government's Harley Street house to find their sons, fourteen-year-old George Washington Adams and John Adams II, nearly twelve, waiting for them. It had been six years since their parents had seen them, and Louisa burst into uncontrollable sobs, clasping her two boys in her arms. Eight-year-old Charles Francis was just turning two when he had last seen his brothers and, of course, had no recollection of either of them. Neither parent recognized George. Without a word about his own feelings, John

Quincy confided to his diary that Louisa had been "so much overcome by . . . the agitation of meeting so unexpectedly her long absent children that she . . . twice fainted. She was relieved by a warm bath."[6]

Also waiting for John Quincy in London were his old friends from Ghent, Henry Clay and Albert Gallatin. Both were there to join him in negotiating a new Anglo-American treaty of commerce and maritime law—a logical outcome of peace. The United States had been Britain's largest source of raw materials for two centuries, and Britain had been the largest supplier of finished and manufactured goods to settlers. With the economies of the two lands so interdependent, both governments were eager to resume trade relations.

Treaty negotiations had only just gotten under way when the Duke of Wellington triumphed at Waterloo in mid-June, ending Napoléon's one-hundred-day reign and provoking a stiffer British attitude toward the Americans at the negotiating table—until news arrived of American Captain Stephen Decatur's spectacular naval victories over the Algerines in the Mediterranean. During the Anglo-American War of 1812, the dey of Algiers had declared war against the United States, demanding tribute for the right to sail the Mediterranean, seizing American ships, enslaving their seamen and passengers, and selling most of the ships to the British. When American hostilities with Britain ended, Congress authorized Decatur to lead a ten-vessel fleet to attack the Algerines. In mid-June, over the course of two days, Decatur's fleet captured two Algerine frigates, one with forty-four guns, the other with twenty-two; he then sailed into Algiers Harbor and forced the dey to release U.S. prisoners, end his depredations against American ships, and withdraw his demands for tribute. Decatur would go on to similar successes against Tunis and Tripoli, which, together with Algiers, agreed to pay the U.S. compensation for the vessels they had seized.

Decatur's impressive display of American naval power surprised the British government, which immediately softened its tone at the talks with John Quincy and his colleagues. British foreign secretary Viscount Castlereagh even went out of his way to send a warm personal note to notify John

Quincy of Wellington's victory. Instead of locking horns over terms of a formal treaty, Castlereagh and John Quincy worked out a less formal, but far broader, four-year, renewable commercial "convention." It allowed reciprocal establishment of consuls and free commerce by the ships of both nations between the United States and Britain and all British territories, with all products, ships, citizens, and subjects of both nations granted equal status in all ports of both nations. The convention also banned discriminatory duties and port fees and allowed Americans to trade directly in British East Indies ports—Calcutta, Madras, Bombay, and so forth—as a most favored nation, thus eliminating costly markups by British intermediaries in England. The convention, with its nondiscrimination provision, would serve as a framework for U.S. trade with all other nations for decades thereafter.

When the time came to approve the finished convention, however, John Quincy balked suddenly, saying the documents had not provided for the *alternat*—a French diplomatic term defining the order of appearance of participating parties in the texts of international agreements and of the signatures at the bottom of such agreements. Under the *alternat* protocol, the order of participating nations and their signatories alternates with each copy of the treaty, with, for example, "Great Britain and the United States" in the British copy appearing as "the United States and Great Britain" in the American copy. Until that moment, the name of U.S. signatories had always appeared after "His Most Christian Majesty," in the case of U.S. agreements with France, or "His Most Britannic Majesty," in the case of the peace treaty with Britain in 1783. When time came to approve the new convention with Britain, however, John Quincy found that the document "named the British government and plenipotentiaries first, which was right for *their copy*."

> But at the close they had put "done in *duplicate*," which was improper. . . . I . . . directed that our copy should be made out, taking the alternative throughout the whole treaty, always naming the American government and plenipotentiaries first, but without any change either in substance or in the words.[7]

Fearing John Quincy's demand might scuttle the entire agreement, Gallatin called the *alternat* protocol "a matter of no importance," and Clay agreed, but America's July 4 Independence Day was just days away, and John Quincy refused to yield. He reiterated his father's furious demand to the arrogant French prime minister Talleyrand seventeen years earlier that the United States be treated with "the respect due to . . . a free, independent, and powerful nation."[8]

"It will throw the business into confusion," Gallatin insisted.

"Mr. Gallatin," John Quincy replied angrily, "you and Mr. Clay may do as you please, but I will not sign the treaty without the alternative [*alternat*] observed throughout."

"Now don't fly off in this manner," Gallatin countered.

"Indeed, sir," John Quincy continued growling, "I will not sign the treaty in any other form."

> I am so far from thinking with Mr. Clay that it is of no importance that I think it by much the most important thing that we shall obtain by this treaty. The treaty itself I very much dislike, and it is only out of deference to you and Mr. Clay that I consent to sign it at all. I should infinitely prefer to sign no treaty at all, being perfectly convinced that we obtain nothing by it but what we should obtain by the regulations of this government without it.[9]

On July 3, 1815, the signatories penned their names on the final documents, and John Quincy Adams savored the joy of having ensured the appearance of his nation's name first on one of the copies of an international document as a full equal with Great Britain for the first time in history. He then went to celebrate his nation's Independence Day with his wife and children.

As minister plenipotentiary, John Quincy next turned to the task of improving his nation's relations with Britain. To everyone's surprise in London's diplomatic circles, John Quincy established a solid working relationship with Britain's brilliant, politically powerful foreign secretary

Robert Stewart, Viscount Castlereagh. Castlereagh had organized the grand alliance of European nations that defeated Napoléon, then organized the Congress of Vienna, where he effectively dictated terms of a common peace settlement. In organizing the so-called Concert of Europe, he established a precedent that presaged the intra-European ties of the late twentieth and early twenty-first centuries. Two years younger than John Quincy, he was too young to harbor any of the deep antagonisms born of the Anglo-American disputes of the previous century. Raised in wealth and educated at Cambridge, he commanded the same erudition as John Quincy and was an equally skilled diplomat.

Wellington's army had been the dominant force at Waterloo, and Castlereagh again dictated terms of peace to ensure Europe's return to pre-Napoleonic borders, thus preventing Russia from swallowing Poland and Prussia from seizing Saxony. In an expansive mood after his diplomatic triumphs in Europe, Castlereagh showed great respect for John Quincy—not only because of the latter's position in the American political world and his experience in international diplomacy but because of John Quincy's breathtaking erudition. As Czar Alexander I had learned, few Western diplomats could match John Quincy's mastery of classical literature, history, and modern languages. And unlike most diplomats, John Quincy never felt the need to equivocate. From the first, he made it clear that his primary goal was to ensure his nation's territorial integrity and the safety of her ships and men at sea. He could not have arrived in London at a better time to do just that. With Waterloo and the exile of Napoléon to a volcanic island in the Atlantic where he could bother no one, Europe settled into an unearthly peace after centuries of constant war. "The world of Europe is in a glassy calm," John Quincy wrote to his father. "Not a breath of wind or a ripple of water is moving."[10]

Like John Quincy, Lord Castlereagh embraced the concept of Anglo-American reconciliation, and at John Quincy's suggestion, he agreed in principle to total disarmament on the Great Lakes, pledging, "I will propose it to the government for consideration."[11] While the government considered, both men agreed to freeze armaments at then-current levels. A year later, both nations agreed to reduce naval armaments on the Great Lakes to four ships each, armed only enough to enforce customs regulations—a landmark voluntary agreement for reciprocal naval disarmament that would become the longest-lasting and most successful agreement of its kind in the world.

With the Great Lakes eliminated as a danger zone, John Quincy addressed other issues that had soured Anglo-American relations in the years after the Revolutionary War: impressment, American access to fisheries off the Canadian Atlantic coast, and the return of slaves who had fled to the British West Indies with the British after the war. Castlereagh brushed each of them aside, however, saying they were best postponed until reconciliation between the two countries had progressed and each could address emotional issues more objectively. In the matter of impressment, for example, Castlereagh pointed out the difficulties of determining the true citizenship of seamen not born in one country or the other. As for returning slaves to their owners, he deferred to Prime Minister Charles Jenkinson, the Earl of Liverpool, who asserted as diplomatically as he knew how, "I do not think they can be considered precisely under the general denomination of private property. A table or a chair, for instance, might be taken and restored without changing its condition; but a living human being is entitled to other considerations."

Although he insisted that the treaty ending the Revolutionary War had made no such distinction, John Quincy relented, admitting the validity of Liverpool's point. "Most certainly a living, sentient being, and still more a human being, was to be regarded in a different light from the inanimate matter of which other private property might consist."[12]

Convinced by the arguments of Castlereagh and Liverpool, John Quincy stopped discussing unresolved issues that had no evident solutions and turned his attention to reconciliation between the two governments and the two peoples. "My social duty at present," John Quincy explained to his father, "is to preach peace. And from the bottom of my soul I do preach it as well to those to whom as to those from whom I am sent. I am deeply convinced that peace is the state best adapted to the interest and the happiness of both nations."[13]

Becoming the consummate ambassador of goodwill, he and, when appropriate, Louisa attended every public function and accepted every invitation they could, including the dinner of London's lord mayor in the spring of 1816 to honor the Duke of Wellington. After presenting Wellington to John Quincy, the lord mayor toasted "the President of the United States." John Quincy responded, "My lord, I pray your lordship to accept my hearty thanks for the honor you have done my country. . . . To promote peace, harmony, and friendship between Great Britain and the United States is the first duty of my station. It is the first wish of my heart. It is my first prayer to God."[14]

The all-pervasive peace in the Western world left John Quincy and other diplomats with few, if any, formal negotiations. They and he spent much of their time creating and improving personal ties to each other at receptions, dinners, and balls, and John Quincy established warm—and, as it turned out, lasting—relationships with both Lord Liverpool and Viscount Castlereagh and many others of note. "The Duke of Wellington called in person," John Quincy enthused in his diary, "and invited me and Mrs. Adams to the wedding in his house. . . . The duchess afterwards called and left her card."[15] John Quincy sought out and befriended as many academic leaders, jurists, and thinkers as possible and established a close friendship with jurist and philosopher Jeremy Bentham, who pioneered penal reform in England and with whom John Quincy often walked and talked for hours.

With so little official work to do in London, John Quincy moved his family into a rented house in rural Ealing, about eight miles from his London quarters. John Quincy called the house "one of the most delightful spots upon which I ever resided."[16] He enrolled the two older boys in a local private school, then supplemented George's daily academic chores with advanced work in Greek, Latin, and history—essentials for entrance into

Harvard. He and Louisa occasionally went into town to the opera—they both loved Mozart's *Don Giovanni*—and he took John II to see several debates in Parliament. But he spent most of his time at Ealing.

At night, he and the boys gazed at the heavens, and he took time to write long, intimate letters to his father, often digressing into complex discussions of political philosophy. Louisa, meanwhile, began writing Abigail, and the two ladies, often cool to each other during the first years of Louisa's marriage, established a deep and warm mother-daughter relationship. To Abigail's delight, Louisa described her sorties to the opera, theater, and formal dinners in London and details of her activities with the boys in Ealing. She was particularly generous in describing the progress of the boys—knowing, of course, how much Abigail and John Adams missed their grandchildren.

"How delighted I should be to have them all about me," John Adams wrote in one of his increasingly emotional letters to John Quincy. "Yet they would devour all my strawberries, raspberries, cherries, currants, plums, peaches, pears and apples. And what is worse, they would get into my bedchamber and disarrange all the papers on my writing table."[17] The elder Adamses also missed their son. "A man should be in his own country," the former President admonished John Quincy.

Inspired perhaps by his nightly studies of the stars, John Quincy started writing poetry again—serious poetry. He had harbored ambitions of writing poetry since his days in Newburyport, when he wrote rhymes to ease the boredom of reading law. "Could I have chosen my own genius and condition," he now thought to himself, "I should have made myself a great poet."[18] John Quincy often read some of his poems to his family and neighborhood friends, after which they all gathered about Louisa and her harp to sing. While at Ealing, Louisa assumed chores as her husband's private secretary, writing and answering routine letters—mostly from Americans in Britain needing or complaining about one thing or another—or, too often, stranded without money.

While Louisa replied to his letters, John Quincy was writing

"Man wants but little here below,
Nor wants that little long."*
'Tis not with me exactly so,
But 'tis so in the song.
My wants are many, and if told
Would muster many a score;
And were each wish a mint of gold,
I still should long for more.[19]

In 1816, Secretary of State James Monroe rode a wave of popularity for his wartime successes to an easy election victory to succeed his friend James Madison as President. Next to the President himself, the secretary of state held the most important and powerful post in any administration, with a portfolio that included far more than simple foreign relations. In modern terms, the secretary of state in the early 1800s controlled many functions of today's Secret Service, Central Intelligence Agency, Department of Interior, Department of Commerce, Department of Agriculture, Department of Transportation, and a number of agencies such as the Bureau of Indian Affairs. Given the secretary of state's range of executive authority, it was no coincidence that the American electorate had chosen three successive secretaries of state to succeed the Presidents they had served—Thomas Jefferson, James Madison, and, in 1816, Monroe. Two days after his inauguration, President Monroe named John Quincy Adams of Massachusetts to be secretary of state—the first sign of a break in the Virginia dynasty that had provided four of the first five Presidents.

Despite widespread calm in the Western world, the United States remained surrounded on land and sea by powerful foreign powers, each greedily eyeing the rich resources of the American continent and ready to pounce if an opportunity arose. The secretary of state and his overseas

---

* Oliver Goldsmith's "The Hermit."

envoys were therefore central to the nation's survival, tiptoeing away from military confrontations while maintaining trade relations essential to the American economy. John Quincy had been the most visible and most eloquent American diplomat in Europe for seven years and, like Monroe himself, had proved himself the most skillful—parrying and thrusting delicately and effectively, taking a stand or not, as the situation required, to extract the best terms he could realistically obtain, given his nation's relatively weak military and naval posture.

"The question whether I ought to accept the place . . . is not without difficulties in my mind," John Quincy wrote about his new appointment. "A doubt of my competency for it is very seriously entertained."[20] Former President John Adams had sensed his son's fatigue with public service and his infatuation with the poet's quiet life in Ealing. Fearing his son might reject the appointment—as he had the Supreme Court—he urged John Quincy to

> accept without hesitation and share the fortunes of your country whatever they may be. You are now fifty years of age. In my opinion you must return to it or renounce it forever. I am well aware of the critical situation you will be in. I know you have not the command of your feelings or the im-mutable taciturnity of Franklin and Washington, but you must risk all.[21]

Abigail added her voice to her husband's appeal, saying that American political leaders were already pointing to him as "worthy to preside over the councils of a great nation."[22] Some of John Adams's colleagues from the Continental Congress of 1774 had indeed written to congratulate him on his son's appointment: "It seems that the office of secretary of state . . . is the stepladder to the presidential chair, at least it has been so in the case of the last three presidents," wrote one of John Adams's friends. "Now, as your son . . . is appointed to that station, if he makes the best advantage of his situation, it is more than probable that he may be the next President of the United States."[23]

As he had in the past, John Quincy yielded to his parents' ambitions and accepted his new assignment. Critics predicted that as a former Federalist, he and the Republican President would soon be at odds over foreign policy, but he scoffed at the allegations, pointing out that he had worked harmoniously under Secretary of State Monroe for eight years. "I have known few of his opinions with which I did not cordially concur. . . . My *duty* will be to *support* and not to counteract or oppose the President's administration."[24]

On June 15, John Quincy Adams abandoned his idyll at Ealing and, with his wife and three sons, set sail for America, taking with him two maids, a household manager, thirty-one trunks, barrels, and boxes, and furniture accumulated in Russia and England. Without any space to spare left on board, he had to sell his 560 bottles of red wine and 298 bottles of champagne before leaving.

After celebrating his fiftieth birthday in mid-ocean, John Quincy Adams stepped on shore in America for the first time in eight years, landing in New York City on August 6, 1817. He immediately sent word to his parents of his and his family's safe arrival.

"Yesterday was one of the most uniformly happy days of my whole life," the ecstatic former President replied to his son. "Kiss all the dear creatures for me, Wife, George, John and Charles. I hope to embrace them all here in a few days. God Almighty bless you all. So prays John Adams."[25]

"God be thanked," an equally joyful Abigail wrote to her son in a separate note. "We now wait in pleasing expectation of welcoming you, one and all, to the old habitation, altered only by the depredation of time, like its ancient inhabitants. Come then all of you; we will make you as comfortable as . . . love and affection can render you."[26]

After attending several functions in New York in his honor, John Quincy and his family left by boat for Boston, and at 10 a.m., on August 18, their carriage pulled up to John and Abigail Adams's house in Quincy. Abigail stood in the door as John Adams II flew from the carriage into his grandmother's arms in tears, with George Washington Adams just behind him crying, "Oh! Gran'! Oh! Gran'!"

Poor little Charles, only ten, held back. He had not seen his grand-parents since he was an infant, didn't know them or what to do or say, and could not yet share their "affection and reverence."[27] He quickly changed his mind, however, as seventy-three-year-old Abigail resumed her role as family governor and hectored all three boys to be diligent, punctual, neat and clean, and so forth. Like his older brothers, he learned that hectoring was the only way his grandmother knew to express her "love and warm affection."[28]

Over the next three weeks, friends, relatives, and enthusiastic Republi-can supporters of President Monroe took turns entertaining John Quincy and Louisa, and they managed to settle briefly into the old house that had been John Quincy's birthplace. His brother, Thomas Boylston Adams, had prospered in Boston. A successful lawyer and father of five, he had won appointment as a judge and, privately, built John Quincy's estate to more than $100,000 in cash and securities and acquired five income-producing residential properties for his brother. But the size of his family was growing uncontrollably, and the strain, it seems, motivated him to begin drinking—a fatal error for anyone with Abigail Adams's genes.

Less than a month after their arrival, John Quincy and Louisa had to leave Quincy for their new home in Washington. They enrolled Charles Francis and his older brother John II in the prestigious Boston Latin School and took George Washington Adams to Cambridge to enroll in Harvard, but the faculty found the boy academically unprepared for ad-mission. John Quincy arranged for him to board with the family of a Harvard faculty member who agreed to tutor the young Adams and pre-pare him for the college curriculum.

Satisfied that he had provided for the education of his sons, John Quincy set off with Louisa for New London, Connecticut, where they stepped aboard a steamboat for the first time in their lives. They "steamed" succes-sively to New Haven, New York, and Philadelphia, covering in a day and a half, in comfortable quarters, a distance that would have taken three times longer by coach—and that produced a collection of bruises. They arrived in Washington on September 20, 1817, and went to stay with another of

Louisa's sisters and her husband until they could find their own property. In accordance with the President's instructions, John Quincy went immediately to confer with Monroe. Because of the thick, gleaming coats of white paint workers had slathered on its blackened exterior after the War of 1812, the presidential mansion had acquired a new name: the White House.

Work on the interior was still progressing when John Quincy arrived to see the President. Out of deference for the secretary of state's first rank in the cabinet, Monroe had awaited John Quincy's arrival to announce his other cabinet appointees. The President had intended to ensure representation of all the nation's regions in his cabinet by naming Kentucky's Henry Clay as secretary of war, Georgia's William H. Crawford as secretary of the Treasury, Maryland's William Wirt as attorney general, and Benjamin Crowninshield of Massachusetts as secretary of the navy. Clay, however, lusted for the presidency—and had sought appointment to head the State Department as his own "stepladder" to the White House. When Monroe appointed John Quincy, Clay decided to remain in his powerful, high-profile post as Speaker of the House rather than recede into semi-obscurity as a peacetime secretary of war. The President named John C. Calhoun of South Carolina instead.

Although John Quincy had expected cabinet members to work as a team, he realized after its first meeting that far from a cooperative venture, James Monroe's cabinet was a hornet's nest of ruthless, politically ambitious adversaries, bent on crushing his chances of becoming President. And beyond the confines of the cabinet meeting room, Henry Clay sat in Congress ready for every opportunity to promote his own candidacy by undermining John Quincy.

> My office of secretary of state makes it the interest of all the partisans of the candidates for the next presidency . . . to decry me as much as possible in the public opinion.
>
> The most conspicuous of these candidates are Crawford . . . Clay . . . and De Witt Clinton, governor of New York. Clay expected himself to have been secretary of state, and he and all his creatures were disappointed

by my appointment. He is therefore coming out as the head of a new opposition in Congress to Mr. Monroe's administration, and he makes no scruples of giving the tone to all his party of running me down.[29]

Indeed, Clay, as Speaker of the House, acted immediately to restrict John Quincy's activities in the State Department with so low a budget that he could barely function. His salary, for example, was a mere $3,500 a year, compared with the more than $75,000 a year that British foreign secretary Lord Castlereagh earned in London. With only eight employees, the State Department had a budget of less than $125,000 a year—one-tenth the budget of the British Foreign Office. Under pressure from President Monroe, Congress raised John Quincy's salary to $6,000 a year in 1819 but gave him no funds to cover his annual entertainment expenses, which totaled about $11,000, or nearly twice his salary.

Monroe himself, of course, had struggled under the same budgetary restrictions as a U.S. minister overseas for six years and as secretary of state for five, and because of his experience in foreign affairs, he involved himself more in State Department business than that of any other executive department—with the warm approval of his secretary of state.

"They were made for each other," Thomas Jefferson declared. "Adams has a pointed pen; Monroe has judgment enough for both and firmness enough to have *his* judgment control."[30] As Jefferson predicted, the two men worked so closely and comfortably together and became such intimate friends that John Quincy could anticipate what the President was thinking before the President himself even knew. The warmth that developed between the two men was evident years later, after the President's retirement, when he told Adams, "It would afford me great satisfaction if we resided near each other and could frequently meet and indulge in that free and confidential communication which it was, during our residence in Washington, our practice to do."[31]

John Quincy was all too aware, of course, how Secretary of State Jefferson's opposition had undermined President George Washington's neutrality policy, and he was even more cognizant of Secretary of State Timothy

Pickering's unconscionable efforts to undermine the John Adams administration. On taking his constitutional oath and assuming office, John Quincy vowed to be a loyal and effective secretary of state—advising the President but allowing him to make all policy decisions and putting those decisions in effect to the best of his ability. "Extend, all-seeing God, thy hand," he prayed in a poem he wrote the night before he took his oath,

> In mercy still decree,
> And make his hand to bless my native land
> An instrument of me.[32]

"From the information given to me," he added, "the path before me is beset with thorns. . . . At two distinct periods of my life heretofore my position has been perilous and full of anxious forecast, but never so critical and precarious as at this time."[33]

As it turned out, Louisa's path was as beset with thorns as her husband's. She still displayed a "continental accent," and Washington's social elite soon referred to the Adamses as "aliens"—especially after John Quincy began walking in the winter weather wearing his exotic Russian fur hat and great coat. To make matters worse, the Adamses decided to forego the long-standing practice of cabinet members' wives paying the first visit to each member of Congress at the start of each session. John Quincy scorned the practice as a waste of time, and Louisa simply saw no point in soiling herself in the mudflows that separated the buildings and homes of the capital. Although they had bought a lovely home, most of Washington City remained a relative wasteland of woods, swamps, cheap brick buildings, and tumbledown shacks. Seams of squalid slave quarters wove through every neighborhood. Streets were still unpaved, and every rain turned them into vermin-infested marshland that often provoked epidemics. Rats and snakes were commonplace, as were cows, horses, pigs, and other livestock, and Louisa hated stepping outside her door. Washington's ladies were outraged by the snub, however, and even complained to the First Lady. Elizabeth Monroe responded by asking Louisa to the White

Cows graze near the Capitol in what was still the undeveloped capital city of the United States. At the time, the Supreme Court met in an area beneath the Senate floor.
(LIBRARY OF CONGRESS)

House—not, as it turned out, to admonish her but to explain the malignity that motivated the custom—namely, the ambitions of cabinet members, who sent their wives to court votes in Congress for their husbands to succeed to the presidency. After Washington's retirement, few in the capital expected any presidential candidate to win a majority of Electoral College votes, thus leaving the final decision to the House of Representatives. As a result, candidates' wives made a show of visiting every representative's wife when she and her husband arrived in town.

"All ladies arriving here as strangers, it seems, expected to be visited by the wives of the heads of departments and even by the President's wife," John Quincy learned. "Mrs. Madison subjected herself to this torture. . . . Mrs. Monroe neither pays nor returns visits. My wife returns all visits but adopts the principle of not visiting first any stranger who arrives, and this is what the ladies have taken in dudgeon." Louisa told the President's wife she had no intention of changing her habits—"not on any question of etiquette," John Quincy emphasized, but simply because "she did not exact of any lady that she should visit her."[34] Surprised by the controversy over Louisa's visits, an editor questioned John Quincy whether "I was determined to do nothing with a view to promote my future election to the presidency as the successor of Mr. Monroe," to which John Quincy replied, "Absolutely nothing!"

> He said that as others would not be so scrupulous, I should not stand upon equal footing with them. I told him that was not my fault—my business was to serve the public to the best of my abilities in the station assigned to me, and not to intrigue for further advancement. I never, by the most distant hint to anyone, expressed a wish for any public office, and I should not now begin to ask for that which of all others ought to be most freely and spontaneously bestowed.[35]

John Quincy said he had accepted his appointment "for the good of my country"—not for the good of his career. Although willing to accept higher office, he was determined that the public should decide on his fitness for any office by his record rather than his words. He would soon learn he had adopted a naive approach fraught with enormous political danger.

CHAPTER 11

The Great and Foul Stain

Although the controversy over Louisa's refusal to visit congressional wives persisted for a while, she gradually calmed the social storm by turning her house into a coveted social destination with elegant receptions for illustrious friends from Europe. Washington's ladies (and their men) soon sought invitations to Louisa's Tuesday evening receptions more than to any other social event in Washington. And most gossip about their "alien" tastes ended abruptly when the Adamses hosted a New Year's ball in January 1818 for three hundred guests, who called it the finest Washington festivity in memory. Louisa sparkled in a magnificent gown and emerged as a gracious and ebullient hostess. John Quincy, on the other hand, was a bit of a grouch. Although brilliant at serious gatherings and conferences, his face turned sour when the music began to play and those around him chitchatted and immersed the scene in badinage.

"I am a silent animal," he grumbled[1]—although he usually exuded cheer with his immediate family in private. After the last guests had left one Christmas ball, he broke into a grin and even danced a reel with Louisa and his sons, who were home for the holidays from college.

At the State Department, John Quincy asserted firm authority over his department from the moment he entered. State Department papers had been in disarray since the War of 1812, so he ordered clerks to create an index of diplomatic correspondence and cross-reference every topic in every dispatch and letter to and from overseas consulates and ministries, foreign ministers, and foreign consuls. He then organized and expanded the State Department Library, which became one of the world's largest collections of references and other works relating to foreign affairs. He also assumed an 1817 congressional mandate that directed the secretary of state to report on the systems of weights and measures of various states and foreign countries and to use these to propose a uniform system for the United States. His *Report on Weights and Measures* would take three years to complete, but it became a classic in its field and led to the establishment of the Bureau of Weights and Measures and was the basis for the uniform system that still exists in the United States.

When he finished the tasks of office management, he turned to foreign affairs policies. Always careful to obtain presidential approval, he issued a standing order that all U.S. ministers abroad adhere firmly to the *alternat* protocol he had championed in London, ensuring that the name of the United States appeared ahead of the other nation on alternating copies of international agreements.*

Despite peaceful relations with the world's great powers, many stretches along the United States' frontiers seemed at war. Pirates repeatedly attacked American shipping from encampments on Amelia Island in the Atlantic Ocean on the Florida side of the Florida-Georgia border and on Galveston Island in the Gulf of Mexico off the Texas coast. In addition, runaway slaves and Seminole Indians encamped in Spanish Florida were raiding and burning farms and settlements across the border in Georgia. In the North, the British had blocked American access to rich fisheries in and about the Gulf of Saint Lawrence between Newfoundland and the Canadian coast.

---

*In multinational treaties, names of signatory countries usually appear alphabetically.

*John Quincy Adams as secretary of state, an office
considered "the stepladder to the presidential chair."*
(AFTER THOMAS SULLY AND GILBERT STUART,
NATIONAL PARKS SERVICE, ADAMS NATIONAL
HISTORICAL PARK)

Other unsettled issues between Britain and the United States included impressment and Britain's compensation for slaves who had fled to the West
Indies at the end of the Revolutionary War.

By the time John Quincy was ready to return to America, he and Lord
Castlereagh had grown closer and learned to trust each other enough to
discuss most remaining issues between their two nations—and both were
eager to reach agreement. Britain wanted to focus on European affairs
without fear of friction with the Americans, and the United States, in
turn, needed to deal with the Spanish menace in the south without fear of
a British attack in the north. After several months of complicated give-
and-take on both sides, John Quincy Adams and Richard Rush, the new

American minister in London, finally worked out an agreement with the British that solved a few things, postponed others, and, most importantly, produced lasting peace between the two nations.

Under the agreement signed in 1818, the British agreed to ban impressment for ten years, restore American inland fishing rights along the Canadian coast, and allow Czar Alexander I of Russia to mediate the slave-compensation issue.* The historic treaty also fixed, for the first time, the American-Canadian frontier from the Great Lakes to the Rocky Mountains, giving the United States undisputed sovereignty over the so-called Adams Strip. By extending the boundary line along the Forty-ninth Parallel westward from the northwesternmost tip of Lake of the Woods in northern Minnesota to the Rocky Mountains, the Americans acquired a 150-mile-wide strip across northern Minnesota, North Dakota, and Montana. (See map on page 134.) Recognition of the Adams Strip as American territory established a precedent for eventually extending the northern border line to the Pacific Ocean, giving the United States sovereignty over Puget Sound and the mouth of the Columbia River. In the meantime the Oregon Territory west of the Rockies would remain open to both English and Americans, to trade with each other freely and come and go as they pleased, with neither nation claiming sovereignty over them or their lands.

In a subsequent discussion with John Quincy, however, Stratford Canning, the British minister to the United States, seemed to dismiss the agreement by claiming British ownership of the mouth of the Columbia River. When John Quincy disagreed, Canning replied sharply, "Why? Do you not *know* we have a claim?"

"I do not *know* what you claim nor what you do not claim," John Quincy snapped back. "You claim India, you claim Africa—"

---

*Four years later, the czar found in favor of the United States and ordered two commissions to determine the number of slaves and value of each due to the United States. In 1826, Britain agreed to pay the United States a total of $1,204,960 in full compensation for all the slaves.

"Perhaps," Canning interrupted, "a piece of the moon."

"No," John Quincy replied angrily. "I have not heard that you claim exclusively any part of the moon; but there is not a spot on *this* habitable globe that I could affirm you do not claim, and there is none which you may not claim with as much color of light as you can have to Columbia River or its mouth."

"And how far would you consider this exclusion of right to extend?" Canning asked.

"To all the shores of the South Sea [Pacific Ocean]," John Quincy asserted.[2]

In the end, the British Foreign Office disavowed Canning's claim of British sovereignty at the mouth of the Columbia River, thus ensuring peace along the U.S. frontier with Britain. Free to turn its attention to the conflict with Spain, the Monroe administration ordered Secretary of War John C. Calhoun to organize two military expeditions—one to crush pirates on Amelia Island and another to pursue and attack Indians and renegade slaves in Florida.

Two weeks later, General Edmund P. Gaines led troops to Amelia Island, while Tennessee militia commander General Andrew Jackson led a campaign into northern Florida, with President Monroe exhorting Jackson that "great interests are at issue, and until our course is carried through triumphantly . . . you ought not to withdraw your active support from it."[3] The President made it clear that he considered acquisition of the Floridas essential to the security of the United States. With the Spanish army attempting to suppress wars of independence in Chile, Colombia, Venezuela, and Panama, President Monroe did not believe Spain would be able to spare enough troops to defend the Floridas.

Aware that his mission was a de facto declaration of war, Jackson at first refused to violate the Constitution by warring against another nation without a congressional mandate. Before setting out for Florida, he demanded a letter from the President clarifying his mission, but he never received one and invaded Florida without it. After seizing Spanish posts at St. Marks,

about forty miles south of the Georgia border, he and his men swept eastward to the Sewanee River, where he captured the Seminole village of Bow-
leg's Town and burned three hundred houses. He then marched his force
westward across the panhandle, leveling every Seminole fort and black village he could find. To terrify the population into submission, he hanged
two captured Creek chieftains.

"They will foment war no more," Jackson declared.[4]

On May 24, Jackson's troops marched into Spanish-controlled Pen-
sacola, on the Gulf of Mexico near the Alabama border, effectively taking
control of the entire Florida panhandle. He also captured two British
traders, one of them a shipowner, and accused them of aiding the enemy.
He hanged the shipowner from the yardarm of his own ship in front of a
group of terrified Indians and ordered a firing squad to execute the other.
On June 2, Jackson sent a message to Monroe that he had won the Seminole War, and if the President would send him the Fifth Infantry, he
would march his men eastward to deliver Fort St. Augustine. "Add another regiment and one frigate," he boasted, "and I will insure you Cuba
in a few days."[5]

"The President and all the members of the cabinet except myself," John
Quincy was surprised to find, "are of opinion that Jackson acted not only
without, but against his instructions; that he has committed war against
Spain. The question is embarrassing and complicated, not only as involv-
ing an actual war with Spain, but that of the executive power to authorize
hostilities without a declaration of war by Congress." John Quincy stood
alone in disagreement, arguing that Jackson's actions were "justified by the
necessity of the case and by the misconduct of the Spanish commanding
officers in Florida." John Quincy insisted that Jackson "was authorized to
cross the Spanish line in pursuit of the Indian enemy" and that the Constitution authorized the executive to wage "defensive acts of hostility" without notifying Congress.

Although John Quincy failed to convince the rest of the cabinet, he
convinced the President that Jackson had actually strengthened America's
international standing by demonstrating a will to defend national inter-

ests. Switching to John Quincy's position, Monroe rewarded Jackson by naming him governor of Florida—to the cheers of the overwhelming majority of Americans. The Spanish king, of course, protested, as did English and European government leaders and newspapers, all condemning Jackson's invasion of Florida as brutal, runaway imperialism.

On June 13, Speaker of the House Henry Clay added his voice to the chorus of criticisms, charging Jackson with undermining the constitutional authority of Congress to declare war. "Efforts were forthwith made in Congress," John Quincy explained, "to procure a vote censuring the conduct of General Jackson, whose fast increasing popularity had, in all probability excited the envy of politicians . . . but the President himself, and Mr. Adams . . . warmly espoused the cause of the American commander."[6]

With President Monroe now giving him free rein on the Florida issue, John Quincy sent instructions to the American minister in Madrid to present the Spanish government with an ultimatum: cede Florida or act decisively to prevent further attacks on American territory by Florida-based renegades. John Quincy then called Spanish minister Don Luis de Onis y Gonzales to the State Department. He did not like the fifty-five-year-old Spaniard, called him "wily Don" in private, and disparaged him as "cold, calculating . . . supple and cunning . . . overbearing . . . careless of what he asserts or how grossly it is proved to be unfounded."

I had an hour's conversation with him. . . . I mentioned the hostilities of the Seminole Indians upon our frontiers, and I urged that if we should not come to an early conclusion of the Florida negotiation, Spain would not have the possession of Florida to give us.[7]

President Monroe then prepared to go before Congress for his second annual address, in which he planned to answer his critics. He instructed John Quincy to prepare a single policy statement that would respond to the king of Spain, to critics in England and Europe, and to the American Congress. John Quincy had no sooner started working on a draft, however, when a letter arrived from his son John II that left him all but prostrate with shock and grief: Abigail Adams had died on October 28, 1818, two weeks short of her seventy-fourth birthday.

"Oh, God!" he cried out, tears streaming down his face. "Oh, God! My mother, beloved and lamented more than language can express, yielded up her pure and gentle spirit to its creator."

> Oh, God! Never have I known another human being the perpetual object of whose life was so unremittingly to do good. . . . There is no virtue in the female heart . . . [that] was not the ornament of hers. . . . She had been, during the war of our Revolution, an ardent patriot, and the earliest lesson of unbounded devotion to the cause of their country that her children received was from her.[8]

After recovering his composure, he wrote to his "Ever Dear and Revered Father":

> By a letter from my son John, I have . . . been apprised of that afflictive dispensation of Providence which has bereft you of the partner of your life; me of the tenderest and most affectionate of Mothers. . . . How shall I offer you consolation for your loss when I feel that my own is irreparable? . . . Let me hear from you, my dearest father, let me hear from you soon. And may the blessing of that God whose tender mercies are over all his works still shed rays of heavenly hope and comfort over the remainder of your days.

He signed it, "Your distressed but ever affectionate and dutiful son."[9]

Although President Monroe was deeply sympathetic, only a few days remained before he would have to justify the attack and seizure of Florida to the world and obtain retroactive approval from Congress. As Thomas Jefferson had predicted of the Monroe-Quincy relationship, John Quincy's "pointed pen"—despite the sorrow of its holder—prepared a response that articulated the President's thoughts better than the President could have done himself. Using John Quincy's carefully considered words, the President hailed Jackson's attack as "an act of patriotism, essential to the honor and interests of your country." Brushing aside constitutional issues, Monroe declared that

> the United States stand justified in ordering their troops into Florida in pursuit of their enemy. They have this right by the law of nations if the Seminoles were inhabitants of another country and had entered Florida to elude pursuit. It is not an act of hostility to Spain. It is the less so, because her government is bound by treaty to restrain . . . the Indians there from committing hostilities against the United States.[10]

The message scoffed at the Spanish king's portrayal of Jackson's assault as an outrage and Jackson himself as lacking "honor and dignity." Monroe then quoted a letter from a survivor of one of the Indian attacks on settlers.

> There was a boat that was taken . . . that had in it thirty men, seven women, and four small children. There were six of the men got clear, and one woman saved, and all the rest of them got killed. The children were taken by the leg and their brains dashed out against the boat. . . . Should inquiry be made why . . . after this event the savage Hamathli-Meico [the Creek chieftain] upon being taken by the American troops was by order of their commander immediately hung, let it be told that that savage was the commander of the party by whom those women were butchered and those helpless infants dashed against the boat.[11]

President Monroe went on to cite the law of nations [*le droit des gens*] as drafted by Swiss jurist Emmerich von Vattel, who wrote, "When at war with a ferocious nation which observes no rule and grants no quarter, they may be chastised by the persons of them who may be taken."[12] As for the Englishmen that Jackson ordered hung, John Quincy's response for the President called them "accomplices of savages, and, sinning against their better knowledge, worse than savages."

General Jackson, possessed of their persons and of the proofs of their guilt, might, by the lawful and ordinary usages of war, have hung them both without formality of a trial. . . . He gave them the benefit of trial by a court-martial of highly respectable officers. . . . The defense of one consisted . . . of technical cavils at the nature of part of the evidence against him, and the other confessed his guilt.[13]

John Quincy's text then addressed Henry Clay's criticisms: "The President will neither inflict punishment nor pass a censure on General Jackson for that conduct, the motives of which were founded in the purest patriotism . . . and the vindication of which is written on every page of the law of nations as well as in the first law of nature—self-defense."

And finally, the presidential address referred to John Quincy's negotiations with Don Luis de Onis, saying that the restoration of Florida to Spanish sovereignty was based on the President's confidence that Spain would

restrain by force the Indians of Florida from all hostilities against the United States . . . that there will be no more murders, no more robberies . . . by savages prowling along the Spanish line, seeking shelter within it to display in their villages the scalps of our women and children and to sell with shameless effrontery the plunder from our citizens in Spanish forts and cities. . . . The duty of this government to protect the persons and property of our fellow citizens on the borders of the United States is imperative. It must be discharged. And if, after all the warnings Spain has had . . . the necessities of self-defense should again compel the United States to take possession of the Spanish forts and places in Florida . . . restoration of them must not be expected.[14]

Faced with revolts across South America and terrified of again confronting the man they called "the Napoléon of the woods [Jackson],"[15] the Spaniards capitulated. In the negotiations that followed, John Quincy let the Spanish government save face by asking the secretary of war to withdraw American troops from Florida and restore nominal sovereignty over the Florida panhandle to Spain. Spain then ceded both East and West Florida to the United States and renounced all claims to both territories. The United States, in turn, renounced all claims to Texas and used the $5 million owed to Spain for the Florida acquisition to settle claims of American citizens against Spain for Indian depredations. In addition to ceding the Floridas, the Adams-Onis agreement, or Transcontinental Treaty, defined the western limits of the Louisiana Territory, with the Spanish ceding all claims to the Pacific Northwest and extending nominal U.S. sovereignty to the Pacific coast.

Cowed by the President's annual address, Henry Clay and the Senate approved the Adams-Onis treaty. Together with the rest of the Louisiana Purchase and the Florida conquest, the treaty expanded the small, East Coast nation that George Washington had governed into a vast, rich, and powerful empire, within a relatively impregnable wall of natural defenses.

On February 22, 1821, George Washington's birthday, John Quincy Adams effected the exchange of treaties ceding Florida to the United States—a transaction he called "the most important of my life . . . an event of magnitude in the history of this Union."

> Let my sons, if they ever consult this record of their father's life . . . remark the workings of private interests, of perfidious fraud, of sordid intrigues, of royal treachery, of malignant rivalry, and of envy masked with patriotism . . . all combined to destroy this treaty. Under the petals of this garland of roses . . . Onis had hidden a viper . . . and all the calculations of my downfall by the Spanish negotiation has left me with credit rather augmented . . . by the result.[16]

Stung by their attempts to censure him, Jackson rode over the mountains to Washington City to confront his congressional challengers. An adoring public intervened. "Whenever the General went into the streets," one newspaper reported, "it was difficult to find a passage through, so great was the desire of people to see him. . . . Among the people . . . his popularity is unbounded—old and young speak of him with rapture."[17]

Congress responded to the public euphoria by overwhelmingly defeating Clay's proposed censures, and when Clay went to Jackson's hotel to apologize, the general had already left for New York.

In addition to silencing Clay, John Quincy's masterful policy statements silenced the British press and government. Jackson's execution of two British subjects would, a few years earlier, have provoked a British naval attack, but after reading John Quincy's paper, Lord Castlereagh agreed, "It is impossible not to admit that the unfortunate sufferers . . . had been engaged in unauthorized practices of such a description as to have deprived them of any claim on their own government for interference in their behalf." He ordered the British minister in Washington not to take "any further step in the business."[18]

In the fall of 1819, John Quincy and Louisa returned to Quincy to visit John Adams—only to find that John Quincy's beloved brother Thomas Boylston's occasional drinking had become chronic. Not only had his law practice deteriorated, he had allowed John Quincy's affairs to fall into disarray. Although Thomas promised to reform, John Quincy had no choice but to transfer his estate to another firm. By 1820, its attorneys had restored enough order to his investments for him to buy a large new double-house in Washington—on present-day F Street at Thirteenth, at the time within view of the White House. It came with a second-floor ballroom for Louisa's huge Christmas assemblies, and its proximity to the Potomac allowed John Quincy to add a swim to his regular regime of daily walks. Bathing suits having not yet been invented, he simply left his clothes on a rock at the shore and waded in stark naked—and no one paid attention.

To break the routine of diplomatic paperwork, John Quincy returned to his old reading habits—Tacitus, Alexander Pope, scientific journals, and, of course, the Bible. He became president of the American Bible Society and, in 1820, president of the American Academy of Arts and Sciences, which his father had helped found.

To John Quincy's dismay, the Adams-Onis treaty he had negotiated created almost as many problems as it solved. Although it opened the West

to settlement and promised an unprecedented period of growth and prosperity, it also extended the problem of slavery far beyond the confines of
southern slave states. At the end of 1819, the Missouri Territory applied
for statehood, provoking a motion in Congress to exclude slavery from
new states. Although John Quincy had despised slavery since his first encounter with it in Germany as a youngster, he had never before involved
himself politically in disputes over the issue because it was virtually non-
existent in his native New England and seldom a topic of discussion
there—certainly not in Quincy.

"I take it for granted," he now realized, "that the present question [of
slavery] is a mere preamble—a title page to a great tragic volume." As he
further studied the issue, he concluded, "This is a question between the
rights of human nature and the Constitution of the United States. Probably both will suffer by the issue of the controversy."[19]

The controversy divided Congress—and, indeed, the nation—for political and economic reasons as well as moral. The North feared Missouri's
entry into the Union as a slave state would alter the free-state/slave-state balance in the Senate, where a succession of northern vice presidents had invariably tilted tie votes in favor of northern interests. When Alabama—a slave
state—won admission as the twenty-first state, the admission of Illinois—a
free state—restored senatorial balance. There was no semblance of balance
in the House of Representatives, however. In the years since ratification of
the Constitution, the population of the North had grown faster than that of
the South. Free states counted about 5.2 million people, with 105 House
votes, by 1819, while the population of slave states totaled about 4.5 million, with only 81 House votes. With Missouri's admission, the South saw
the opportunity to gain a one-state majority in the Senate to compensate for
its minority status in the House of Representatives.

Monroe had formed his cabinet with members from each region, and he
ordered them not to involve themselves—or him—in the controversy. The
dispute over slavery in the Missouri Territory, however, grew too widespread to ignore, and the more John Quincy heard cabinet members from

the South defend slavery, the more convinced he became that it was "false and heartless." Slavery, he asserted, made "the first and holiest rights of humanity depend upon the color of the skin."

> It perverts human reason . . . to maintain that slavery is sanctioned by the Christian religion, that slaves are happy and contented in their condition, that between master and slave there are ties of mutual attachment and affection, that the virtues of the master are refined and exalted by the degradation of the slave; while at the same time they vent execrations upon the slave trade, curse Britain for having given them slaves, burn at the stake Negroes convicted of crimes for the terror of the example, and writhe in agonies of fear at the very mention of human rights as applicable to men of color. . . . The bargain between freedom and slavery contained in the Constitution of the United States is morally and politically vicious, inconsistent with the principles upon which alone our Revolution can be justified.[20]

Cabinet members William H. Crawford, from Georgia, and John C. Calhoun, from South Carolina, were both slaveholders, as was the President. Hardly a champion of manumission, Monroe steered clear of the issue—not because of indifference but because the Constitution gave only Congress jurisdiction over the admission of states, and it gave territories the right to become states without restrictions or preconditions. As for his personal views, Monroe had no strong objections to slavery, saying only, "The God who made us, made the black people, and they ought not to be treated with barbarity."[21]

Apart from morality, both sides used the Constitution to press their arguments. Although its power to regulate interstate trade gave Congress the right to prohibit interstate traffic in slaves, the Constitution did not give either Congress or the states powers to abolish slavery in states and territories where it already existed or to establish slavery in states where it did not exist. Although it was not his purview as secretary of state, John Quincy had enough standing as a constitutional scholar to step into the debate to help the President and Congress resolve the issue as it affected Missouri. While admitting he despised slavery as "a sin before the sight of God,"[22] he said his role was not to debate the pros and cons of the institution but solely to determine whether the Constitution gave the federal government power to abolish it without a constitutional amendment. Clearly, it did not.

"For the admission of a state where no slavery exists," John Quincy explained, "Congress may prescribe as a condition that slavery shall never be established in it, as they have done to the states of Ohio, Indiana, and Illinois. But where it exists, as in Missouri and Arkansas, the power of extirpating it is not given to the Congress by the Constitution."[23]

John Quincy's pronouncements, like those of a judge on high, silenced the debaters for a while, and before the end of the year, an opportunity for compromise materialized with a petition from Maine to separate from Massachusetts and join the Union as a new state. When the Sixteenth Congress met in mid-February 1820, it needed only two weeks to admit Maine as a free state and Missouri as a slave state. It then drew a line across the rest of the Louisiana Territory, excluding slavery in all new states above latitude 36°30' and permitting slavery in new states below that line. (See map on page 214.)

The Missouri Compromise solved the problem of admitting new states but postponed the question of abolition for nearly a decade, at which time John Quincy Adams would have no choice but to confront it head-on. "Slavery," he declared presciently,

> is the great and foul stain upon the North American Union, and it is a contemplation worthy of the most exalted soul whether its total abolition is or is not practicable: if practicable, by what means it may be effected . . . at the smallest cost of human sufferance. A dissolution, at least temporary, of the Union as now constituted would be certainly necessary, and the dissolution must be upon a point involving the question of slavery and no other. The Union might then be reorganized on the fundamental principle of emancipation.[24]

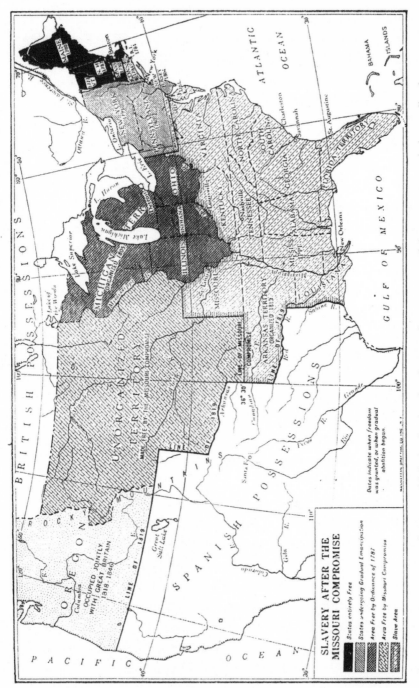

The Missouri Compromise of 1820 established a dividing line between free territory and slave territory, with slavery illegal in any new states in the lands above the line and legal in states formed below the line.

The Missouri Compromise seemed to settle America's future, and when James Monroe stood for reelection at the end of 1820, no one opposed him. Of 235 electoral votes, Monroe received 231, with three abstentions and only one elector casting a dissenting vote to prevent Monroe from matching George Washington as the only President to have won unanimously. "And that vote, to my surprise and mortification, was for me," John Quincy Adams recounted with embarrassment. He was, however, pleased with the election results. "Party conflict has performed its entire revolution," he said with satisfaction, "and that unanimity of choice which began with George Washington has come around again in the person of James Monroe. In the survey of our national history, this latter unanimity is much more remarkable than the first."[25]

Monroe's unopposed reelection, however, marked the end of the Federalist Party and left his own Republican Party in disarray, with leaders in each state casting greedy eyes on the President's chair if and when Monroe decided to vacate it. John Quincy warned the President that "as the first term . . . has hitherto been the period of the greatest national tranquility . . . it appears to me scarcely avoidable that the second term will be among the most stormy and violent. I told him that I thought the difficulties before him were thickening and becoming hourly more and more formidable."[26]

In 1821, a rising tide of populist sentiment swept in from the West, where, in a monumental clash of generations, frontiersmen and settlers rejected property ownership as a qualification for voting and holding office in the new states they founded. A concept that dated back to eighteenth-century colonial rule, when land ownership depended on royal grants from Britain, property qualifications for voting were alien to young, free-spirited, nineteenth-century frontiersmen. Kentucky, Indiana, Illinois, and other western states, therefore, rejected the concept in writing their constitutions, providing instead for white manhood suffrage. Although New Jersey had expanded suffrage in 1807 and Maryland in 1810, Connecticut waited until 1818 to eliminate property requirements for voting, with Massachusetts following in 1820 and New York in 1821.

In addition to demands for greater democracy at home, western populists embraced the spread of democracy abroad, with Speaker Henry Clay asking Congress in 1818 to recognize the growing number of revolutionary governments in Spanish America. The House expressed its sympathy with the Latin Americans and pledged to support the President if he recognized any of the new regimes. Inspired by America's Revolutionary War, South America's wars of independence had broken out in 1810, but James Madison's administration, and Monroe himself during his first term in office, had treated the conflicts as civil wars and, in the tradition of George Washington, kept the United States neutral.

In March 1822, President Monroe was ready to assert America's voice as a world power and asked Congress to recognize Latin American republics that had declared independence from Spain. It was, he said, "manifest that all those provinces are not only in the full enjoyment of their independence, but . . . that there is not the most remote prospect of their being deprived of it." The new governments, he asserted, "have a claim to recognition by other powers" and the United States "owe it to their station and character in the world, as well as to their essential interests," to recognize them.[27] Led by Speaker Henry Clay, Congress supported the President, and the United States recognized Colombia and Mexico as independent nations.*

Although Monroe believed Spain unable "to produce any change . . . in the present condition" of its former South American colonies, French king Louis XVIII led an alliance of absolute monarchs in pledging to send troops to his Bourbon cousin, Spanish king Ferdinand VII, to help him recapture his rich South American colonies. After decades of war against Napoléon to prevent French expansion, Britain threatened to resume her war with France rather than tolerate French military expeditions to South America—and asked the United States to join her.

---

*The United States would recognize Chile and Argentina in January 1823, Brazil in May 1824, the United Provinces of Central America (now Guatemala, Honduras, El Salvador, Costa Rica, and Nicaragua) in August 1824, and Peru in May 1826.

When they learned of the European threats to suppress South American independence movements, former Presidents Jefferson and Madison intruded into the political picture by urging President Monroe to accept England's invitation, as did Secretary of War Calhoun and Speaker of the House Clay and his legion of congressional war hawks. John Quincy stood alone, arguing against any American ties to England or entangling alliances with any other foreign nation, for that matter. Like his father, he believed that even the slightest subservience to a foreign power represented a loss of independence—symbolically if not materially, but probably both. Still the champion of George Washington's policies, John Quincy called "the principle of neutrality in *all* foreign wars fundamental to the continuance of our liberties and of our Union."

> So far as [South Americans] were contending for independence, I wished well to their cause, but I have seen and yet see no prospect that they would establish free or liberal institutions of government. They are not likely to promote the spirit either of freedom or order by their example. They have not the first element of good or free government. Arbitrary power, military and ecclesiastical, was stamped upon their education, upon their habits, and upon their institutions.[28]

Proclaiming a policy the President would later claim as his own, John Quincy urged the President to disclaim any intention of "interference with the political affairs of Europe" so that the United States could hold the "expectation and hope that European powers will equally abstain from the attempt to spread their principles in the American hemisphere or to subjugate by force any part of these continents to their will."[29]

No sooner had he spoken than his friend Russian czar Alexander I extended his nation's claims along the Pacific coast of North America to the Fifty-first Parallel in the middle of the Oregon Territory and closed the waters of the Bering Strait to commercial fishing by other nations. John Quincy urged the President to "contest the right of Russia to any territorial establishment on this continent" and to "assume . . . the principle that the American continents are no longer subjects for any new European colonial establishments."[30]

Just at that time, John Quincy learned that Britain intended claiming Graham Land, an island rich in seals that American hunters had discovered off the northern section of the Antarctic Peninsula. At John Quincy's urging, President Monroe ordered a U.S. Navy frigate to sail around Cape Horn to claim Graham Land before the British. With the Russian attempt to claim the Oregon coast, he ordered a second warship to join the one at Graham Land and sail to Oregon. Although Monroe once again flirted with an unconstitutional de facto declaration of war, the Russians relented and agreed to move the boundary of the lands they claimed three hundred miles to the north and to remove all maritime restrictions on the surrounding seas. In effect, President Monroe successfully extended the United States' sphere of influence beyond its western boundaries into the rich Pacific Ocean fisheries.

With American warships showing the flag in all parts of the world—from the Mediterranean coast of North Africa to the Pacific coast of North America—the President decided to explain America's intentions to the world. He asked cabinet members for written and oral suggestions for a policy statement that he would include in his annual message to Congress. "The ground I wish to take," he told them, "is that of earnest remonstrance against the interference of the European powers by force with South America, but to disclaim all interference on our part with Europe, to make an American cause, and adhere inflexibly to that."[31]

John Quincy submitted a proposal that "the American continents by the free and independent condition which they have assumed, and maintain, are henceforth not to be considered as subject for future colonization by any European power."[32] The President included it verbatim in his annual message, later called the Monroe Doctrine.

In his two-hour address—aimed at foreign leaders as well as Congress and the American people—Monroe embraced John Quincy's political philosophy and formally closed the Western Hemisphere to further colonization. He explained that America's political system differed substantially from Europe's and that the United States would consider any European attempts to extend its system anywhere in the Western Hemisphere as a threat to the United States. From its origins, he said, the United States had sought nothing but peace—for its citizens to fish, hunt, and plow their fields unmolested. The United States had never interfered in Europe's internal affairs and would not do so—indeed, it wanted no part of Europe's incessant wars. To that end, he pledged not to interfere with Europe's existing colonies in the New World. But he declared it to be "a principle in which the rights and interests of the United States are involved" that "the American continents, by the free and independent condition which they have assumed and maintain, are henceforth not to be considered as subjects for future colonization by any European powers." He warned that the United States would view "any interposition . . . by any European power . . . as the manifestation of an unfriendly disposition toward the United States"—in effect, a declaration of war.[33]

Monroe's new "doctrine" drew universal acclaim across America. Although much of the European press and some European leaders condemned it, few European powers had not learned the lessons of the British in the American Revolutionary War and, more recently, of the French in Russia. As the Duke of Wellington had warned, no nation on earth was powerful enough to sustain military supply lines long enough to challenge American hegemony in the Western Hemisphere. With the Monroe Doctrine, most European leaders realized it would be far less costly to trade with Americans than to try to subjugate them.

"I went to the President's," John Quincy described the hours following delivery of the Monroe Doctrine, "and found Gales, the half-editor of the *National Intelligencer,* there. He said the message was called a war message and spoke of newspapers from Europe announcing that an army of twelve thousand Spaniards was to embark immediately to subdue South America."

John Quincy all but laughed in the half-editor's face, calling the reports absurd. "The same newspapers," John Quincy scoffed, "announced . . . the disbanding of the Spanish army."[34]

As the Monroe Doctrine quelled European ambitions for new conquests in the Americas, it also dispelled American fears of imminent attack by foreign powers and unleashed a surge of popular energy that strengthened the nation economically and militarily. State governments worked with builders and visionaries to cover the Atlantic states with networks of canals, free roads, and toll roads, or turnpikes, that generated revenues from user fees to pay the costs of maintenance and expansion. The Lancaster Pike tied Philadelphia to Gettysburg; the Boston Post Road connected Worcester to Springfield and Boston to Providence; and work began to extend the great Cumberland Road—then often called the National Road—from Baltimore to the Mississippi River. Speaker Henry Clay envisioned its eventual extension to the Pacific Ocean. In New York State, continuing construction on the great Erie Canal extended the link between Rome and Utica westward to Seneca Lake. Already tied to the Atlantic Ocean by the Mohawk and Hudson Rivers, the canal's western tip stood only 120 miles from Buffalo and the entrance to the Great Lakes. Plans for other roads, turnpikes, and canals were legion. One proposed canal was to stretch from Boston to Savannah, while a turnpike out of Washington was to reach New Orleans.

Economic expansion spurred advances in the arts and education, as well as industry and agriculture. The works of American writers—Washington Irving, James Fenimore Cooper, and others—replaced English literature as the most widely read in the United States. In addition to female academies, free schools open to all children sprouted in New York, Pennsylvania, Massachusetts, and Connecticut. Boston opened the nation's first "high school" in 1821, and Massachusetts passed a law requiring every town of five hundred families to establish a high school for their children. Institutions for adult education appeared as well, with 3,000 "lyceums" in fifteen states offering adult education and self-improvement courses.

The apparent end to threats from abroad and the boundless opportunities at home left the Monroe administration with few major projects to pursue in the time it had left in office, thus freeing cabinet members to pursue personal ambitions. In the naive assumption that his cabinet and other government leaders would serve the nation as selflessly as he, Monroe emulated his presidential predecessors and announced early in his second term that he would limit himself to two terms in office. With the exception of John Quincy, cabinet members all but renounced their oaths of office and personal pledges to the President and launched a bitter struggle for political power that left the President impotent—and ended what a Boston newspaper had labeled the "Era of Good Feelings."[35]

The frenetic activity of the Monroe years had left John Quincy exhausted and without the physical, let alone emotional, energy to seek the presidency himself. Although based in his native country after so many years overseas, his time as secretary of state had left him few moments to spend with his wife and family, and he was simply too tired and, in effect, lonely for family life to concern himself with the forthcoming elections. Not so the other cabinet members and presidential aspirants.

When budget restrictions forced a reduction in the number of army officers, Treasury Secretary Crawford pressed Monroe not to dismiss any Crawford confederates. When the President ignored the request, Crawford went to the White House in a rage, calling the President an "infernal scoundrel" and raising his cane as if to assault him. According to Navy Secretary Samuel L. Southard, who witnessed the confrontation, "Mr. Monroe seized the tongs and ordered him instantly to leave the room or he would chastise him, and he rang the bell for the servant."[36] Realizing how closely he had flirted with treason, Crawford left and never again set foot in the White House during Monroe's presidency.

In Florida, meanwhile, Andrew Jackson, whom President Monroe had appointed governor, embarrassed the administration by violating the outgoing Spanish governor's diplomatic immunity and arresting him for failing to surrender documents needed in a legal proceeding. The arrest caused a furor in the press, which assailed Jackson as a would-be dictator. Jackson resigned in a rage, went home to Tennessee, won election as senator, and returned to Washington to wreak havoc on his political enemies.

As cabinet members and other presidential aspirants turned on the President or on each other, the vicious rhetoric created political schisms

Secretary of the Treasury William H. Crawford of Georgia had ambitions to succeed James Monroe as President but suffered a paralytic stroke before the elections. (LIBRARY OF CONGRESS)

in Congress not seen since the days of the Confederation of American States. "I have never known such a state of things," Monroe lamented to his predecessor in office, James Madison, "nor have I personally ever experienced so much embarrassment and mortification."

> Where there is an open contest with a foreign enemy . . . the course is plain and you have something to cheer and animate you to action, but we are now blessed with peace. . . . There being three avowed candidates in the administration is a circumstance which increases the embarrassment. The friends of each endeavor to annoy the others. . . . In many cases the attacks are personal, directed against the individual.[37]

Only one candidate remained silent and above the fray. John Quincy, the most obvious and logical choice to succeed President Monroe, refused to state whether he even wanted the office. Raised in a society where the ignorant deferred to the educated propertied class, he hewed to what his grandson Henry Adams would later call "the Ciceronian idea of government by *the best*," selected by an elevated class of educated, propertied professionals who "chose men to represent them because they wanted to be well represented and they chose the best they had." Those selected did not accept "pay" for their services but "honoraria." Those who accepted public office were "statesmen, not politicians; they guided public opinion but were little guided by it."[38]

Clearly alarmed by John Quincy's reticence, former congressman Joseph Hopkinson, a close family friend and prominent Philadelphia lawyer, wrote to Louisa,

> I think our friend Mr. A. is too fastidious and reserved on a certain subject as interesting to the country as it is to himself. . . . His conduct seems to me, as it does to others, to be calculated to chill and depress the kind feeling and fair exertions of his friends. They are discouraged when they see a total indifference assumed on his part. . . . Now, my dear madam, this won't do. The Macbeth policy—"if chance will make me king, why chance may crown me"—will not answer where little is left to chance or merit. Kings are made by politicians and newspapers, and the man who sits down waiting to be crowned, either by chance or just right, will go bareheaded all his life.[39]

Louisa, of course, showed Hopkinson's letter to her husband and urged him to campaign more aggressively. "Do for once gratify me," she pleaded. "Show yourself if only for a week . . . and if harm comes of it I promise never to advise you again."[40] But John Quincy was adamant, insisting that the presidency "is not in my opinion an office to be either solicited or declined. . . . The principle of the Constitution in its purity is that the duty shall be assigned to the most able and the most worthy."

The law of friendship is a reciprocation of good offices. He who asks or accepts the offer of friendly service contracts the obligation of meeting it with a suitable return. He who asks or accepts the offer of aid to promote his own views necessarily binds himself to promote the views of him from whom he receives it. . . . Between the principle . . . that a President of the United States must remember to whom he owes his elevation and the principle of accepting no aid on the score of friendship or personal kindness to him, there is no alternative. The former . . . I deem to be essentially and vitally corrupt. The latter is the only principle to which no exception can be taken.[41]

For one of the few times in their marriage, Louisa decided to ignore her husband and take matters into her own hands. Aware of his ambitions and fearful of the effects of a loss on his spirit, she decided to compete with wives of other candidates by expanding the scope of her popular Tuesday evening receptions. "My Tuesday evenings appear to have some attractions," she realized.

At least they afford the probable certainty of giving opportunity for amusement throughout the winter and in this consists the charm. . . . If Mr. A instead of keeping me back when I was a young woman had urged me forward in the world I should have better understood the maneuvering part of my situation. But instead of this I find myself almost a stranger to the little arts and intrigues of the world in which I move.[42]

Louisa learned quickly, however, realizing that "wine maketh the heart glad" and gradually enlarging the number of guests she invited. One party drew one hundred guests; another, "one hundred and thirty odd persons all very sociable and good humored. The young ladies danced, played, and sang and were very merry. . . . I am very willing to show that I am the public servant." As she enlarged her parties, she hired the Marine Band for a fee of "five dollars to each performer plus wine and supper." She then organized a party for 252—"ladies being a much larger proportion than we have had this winter." Although William H. Crawford's wife, Susanna, sent six hundred invitations to a ball she sponsored, Louisa, not surprisingly, found it "dull and uncomfortable, and we left before ten o'clock."[43]

Consciously or unconsciously, John Quincy refused to help Louisa plan the parties she hosted for his campaign, acting disinterested at times and even failing to appear at some events. She, in turn, suppressed her growing irritation at her husband and simply threw herself into organizing her entertainments. Her ambitions seemed to surpass those of her husband. "My whole morning was occupied with visits and writing cards of invitation," she smiled. "We have had forty or more members of Congress already here and all who call I invite to my evenings. If I can help it I will invite only those who call, lest it should be said I am courting them to further a political purpose."[44]

With the approach of summer, Louisa curtailed her campaign work, and John Quincy left for Cambridge to enroll their youngest son, Charles Francis, in Harvard—and to attend the graduation of his oldest son, George Washington Adams. Once at his beloved alma mater, however, he met with nothing but disappointment. Although George did graduate, he finished only thirtieth in his class of eighty-five. Then, to John Quincy's dismay, he learned that his middle boy, John II, in his next-to-last year at the school, ranked even lower—forty-fifth in a class of eighty-five. To compound John Quincy's disappointment, fourteen-year-old Charles Francis did so poorly on his Latin entrance examination that the college granted him only a conditional admission. He had spent years teaching Charles Francis his Latin and erupted in anger, storming into President John Kirkland's office charging that his son had been unfairly treated. In no mood for a confrontation with the man likely to be the next President of the United States, Kirkland ordered Charles Francis retested, and to every one's relief, the boy passed and gained unconditional entry into his father's alma mater.

John Quincy sensed, however, that his troubles with the boys were just beginning. "I find them all three coming to manhood with indolent minds, flinching from study whenever they can."[45] He could not and would not allow what he deemed the indolence of the boys to go unpunished and told them they could not return to Washington for Christmas. Instead of enjoying holiday balls and lavish White House dinners, they would have to spend Christmas and New Year's in the somber mansion of their grandfather in Quincy—studying. Not until they ranked among the top ten students in their classes would he allow John II and Charles Francis to enjoy holidays with their parents. In the meantime, he sent George to study law with Daniel Webster in Boston.

A few months later, John Quincy's discipline produced the opposite of its intended effects: John II joined a student riot, Harvard expelled him, and he returned to his parents in total disgrace. The boy could not have returned home at a worse time. The Adamses were already caring for Louisa's sister's three orphaned children—two boys, Johnson and Thomas, who were proving more difficult than the Adamses own sons, and the flirty Mary Catherine. John Quincy had paid for Thomas to attend Phillips Academy at Exeter, New Hampshire, then Harvard, but he dropped out and returned to Washington to loaf in the Adams home—without a degree, a skill, or a job. His older brother, Johnson, did not even bother enrolling in Harvard. From the first, he preferred loafing.

Young Charles Francis, meanwhile, fell in love with Mary Catherine, but the two were both too young to marry, and when Charles Francis went off to Harvard, their relationship cooled. When George Washington arrived for a visit, however, he took his brother's place in Mary Catherine's heart. John Quincy put a quick end to the relationship, sending George back to Boston to finish his legal studies with Daniel Webster.

Depressed by his sons' failure at Harvard, John Quincy resigned himself to failure in the presidential race and returned to his boyhood home in Quincy to spend time with his aging father and to look at farming as a possible occupation after he retired from public office. Not only his father but three previous generations of the Adamses had farmed the land in Quincy successfully, and he concluded that, once out of government, he might have to do the same. He soon realized, however, that a life in diplomacy had not prepared him for the physical demands of farm life. His only skills lay in the law, but he feared he had made too many political enemies in Boston's powerful Federalist community to ensure much success.

A run for the presidency was clearly the most logical next step in his career, but he stubbornly refused to demean himself, the American people, or the office of the presidency by actively campaigning. He believed that merit alone, not party or political campaign rhetoric, should determine the choice of the American people—a unique concept voiced only once before, by George Washington, but never since.

"My career," John Quincy proclaimed, "has attached no party to me precisely because it has been independent of all party . . . and the consequence has been that all parties disown me."

> I have followed the convictions of my own mind with a single eye to the interests of the whole nation. . . . If I am to be a candidate, it must be by the wishes . . . of others, not by mine. If my countrymen prefer others to me, I must not repine at their choice. Indifference at the heart is not to be won by . . . the loudest trumpet. Merit and just right in this country will be heard. And in my case, if they are not heard without my stir, I shall acquiesce in the conclusion that it is because they do not exist.[46]

As his opponents resorted to every ruse they could invent to win votes, John Quincy refused to compromise his values and political beliefs—even if, as seemed likely, those values doomed him to defeat in his lifelong quest for national leadership.

CHAPTER 12

The End of the Beginning

Although President James Monroe believed John Quincy was the most qualified candidate for the presidency, he remained silent. "He thought it incumbent on him to have nothing to do with party politics," explained Egbert R. Watson, Monroe's private secretary. Watson said Monroe considered it "beneath the dignity" of an outgoing President and "unjust to the people . . . to throw the weight of his name and character on either side of any contest."[1]

Having no organizational structure, political parties held no nominating conventions, leaving it to state legislatures to nominate presidential candidates—so-called favorite sons. To find qualified candidates, however, states often had to adopt sons of other states. The Tennessee legislature nominated Carolina-born Andrew Jackson, while Kentucky nominated Virginia-born Henry Clay. The Massachusetts legislature stood alone in nominating a true native son, John Quincy Adams. A group of rogue Republicans in Congress ignored the Georgia legislature and nominated that state's William H. Crawford, while John C. Calhoun of South Carolina snubbed his state legislature and nominated himself. With little national support, however, Calhoun withdrew from the presidential race and ran

Secretary of War John C. Calhoun, of South Carolina,
recognized he lacked the support to contend for the
presidency and ran for vice president instead. (LIBRARY
OF CONGRESS)

for vice president—a post he knew no one else would seek. To ensure his
securing the office, he ran on both the Adams and Jackson tickets.

In September 1823, Crawford suffered a paralytic stroke, leaving Adams,
Jackson, and Clay as the only active presidential contenders. Adams was the
clear early favorite.

By the end of 1823, however, Andrew Jackson had made enough inroads
in the Northeast to threaten John Quincy's lead in the presidential race. Surprisingly, John Quincy asked Louisa to throw a ball to honor the popular
western candidate. Privately, John Quincy called Jackson "a barbarian and
savage who could scarcely spell his own name,"[2] and he feared a Jackson
presidency as a danger to the nation. The only way he saw to block such an
outcome was to win the presidency himself and relegate Jackson to political

impotence as vice president. Louisa's ball was to serve as an opportunity to invite Jackson to be his running mate—a partnership that would ensure John Quincy the support of the many Jackson followers in the East and a huge bloc of Jacksonians in the West, while leaving Jackson in the political doldrums. Although the general was too skilled a leader not to suspect John Quincy's motives, he nonetheless accepted, and Louisa's ball proved one of the most brilliant, most memorable social events in capital history.

More than 1,000 guests—bejeweled ladies in flowing gowns, men in smart suits and uniforms—poured into Louisa's sparkling mansion. They dined, drank, and danced until early morning, paying homage to what seemed like the ideal political union between the brilliant statesman from Boston and the heroic soldier and general from Tennessee. Anticipating the huge turnout, John Quincy had the foresight to order pillars wedged under the floor to add support to the second-floor ballroom.

"The floor of the ballroom was chalked with spread-eagles, flags, and the motto 'Welcome to the hero of New Orleans,'" according to John Quincy's niece. "The pillars were festooned with laurel and wintergreen, while wreathings of evergreens and roses interspersed with small, variegated lamps, with a lustre in the center." Jackson stood next to Louisa, with guests entering in pairs and bowing.

> Officers of the army and navy and the diplomatic corps appeared in regimentals and regalia, while plain citizens disported themselves in pumps, silk stockings, ruffled cravats . . . with gold buckles and a big seal of topaz or carnelian, regulation frock coats of green or claret colored cloth . . . gilded buttons, and Hessian top-boots with gold tassels. . . .
>
> In striking contrast with the diplomatic corps . . . were gentlemen and representatives from the Far West, who had not lost the free stride of the forest and the prairie or its freedom of speech and manner. No more remarkable was the sight of Pushmataha, the "Eagle of the Choctaws" . . . than that of the woodsman and Indian fighter David Crockett . . . besides such fellow representatives from Tennessee as James K. Polk and John Bell.[3]

With all of Washington society in or around the Adamses' F Street mansion, some wag with a poetic bent created lines that every one in the capital sang in unison:

> Wend your way with the world tonight.
> Sixty gray and giddy twenty,
> Flirts that court and prudes that slight,
> State coquettes and spinsters plenty,
> Belles and matrons, maids and madames,
> All are gone to Mrs. Adams.[4]

The poet went on to incorporate names of the Washington elite in subsequent verses, all of which ended,

> Belles and matrons, maids and madames,
> All are gone to Mrs. Adams.

The ball was indeed a spectacle and a lasting social triumph for Louisa, if not for John Quincy.

Andrew Jackson did nothing to unsettle the joy of Louisa's extravaganza—or to dispel the notion of an Adams-Jackson political alliance. The hero of New Orleans even raised his glass and delivered a warm and gracious toast to his hostess and left all the guests convinced that he and John Quincy had formed the most perfect political tandem since the Washington-Adams ticket of 1789.

Jackson, however, soon dispelled the notion and announced his intention to seek the presidency himself. Within days, he, Calhoun, Clay, and Crawford launched a bitter campaign of charges and countercharges about each other's views on slavery, banking, tariffs, and other issues, and although John Quincy tried to remain above the fray, they dragged him into it. "Every liar and calumniator in the country," John Quincy complained, "was at work day and night to destroy my character . . . run down my reputation . . . defame and disgrace me."[5]

Andrew Jackson of Tennessee, the hero of the Battle
of New Orleans in the War of 1812, refused John
Quincy Adams's invitation to be his running mate
in the 1824 presidential election. (LIBRARY OF
CONGRESS)

By midsummer, Jackson's status as the hero of New Orleans made him the popular front-runner among presidential candidates, and an atmosphere of gloom engulfed the house on F Street when both Louisa and John Quincy suddenly abandoned the campaign. Physically and emotionally exhausted by then, Louisa fell victim to a debilitating skin condition called erysipelas, or St. Anthony's Fire—a strep infection that left her feverish, with headaches and burning, gangrenous skin inflammations. Doctors sent her to bathe in mineral waters at a Pennsylvania spa. John Quincy, meanwhile, left for Massachusetts after receiving word that his father was failing. To make matters worse, he was unable to elicit any information from his son George, who was studying law at Daniel Webster's Boston office and was responsible for overseeing family affairs. When

*George Washington Adams, firstborn son of John
Quincy and Louisa Catherine Adams, graduated
from Harvard and practiced law in Boston before
succumbing to alcoholism.* (NATIONAL PARKS SERVICE,
ADAMS NATIONAL HISTORICAL PARK)

John Quincy reached Quincy, he found his father unattended—crippled
by arthritis and nearly blind. Adding to his shock, his son George Washington was drunk and unconscious. Like many of his forebears, he had
started drinking in his idle time and fell prey to chronic alcoholism. Even
worse, he turned to gambling to pay for his habit and fell deeply in debt.

Helpless to rein in the sins of his son, John Quincy tended to his father,
arranged for permanent nursing care, and returned to Washington, deeply
discouraged and resigned to putting State Department affairs in good order
for his successor while awaiting what he believed would be his inevitable
loss in the presidential election. In anticipation of defeat, John Quincy had
kept alert for a business opportunity in the private sector to occupy his time
after he left the White House. In July 1823, Louisa's fast-talking cousin

George Johnson sold John Quincy what he said was a stable, profitable local flour business, Columbian Mills, for $32,000. Within weeks, John Quincy discovered that Columbian Mills had been operating at a loss. Worse, Johnson had not only doctored the books but disguised structural damage at the plant, and John Quincy found he would have to invest an additional $12,000 to restore the building and replace or repair aging machinery.

As his new business faced financial collapse, John Quincy's political life seemed destined for the same fate. Andrew Jackson won far more popular votes than his rivals—just under 153,000, compared with 114,000 for John Quincy and about 47,000 each for Clay and Crawford. None of the candidates had a majority of Electoral College votes, however, with Jackson winning ninety-nine; John Quincy, eighty-four; Crawford, forty-one; and Clay, thirty-seven. Under the Constitution, the House of Representatives had to decide the election, with each state casting one vote under a unit rule.

By then, however, the states had ratified the Twelfth Amendment to the Constitution limiting the number of presidential candidates in a House runoff to three. Although Clay had more popular votes than Crawford, they came from states with fewer Electoral College votes and forced Clay out of the race. He nonetheless retained enough political influence to throw the votes of the three states he had won to the candidate of his choice. Apart from their personal dislike for each other, Clay balked at ceding the highest-ranking civilian post to a military man, while Jackson had never forgiven Clay for condemning the Tennessean's military campaign in Florida as a usurpation of congressional war-making powers.

At 6 p.m. on January 9, 1825, Henry Clay arrived at the house on F Street and, according to John Quincy, "spent the evening with me in a long conversation."

He said that the time was drawing near when the choice must be made in the House of Representatives of a President . . . that he had been much urged and solicited with regard to the part in that transaction that he should take. . . . The time had now come at which he might be explicit in his communication with me and he had for that purpose asked this confidential interview. He wished me as far as I might think proper to satisfy him with regard to some principles of great public importance, but without any personal considerations for himself. In the question to come before the House between General Jackson, Mr. Crawford and myself, he had no hesitation in saying that his preference would be for me.[6]

Clay had good reasons for supporting John Quincy. Not only had they worked well together at Ghent, but Clay had an intimate knowledge of John Quincy's thinking. Both were fervent nationalists with a deep belief in the nation's "manifest destiny" and the necessity of building a federally financed network of highways and canals. John Quincy favored Clay's "American System," and Clay had always supported John Quincy's foreign policy of American neutrality and noninvolvement in foreign wars. Neither wanted to see a man as reckless and uneducated as Jackson sitting in the White House. Although John Quincy intended to retain the entire Monroe cabinet, if elected President he would have to name a new secretary of state to replace himself and a secretary of war to replace William Crawford. Even if he and Clay, as they claimed, did not discuss filling the two posts, there was no need for them to do so. Clay had made it clear, when he rejected the War Department post eight years earlier, that his lust for the presidency made the State Department post the only cabinet position he would ever accept.

On January 24, Clay's Kentucky delegation announced it would cast its vote for Adams, despite express instructions from the state legislature to vote for Jackson. Jackson had scored an overwhelming popular victory in Kentucky's popular election, while John Quincy had failed to win even a single vote. All votes had gone to Clay and Jackson. Congressional delegates from Ohio and Missouri—the other states Clay had won—also cast their votes for John Quincy, and on February 9, after only one House ballot, John Quincy Adams won election as the nation's sixth President. In doing so, he became the first non-Virginian to win the presidency since

House Speaker Henry Clay of Tennessee finished fourth in the presidential election of 1824 and threw his votes to John Quincy Adams, who named Clay secretary of state. (LIBRARY OF CONGRESS)

his father's election thirty years earlier in 1796. He also became the first son of a Founding Father and President to become the nation's chief executive. For the first time in three decades, northerners flocked to Washington to attend the inauguration of one of their own.

"The city is thronged with strangers," complained the southern-born socialite Sarah Seaton, whose brother published the *National Intelligencer*, "and *Yankees* swarm like the locusts of Egypt in our houses, our beds, and our kneading troughs!"[7]

John Quincy was more enthusiastic than Mrs. Seaton and wrote to his "dear and honored father" to tell him of "the event of this day, upon which I can only offer you my congratulations and ask your blessings and prayers." He signed the letter, "Your affectionate son."[8]

The ailing former President answered immediately:

I have received your letter of the 9th. Never did I feel so much solemnity as upon this occasion. The multitude of my thoughts and the intensity of my feelings are too much for a mind like mine, in its ninetieth year. May the blessing of God Almighty continue to protect you to the end of your life, as it has heretofore protected you in so remarkable a manner from your cradle. I offer the same prayer for your lady and your family and am your affectionate father, John Adams.[9]

Contrary to its affect on former President John Adams, John Quincy's victory appalled many American political leaders, who called it "a mockery of representative government."[10] Outraged by what he considered the "monstrous union" of Clay and Adams, Jackson cried out, "I weep for the liberty of my country. The rights of the people have been bartered for promises of office. . . . The voice of the people of the West have been disregarded, and demagogues barter them as sheep in the shambles for their own views and personal aggrandizement."[11]

Few members of the Washington political scene doubted that John Quincy had promised, tacitly or otherwise, to reward Clay for his support, and knowing how Clay lusted for the presidency, all assumed that John Quincy would appoint him secretary of state, the stepladder to the presidency for more than two decades. Rumors of "bargain & sale" swept across the political landscape, with some Jackson supporters growling about possible civil war and secession in the West. The mood in the White House turned less than relaxed a few days after the House vote, as President Monroe hosted a reception for the President-elect. The President was chatting with a guest when Andrew Jackson, still recovering from a debilitating illness, thrust his grim, gaunt face through the doorway. Armed as always with two pistols, he snapped his head from side to side until he spotted John Quincy. As the President and other celebrants collectively held their breath, Jackson bounded forward, broke into a warm smile, and, hand outstretched, offered John Quincy his congratulations.

Five days after his election victory, John Quincy announced his decision to appoint Henry Clay as secretary of state.

"So you see," Andrew Jackson wailed in outrage, "the Judas of the West
has closed the contract and will receive thirty pieces of silver. His end will
be the same. Was there ever witnessed such a bare-faced corruption in any
country before?" Others agreed that John Quincy and Clay had arranged a
"corrupt bargain" that undermined the election process and stripped voters of their chosen candidate. New York senator Martin Van Buren, who
had backed Crawford's candidacy, was as outraged as Jackson, warning a
Kentucky congressman that, in voting for Adams, "you sign Mr. Clay's political death warrant."[12] Corrupt or not, in appointing Henry Clay secretary of state, John Quincy had also signed his own political death warrant
as President.

On March 4, 1825, "after two successive sleepless nights, I [John
Quincy] entered upon this day with a supplication to heaven, first, for my
country, secondly for myself and for those connected with my good name
and fortunes, that the last results of its events may be auspicious and
blessed."[13] At 11:30 a.m. John Quincy rode to the Capitol in a carriage with
his friend Attorney General William Wirt. President Monroe followed in a
second carriage, with several companies of militia escorting the two vehicles,
along with thousands of citizens who, according to custom then, escorted
the President to the inauguration before a joint session of Congress. Missing
was Louisa Catherine Adams, whose entertainments had done more to elect
John Quincy than he had done for himself. Ill in bed, still suffering the
aftereffects of her strep infection, she was unable to face the crowds.

John Quincy began his inauguration address in fine fashion, countering
Jacksonian polemics by proclaiming, "Our political creed is . . . that the will
of the people is the source, and the happiness of the people the end of all
legitimate government upon earth."[14] Greeted with enthusiasm at first, his
speech met with ever increasing disbelief, then outright disapproval, as he
asked that "all constitutional objections . . . be removed" for construction
of interstate roads and canals and other "internal improvement" by the
federal government. As he went on, it became clear that his years in the

President John Quincy Adams proved the most ineffective President in early American history—only to metamorphose into one of the nation's greatest congressmen as a champion of abolition, free speech, and the right of petition. (LIBRARY OF CONGRESS)

foreign service, his scholarly pursuits, and his refusal to campaign had left him woefully out of touch with ordinary Americans, and his references to classical civilizations and ancient republics perplexed almost all the members of Congress.

"The magnificence and splendor of their public works," he waxed in Demosthenic oratory, "are among the imperishable glories of the ancient republics. The roads and aqueducts of Rome have been the admiration of all after ages and have survived thousands of years after all her conquests have been swallowed up in despotism or become the spoil of barbarians." Although some members misunderstood his reference to barbarians, none failed to recognize his clear intention of assuming powers reserved to the states under the Tenth Amendment of the Constitution.

After John Quincy's speech, Chief Justice John Marshall, a heroic soldier in the Revolutionary War whom John Adams had appointed to the court at the end of his administration, swore in the new President. John Quincy had spent his life training for the presidency and now left to review "military companies drawn up in front of the Capitol" before returning home to join Louisa and "a crowd of visitors" for a two-hour reception. Later, John Quincy went to a White House reception and, after dinner at home, attended the inaugural ball. It was to be one of the last joyous moments of his administration.

He and Louisa spent the next six weeks moving, gradually dismantling their home on F Street and settling into the White House, selling furniture they did not need and buying furniture they did need, including a billiard table for John Quincy. The move was not simple. In addition to caring for their own two younger sons, John II and Charles Francis, the Adamses were still caring for Louisa's orphaned niece and two ill-behaved nephews, one of whom raced right into the White House kitchen to flirt with maids. To add to the family's immediate problems, the Marquis de Lafayette, his son George Washington Lafayette, his secretary Auguste Lavasseur, and his valet Bastien arrived at the White House late in July for a huge banquet. The feast climaxed Lafayette's triumphant yearlong U.S. tour as "the nation's guest" to commemorate the fiftieth anniversary of American independence. He had just returned from New England, where he had said farewell to John Adams and now came to bid John Quincy good-bye. The two had known each other since John Quincy was a winsome boy of fifteen living with his father at Benjamin Franklin's residence in Paris. To Louisa's dismay, her husband waxed enthusiastic and insisted that Lafayette and his entourage remain at the White House as his personal guests for the rest of their stay in the United States—all of August into September.

"I admire the old gentleman," Louisa complained, "but no admiration can stand family discomfort. We are all obliged to turn out of our beds to make room for him and his suite."[15]

After celebrating Lafayette's birthday on the night of September 6, John Quincy bid Lafayette an official farewell in the peristyle of the White

*Congress invited sixty-seven-year-old Marquis de Lafayette to
tour America as a "guest of the nation" to celebrate the fiftieth
anniversary of the victory at Yorktown. President John
Quincy Adams invited Lafayette to stay at the White House
during his last weeks in America.* (FROM AN ENGRAVING IN THE
CHÂTEAU DE VERSAILLES, RÉUNION DES MUSÉES NATIONAUX)

House. With his cabinet surrounding him and a huge crowd of Lafayette
well-wishers looking on, the President spoke with deep emotion: "We
shall always look upon you as belonging to us . . . as belonging to our children after us."

> You are ours by more than the patriotic self-devotion with which you flew
> to the aid of our fathers at the crisis of our fate; ours by that unshaken grati-
> tude for your services which is a precious portion of our inheritance; ours
> by that tie . . . which has linked your name for endless ages of time with
> the name of Washington. . . . Speaking in the name of the whole people of
> the United States . . . I bid you a reluctant and affectionate farewell.[16]

"God bless you, sir," Lafayette sobbed. "God bless the American people." He embraced John Quincy and, with tears streaming down his face, rushed back into the White House to collect himself before leaving American shores for the last time.

Lafayette's departure ended the few weeks of civil behavior that the French hero's arrival had provoked among Washington political leaders. Even Vice President Calhoun now turned on John Quincy in a political tidal wave of outrage over what Americans perceived as "the theft of government" and disregard of the popular will. In designating Clay his secretary of state, John Quincy inadvertently provoked the founding of a new political party, with a broad popular base spanning the West and South.

Calling themselves Democrats, the new party set out from the first to cripple John Quincy's administration and ensure his departure after one term. John Quincy tried to forestall the inevitable by offering Jackson a cabinet post as secretary of war, but Jackson all but laughed in his face and refused even to consider serving an administration he was determined to bring down.

While Jackson was building a political party to support his own presidential ambitions, John Quincy held stubbornly to his naive dismissal of political parties as antithetical to union. Even more naively, he refused to take advantage of patronage to put men in office who would support him and his policies. The result was a cabinet and government bureaucracy that, for the most part, worked to undermine both his policies and his chances of winning a second term.

As Jackson and his supporters filled the press with charges headlined "Corrupt Bargain," John Quincy reacted scornfully, calling the Democratic Party a "conspiracy" against national unity. Henry Clay grew so angry at Virginia senator John Randolph's constant references to a "corrupt bargain" that he challenged Randolph to a duel. Although both men emerged unhurt, Clay managed to send a bullet through Randolph's sleeve.

The threat of duels notwithstanding, Jacksonians in Congress stepped up their obstructionist tactics. When a group of newly independent Latin American nations invited the United States to send representatives to a conference in Panama to form a pan-American union, Jacksonian congress-men purposely debated the qualifications of John Quincy's appointees until the conference had ended, leaving the American delegates with no confer-ence to attend.

In addition to his political humiliations in Congress, John Quincy faced unexpected personal humiliation when he and his valet tried rowing across the Potomac River one afternoon, with John Quincy intending to swim back. "Before we got half across," he explained,

> the boat had leaked itself half full and . . . there was nothing on board to scoop up the water. . . . I jumped overboard . . . and lost hold of the boat, which filled with water and drifted away. . . . Antoine, who was naked, had little difficulty. I had much more . . . struggling for life and gasping for breath. . . . The loose sleeves of my shirt . . . filled with water and hung like two fifty-six-pound weights upon my arms.[17]

The President managed to strip and swim ashore, where his son John II pulled him from the water, while Antoine scampered out and dressed as best he could, before running to the Adams house across the bridge to get a carriage. "While Antoine was gone," the President confided to his diary, "John and I were wading and swimming up and down on the other shore, or sitting naked basking on the bank at the margin of the river. . . . The carriage came and took me and Antoine home, half dressed."[18]

Although he escaped injury, the President did not escape a torrent of ridicule, and later in the year, in October, the Tennessee legislature heaped insult on top of ridicule by nominating Jackson for the presidency—three years in advance of the next presidential race in 1828. Jackson immedi-ately resigned his Senate seat to begin a national campaign to unseat John Quincy Adams—sooner or later.

Rather than reinforcing his presidency, John Quincy seemed to go out of his way to undermine it. Apparently unaware of or unable to address the needs of a semiliterate rural population in his speeches, he always appeared to address Harvard scholars or their ilk, insisting that "the great object of civil government is the improvement of the condition of those who are parties to the social compact."

> Roads and canals . . . are among the most important means of improvement. But moral, political and intellectual improvement are duties assigned by the Author of our existence. . . . Among the first . . . instruments for the improvement of the condition of men is knowledge, and to the acquisition of much of the knowledge adapted to the wants, the comforts and enjoyments of human life, public institutions and seminaries of learning are essential.[19]

In what he considered—and what really was—a brilliant, forward-looking address to advance the nation, he called on Congress to promote "the improvement of agriculture, commerce and manufactures, the cultivation and encouragement of the mechanic and of the elegant arts, the advancement of literature, and the progress of the sciences." Among the sciences, he cited astronomy as the most important and called for federal construction of astronomical observatories, or "lighthouses of the sky," to study the heavens. He warned that failure to do so "would be treachery to the most sacred of trusts." If any congressmen still supported his program at that point, he proceeded to lose them all with one of the most politically inept statements of his career: "While foreign nations . . . are advancing with gigantic strides in . . . public improvement, were we to slumber in indolence . . . and proclaim to the world that we are palsied by the will of our constituents, would it not be to . . . doom ourselves to perpetual inferiority?"[20]

Even his most loyal supporters misunderstood the phrase "palsied by the will of our constituents." North Carolina congressman Nathaniel Macon charged that "the message of the President seems to claim all the power to the federal government."[21] And General Edmund Gaines, whom former President Monroe had sent to rid Amelia Island of pirates, predicted that "the planters, farmers and mechanics of the country" would see the next presidential election as "a great contest between the aristocracy and democracy of America."[22]

Jackson thundered a reply that devastated John Quincy, who seemed unaware of the implications of what he had written and said. "When I view . . . the declaration that it would be criminal for the agents of our government to be palsied by the will of their constituents, I shudder for the consequence. . . . The voice of the people . . . must be heard. Instead of building lighthouses in the skies, establishing national universities, and making explorations round the globe . . . pay the national debt . . . then apportion the surplus revenue amongst the several states . . . leaving the superintendence of education to the states."[23]

While newspapers ridiculed John Quincy's "lighthouses in the skies," Jackson addressed the needs and concerns of ordinary people. He called for an end to debtors' prisons, citing a blind man in a Massachusetts prison for a debt of $6 and a Rhode Island woman behind bars for a debt of sixty-eight cents. There were five times as many debtors as criminals in prisons, most of them indigent, with debts of less than $50, and forced to pay for their food in jail—or starve.* Jackson also called for reform of bankruptcy laws to prevent employers from declaring bankruptcy to avoid paying wages.

Although many of his proposals were two centuries ahead of their time, John Quincy was out of touch with his America. In what was clearly a clash of cultures—indeed, a clash of generations—John Quincy saw man in general, and the American man in particular, as having unlimited talents, restrained only by lack of educational opportunities that he believed the federal government could and should provide. In fact, Americans were largely a society of small landowners and laborers, tilling the soil, accepting their lot as all but predestined, and largely intent on meeting their physical rather than any perceived intellectual needs. The average American man yearned not to attend school or college but to own a plot of

---

*Private charities emerged in most of the North to feed them. There is little documentation of their fate in the South.

land—to work its soil, to plant and harvest enough to feed himself and his family, and to sell any surplus at market. John Quincy's proposals were so alien to American thinking of his time that his programs—along with his presidency—met with nothing but ridicule and rejection, his chance for leadership spent, his dream of advancing the nation, culturally and economically, shattered.

Depressed, he moped about the White House, lost weight noticeably, and reduced his presidential routine to early-morning Bible reading, a daily walk or swim in the Potomac, dinner with Louisa and the family, then an evening chat or a game of billiards. In the course of the day, he kept up with newspapers, signed letters, and received occasional visitors, but grew so moody he stopped writing in his diary, unable to understand why and how he had failed to make his countrymen understand what he was trying to do for them and the nation. His depression made Louisa's life miserable.

"There is something in this great, unsocial house which depresses my spirits beyond expression," she complained in her diary. Evidently weary of the burdens of married life, she grumbled that a husband expected his wife to "cook dinner, wash his clothes, gratify his sexual appetites," and then "thank him and love him for permission to drudge through life at the mercy of his caprices."[24] She and her husband grew strangely distant, and when he traveled to Quincy for his usual summer vacation, Louisa went off on her own, up the Hudson Valley and then to New Hampshire. Their estrangement would last for the rest of their stay in the White House, although she appeared at family dinners and public entertainments.

The mood of the country worsened as well. Planters, farmers, craftsmen, and frontiersmen who made up the majority of Americans were independent and self-sufficient—unwilling to brook interference in their lives by a far-off federal government. They developed a deep resentment for the Harvard scholar who suggested he knew better than they what they needed to know and what they needed to do. They wanted less government, not more. They would read and learn what they liked—or not. They would build their own roads if they thought they needed any and grow and hunt what they pleased when they pleased.

English-born First Lady Louisa Catherine Adams despised life in the White House, saying, "There is something in this great, unsocial house which depresses my spirits beyond expression." (LIBRARY OF CONGRESS)

Sensing the outrage of ordinary voters, Congress blocked every Adams proposal and brought federal government to a halt. And still clinging to his belief that the public would recognize merit, John Quincy refused to campaign for his programs, refused to answer critics, refused to explain his vision in terms the public could understand. In short, he refused to lead or fight back—even after journalist Russell Jarvis of the *Daily Telegraph* assaulted his son John II in the rotunda of the Capitol.

Jarvis had attended a White House reception after publishing a vicious attack on the President, and young Adams proclaimed in a loud voice that Jarvis should have shown the propriety not to show his face at the President's home. Jarvis sent John II a letter challenging him to a duel, and when

The second-born son of John Quincy and Louisa Adams, thirty-one-year-old John Adams II. (NATIONAL PARKS SERVICE, ADAMS NATIONAL HISTORICAL PARK)

John II ignored it, Jarvis waited in the Capitol rotunda for the young man to arrive with messages from the President for Congress. He went up to John II, pulled his nose, then slapped his face—the standard, public provocation to duel. Unskilled with swords or pistols, John II faced certain death if he accepted the challenge. He wisely walked away, and John Quincy responded with a letter of protest to the Speaker of the House that his son had been "waylaid and assaulted." He demanded a congressional inquiry.

"Assault Within the Capitol," ran the headline of a pro-Adams newspaper, while Jarvis's *Telegraph* called "the pulling of the Prince's nose . . . a signal chastisement . . . of the Royal puppy." Congress held hearings, questioned both Jarvis and John II, and did nothing. The President never said another word.

Politically impotent, John Quincy recognized that he would be the first chief executive in the nation's short history to contribute nothing to his country. With little else to do, he joined Louisa in breeding silkworms outside his office and lengthened the time he spent walking, swimming, and horseback riding each day.

The political misery that Jacksonians inflicted on John Quincy hurt Louisa as well. Calling the White House a "dull and stately prison," she continually searched for ways to quash rumors that she and her husband had imported the aristocratic grandeur of European palaces to the executive mansion. She opened White House doors to the public and turned her home into a public museum that left her all but imprisoned in her living quarters, making it "impossible," she said, "for me to feel at home or to fancy that I have a home anywhere."[25]

In addition, she resumed the weekly receptions, or "levées,"* that Martha Washington, Dolley Madison, and, for a time, Elizabeth Monroe had held. Like Elizabeth Monroe, Louisa stood under the rotunda as visitors passed before her, one by one, bowing or curtsying—shaking hands was forbidden—acknowledging her welcoming nod and short greeting and passing on to partake of refreshments. "All classes of society mingled in the throng that crowded outside the audience chamber and surged into the great East Room," according to one participant. Diplomats in powdered wigs and high-ranking officers with medals mixed with farmers and hunters in muddy boots and frontiersmen with jingling spurs.

John Quincy's inability to discuss the mundane at public functions, however, often stripped White House parties of the mirth that had filled the mansion during the tenures of some of his predecessors. What provoked John Quincy's laughter—for example, a misinterpretation he had read of Tacitus—left others staring in disbelief without the slightest understanding of what he was talking about. Only Louisa understood.

---

*This French term dates back to King Louis XIV, who invited a select few to witness his rising and dressing each morning in the royal chamber—a ceremony called *la levée du roi,* or "rising of the king."

Going to the White House levée. First Lady Louisa Catherine Adams hosted weekly "levées," or open houses, for the public to visit the presidential mansion and see the President and First Lady. (LIBRARY OF CONGRESS)

"Mrs. Adams, like her husband, had . . . a love of literature," explained one observer of the social scene of that era. "The most scholarly woman who has presided over the White House, she possessed the adaptability of a French woman or of an American and could turn gracefully from her books or her family cares to inaugurate certain much needed reforms in official circles. By her grace, tact, and *savoir faire*, Mrs. Adams did much to neutralize the effect of the President's cold and often forbidding manner."[26]

The President, of course, had no intention of being cold or forbidding—and, indeed, did not realize he was. He could not, after all, alter the lines, shadows, and shape of his face. Though his thoughts often contained a smile, it did not leak onto his face or into his words. "I am by nature," he said repeatedly, "a silent animal, and my mother's constant lesson in childhood, that children in company should be seen and not heard, confirmed me irrevocably in what I now deem a bad habit."[27]

On July 4, 1826, the fiftieth anniversary of America's Declaration of Independence from Britain, John Adams died in Quincy, Massachusetts—an hour after the death at Monticello of his onetime vice president and longtime friend, Thomas Jefferson. George Washington Adams was with his grandfather when he died. John Quincy arrived with John II in time for the funeral and burial at the local churchyard, after which he returned to his father's house and went into his father's bedroom. "That moment was inexpressibly painful," he moaned.

> My father and my mother have departed. The charm which has always made this house to me an abode of enchantment is dissolved; and yet my attachment to it and to the whole region round is stronger than I ever felt before. I feel it is time for me to begin to set my house in order and to prepare for the churchyard myself. . . . I shall within two or three years . . . need a place of retirement. Where else should I go? This will be a safe and pleasant retreat, where I may pursue literary occupations as long and as much as I can take pleasure in them.[28]

His father's death gave John Quincy more work to do than his job as President. John Adams left a complicated will. For John Quincy to assume sole ownership of the ninety-five-acre property, the will required him to establish a trust for his brother, Thomas Boylston, who lived in his father's house with his wife but had grown too dependent on alcohol to support himself. Thomas's drunken orgies so disgusted Louisa that she refused even to visit the Quincy homestead with her husband, and when John Quincy left to spend the summer at his birthplace, she remained at the White House, neither writing letters of any consequence to the other.

Meanwhile, midterm congressional elections only added to the Jacksonian majority and further stifled John Quincy's efforts to serve the nation. Although the best-prepared chief executive in American history at the time, he was the least effective and least popular, and he did not understand why, given his deep love for his country. "I must await my allotted time," he sighed. "My career is closed."[29]

As the new, decidedly hostile Congress assembled in Washington, John Quincy's son John II provided the President and Louisa with a bright moment by marrying Louisa's niece Mary Hellen in the Blue Room of the White House.

"The bride looked very handsome in white satin, orange-blossoms, and pearls," wrote John Quincy's niece, who said that she and the other three bridesmaids had "an amusing time . . . arranging flowers and ribbons." They then "passed the cake . . . [and] cut slices to distribute among their friends."[30] Even the President joined in the festivities that followed the cutting of the cake by entering "with spirit into the mazes of the Virginia reel."[31] After the wedding, Louisa's nephew Thomas, who had loafed about the White House after dropping out of Harvard, ran off with one of the young White House maids and, mercifully, left John Quincy with one less family member to support.

By spring of 1828, the President's daily activities were devoid of consequence for the nation:

> I rise generally before five—frequently before four. Write from one to two hours in this diary. Ride about twelve miles in two hours on horseback with my son John. Return home about nine; breakfast; and from that time till dinner, between five and six, afternoon, I am occupied incessantly with visitors, business, reading letters, dispatches, and newspapers. I spend an hour, sometimes before and sometimes after dinner, in the garden and nursery; an hour of drowsiness on a sofa; and two hours of writing in the evening. Retire usually between eleven and midnight.[32]

The President's political inactivity triggered a barrage of scurrilous attacks by Jacksonian newspapers, which took aim at every member of John Quincy's cabinet as well as John Quincy himself. The attacks left Henry Clay so distraught he took a medical leave of absence. Although John Quincy did not want to allow his enemies to topple him from office without defending himself, everything he tried failed. Invited to preside at a July 4 groundbreaking for the heralded Chesapeake and Ohio Canal, a symbol of the very national improvements he espoused, he addressed a friendly crowd of more than 2,000 spectators, then took a gilded spade to turn the first shovel of dirt—only to feel the shovel clang and rebound sharply, then slip from his hands after hitting a hidden tree stump. As murmurs of disappointment spread through onlookers, the President tried again—and again. Finally, he did something he had never done in public: "I threw off my coat and, resuming the spade, raised a shovelful of the earth, at which a general shout burst forth from the surrounding multitude, and I completed my address."

It was the first time in months that an audience had cheered the President, and he left elated, inviting the officers who escorted him home to join him for drinks in the White House. Although it was too late, John Quincy had evidently learned a lesson about relating to the general public: "My casting off my coat," he wrote later, "struck the eye and fancy of the spectators more than all the flowers of rhetoric in my speech."[33] He was, of course, a master at interrelating with czars, kings, counts, and courtiers, but had simply never had the chance to befriend ordinary citizens—at home or abroad.

Although eager for the first time to enter the election fray, it was all too new to him, and he let others do the electioneering. They attacked Jackson and his allies viciously, with Clay allegedly coaxing the editor of Cincinnati's *Gazette* to charge Jackson with having maintained an adulterous relationship with his wife, Rachel, before she had divorced her first husband. The Jacksonians fired back with equally vicious libels against the Yankee "aristocrat" with an "English wife," who had spent public funds to purchase a billiard table for her husband's amusement in the White House.

In the end, election campaign rhetoric made little difference. The hero of the Battle of New Orleans was simply too popular, and the public was thoroughly convinced that the aristocratic New Englander from Harvard had ignored the will of the people and purchased his election by appointing Henry Clay as secretary of state. Unlike John Quincy, Jackson had formed a new and well-organized political party that operated at both lo-cal and state levels and acquired consummate skills in obtaining news-paper publicity.

As the 1828 election approached, New England textile manufacturers set up a drumbeat of demand for higher protective tariffs. The War of 1812 had cut off cloth imports from England and given New England manufacturers a monopoly. After the war, however, renewed competition from larger, more-efficient British mills saw American markets flooded with less costly, high-quality British cloth, and Congress responded to complaints from New England mills by passing protective tariffs in 1816 and again in 1824. Agricultural interests in the South—especially cotton growers—protested, fearing that their best customers, the British cotton mills, would retaliate and curtail purchases of American cotton. Ignoring such protests, other raw materials producers and manufacturers de-manded similar tariff protection—for wool, cotton, hemp, flax, iron, dis-tilled spirits . . . the list grew endless—with the final bill called a "Tariff of Abomination" by its opponents. Passed by a huge veto-proof congres-sional majority, the bill left John Quincy no choice but to sign it into law. Southern states reacted with outrage, with South Carolina's legislature calling the tariff unconstitutional and blaming John Quincy for not hav-ing vetoed it. Georgia, Mississippi, and Virginia followed suit and cost John Quincy the entire South in the 1828 election.

When the votes were counted on December 3, Jackson had humiliated John Quincy Adams—with 647,276 Americans voting for Jackson and 508,064 for Adams. In the Electoral College, Jackson captured 178 votes, more than twice John Quincy's 83 votes. "The sun of my political life sets in the deepest gloom," John Quincy sighed, "but that of my country shines unclouded." To ease the pain of his loss, he took "a ride of an hour and a half on horseback."[34]

Louisa stepped forward to try to cheer her husband by organizing a huge party to celebrate his return to private life. "The defeated party . . . are more smiling and gracious and agreeable than they ever were before,"

Mrs. Samuel Harrison Smith, wife of the owner of the *National Intelligencer*, wrote to her son.

> At Mrs. Adams's drawing room last week, every one attached to the administration, as well as the members of the cabinet, appeared with their best looks and best dresses. Mrs. Adams never on any former occasion was so social, attentive, and agreeable. Instead of standing in one place, making formal courtesies, she walked through the rooms conversing with every one in the most animated manner. To add to the gaiety and brilliancy of the evening the great audience chamber was lit up, the band of music stationed there, and dancing took place.[35]

Shortly after the election results appeared in the newspapers, Rachel Jackson saw the story alleging her adulterous relationship with Andrew Jackson before she divorced her first husband. Shocked to the core as she read, she collapsed—a stroke, perhaps, or a heart attack. She died several days later and was buried on Christmas Eve without seeing her husband assume the presidency.

On March 4, 1829, Andrew Jackson was inaugurated as seventh President of the United States. Ignoring tradition, John Quincy refused to attend either the inauguration or the new President's White House reception afterwards. "I can yet scarcely realize my situation," he shuddered in disbelief, saying, "posterity will scarcely believe . . . the combination of parties and of public men against my character and reputation such as I believe never before was exhibited against any man since this Union existed." He continued:

> This combination against me has been formed and is now exulting in triumph over me, for the devotion of my life and of all the faculties of my soul to the Union and to the improvement, physical, moral and intellectual, of my country. The North assails me for my fidelity to the Union; the South, for my ardent aspirations of improvement. Yet . . . passion,

prejudice, envy, and jealousy will pass. The cause of Union and of improvement will remain, and I have duties to it and to my country yet to discharge.[36]

Although the vast majority of American voters had rejected John Quincy and his vision for America, he refused to accept their judgment and vowed to continue his struggle to lead them and the nation to greatness. His only uncertainty was how to do it.

CHAPTER 13

A New Beginning

After his 1828 defeat, President John Quincy Adams prepared to return to his father's house in Quincy, Massachusetts, resigned to a life of semiretirement, puttering about the farm a bit, but focused on writing a biography of his father and practicing law part time. John Quincy and Louisa were waiting for George Washington Adams to arrive from Boston to help them move back to Quincy, when a messenger delivered a thunderbolt:

Their firstborn son was dead at twenty-eight.

George Washington Adams had been en route to Washington on a steamboat from Providence to New York. On April 30, at 3 a.m., after a night of heavy drinking, he turned irrational, demanding that the captain stop the ship to let him off. When the captain refused, he went topside by himself and either jumped or fell overboard, leaving only his cloak and hat on board—and no note. In the weeks before his death, his drinking and gambling had not abated, and his work had suffered. Still worse, a maid working for the family where he was living had given birth to his child and was blackmailing him.*

---

*His remains washed ashore a month after his death, and his father buried him in the family vault in Quincy.

After learning of her son's death, Louisa decided to remain in Washington apart from her husband. She was too despondent to cope with her husband's moodiness and his brother's drunkenness. John Quincy bought a home two miles from the Capitol and left her there.

"The parting from my wife was distressing to her and to me," he confided to his diary. "The afflictions with which we have been visited—especially the last—has so weakened us in body and mind that our dejection of spirit seems irrecoverable. We parted with anguish that I cannot describe."[1]

Early in September, John Quincy's youngest son, Charles Francis—by then his and Louisa's brightest hope—married Abigail Brooks, whose sister had married Massachusetts congressman Edward Everett.* Everett's brother Alexander had trained in the law with John Quincy and served in his St. Petersburg legation for a year. Although John Quincy attended his son's wedding, Louisa was still too distraught from the death of her oldest son to travel to Boston.

Later that fall, John Quincy rejoined Louisa in Washington, spending his time on walks, swimming in the Potomac, and writing articles on international affairs that found their way into scholarly journals. In the spring of 1830, he returned to Quincy, this time with Louisa, leaving John II in Washington to try to extract profits from the Columbian Mills flour business.

As the summer progressed, however, John Quincy fell deeper into depression, finding his only pleasures in walking and swimming, reading the Bible and Cicero's *Orations*, planting fruit trees, and tending a garden of

---

*Edward Everett graduated from Harvard at the top of his class in 1811 and went on to become a Massachusetts congressman and governor, secretary of state, and senator. One of the nation's great orators, he gave the two-hour-long address at the dedication of the Gettysburg cemetery, only to be upstaged by Abraham Lincoln's short address. "I should be glad," he wrote to President Lincoln the next day, "if I could flatter myself that I came as near the central idea of the occasion in two hours as you did in two minutes" (from *Webster's American Biographies*).

peas, beans, corn, and other vegetables. He made halfhearted attempts at organizing his father's papers, rummaging through boxes and finding some mementos of his youth—largely books, such as a fondly remembered edition of *Arabian Nights*. "The more there was in them of invention, the more pleasing they were," he recalled. "My imagination pictured them all as realities, and I dreamed of enchantments as if there was a world in which they existed."[2] Charles Francis and his wife visited regularly for family clambakes, John II came up from Washington for two short visits, and the summer slipped away.

As ill disposed as he was to public functions, he agreed to attend the bicentennial celebration of the founding of Boston on September 17, and to his surprise, two honorary marshals escorted him from the State House to the Old South Church. Well-wishers hailed him as he passed, and even former Federalist adversaries approached with warm salutations. At the end of the day, he attended a reception at the lieutenant governor's residence, where his friends, the Everett brothers and the editor of the Boston *Patriot,* were huddling with Quincy congressman Reverend Joseph Richardson. After greeting the former President, they asked if they could visit him the following day. He agreed, and at the appointed time, they informed him that Richardson's parishioners had pleaded with him to retire from Congress to devote himself full time to his church, and he had agreed. The Everetts then asked John Quincy to run for Richardson's seat, assuring him that he would win without opposition and flattering him with the notion of "ennobling" the House of Representatives with the presence of a former President.

Always in character, John Quincy feigned disinterest, saying he would do nothing to support his own candidacy. Explaining his familiar position on political campaigns, he asserted that if the people called on him of their own volition, he "might deem it my duty to serve. . . . I want the people to act spontaneously."[3] He made it clear, however, that he would remain independent of party affiliations and represent the whole nation, with his only political loyalty tied to national independence from all foreign entanglements and preservation of the Union.

Both Louisa and Charles Francis were appalled that John Quincy would even consider returning to politics after the humiliation he had suffered. Louisa threatened not to accompany him if he returned to Washington—to no avail. Quincy voted overwhelmingly to return their former President to Washington, giving him 1,817 votes, while the two other candidates garnered a combined total of only 552 votes.

"I am a member-elect of the Twenty-Second Congress," he wrote in joyful disbelief that night, and nothing Louisa could say could detract from his satisfaction. "My return to public life . . . is disagreeable to my family," he admitted, "yet I can not withhold my grateful acknowledgment to the Disposer of human events and to the people of my native region for this unexpected testimonial of their continued confidence."

It seemed as if I was deserted by all mankind. . . . In the French opera of *Richard Coeur-de-Lion*, the minstrel Blondel sings under the walls of his prison a song, beginning:

O, Richard! O, mon Roi!

L'univers t'abandonne.*

When I first heard this song, forty-five years ago . . . it made an indelible impression upon my memory, without imagining that I should ever feel its force so much closer to home. But this call upon me by the people of the district in which I reside, to represent them in Congress, has been spontaneous. . . . My election as President of the United States was not half so gratifying to my inmost soul. No election or appointment conferred upon me ever gave me so much pleasure.[4]

As his spirits revived, he finally coaxed Louisa into returning to Washington, and the two left in December. Along the way, he showed himself still a champion of public improvements by being among the first to ride on the new steam-driven train between Baltimore and Washington. And

---

*"O, Richard, my king, the world abandons thee."

to his delight and Louisa's amazement, a crowd awaited to greet them on their return. Although he would not take his seat until 1832, three hundred callers came to their house on New Year's Day 1831, buoying his spirits still more and spurring him to seek out and meet members of Congress to determine their political views. He attended the House of Representatives to learn the rules and study member quirks and tics, and as he soaked up the thinking of his future colleagues, the joy of his return to politics spurred a renewed interest in scholarly pursuits, including poetry. By spring, when the time came to return to Quincy, he had reread *Childe Harold, Don Juan*, and other works of Lord Byron—and written his own epic, 2,000-line poem titled *Dermot MacMorrogh*, on Henry II's conquest of Ireland. He considered it his finest work and at least one publisher agreed, producing three successive editions.* On the way north, he stopped to see former President James Monroe, who was gravely ill in New York and destitute, living off the charity of his daughter and son-in-law at their New York City home.

After his return to Quincy, town officials invited him to give the July 4 oration, and he set to work drafting a fierce attack on the doctrine of "nullification," which had regained currency in the South in response to high federal tariffs on cotton goods. Thomas Jefferson had fathered the concept in 1798, when he was vice president and opposed the Alien and Sedition Acts of President John Adams. Declaring the Constitution only "a compact" among sovereign states, Jefferson insisted that the states retained authority to restrain actions by the federal government that exceeded its constitutional mandate. Jefferson persuaded the Kentucky legislature to approve a resolution allowing it to declare unconstitutional any federal government exercise of powers not specifically delegated by the Constitution. His protégé, James Madison, marched in lockstep and convinced the Virginia legislature "to interpose" its authority to prevent federal "exercise

---

*Dermot MacMorrogh, or the Conquest of Ireland: An Historical Tale of the Twelfth Century, in Four Cantos (Boston: Carter Hendee, 1832; 1832; Columbus, OH: I. N. Whiting, 1834).

of . . . powers" not granted by the Constitution.[5] Federalist legislatures in other states, however, declared the Virginia and Kentucky resolutions "mad and rebellious" and rejected them by declaring U.S. courts to be the sole judges of constitutionality.

Vice President John C. Calhoun subsequently revived southern interest in the concept with an essay he called "South Carolina Exposition and Protest." In it, he insisted that the Tenth Amendment gave every state the right to nullify a federal act that it deemed a violation of the Constitution. In his July 4 oration in Quincy, John Quincy countered by labeling the concept of state sovereignty a "hallucination" and nothing "less than treason"— a fierce charge that resounded across the country after an enterprising printer distributed more than 4,000 copies of his speech nationwide.

As John Quincy delivered his oration, the President he had served for eight years died in New York—joining John Adams and Thomas Jefferson as the third of the first five Presidents to die on July 4. Asked to deliver a eulogy for Monroe at Boston's Old South Church, John Quincy produced a stirring reminder of Monroe's courage as an officer during the Revolution, "weltering in his blood on the field of Trenton for the cause of his country." Then John Quincy turned to his own—and Monroe's—favorite subject: public improvements. He urged mourners to "look at the map of United North America, as it was . . . in 1783. Compare it with the map of that same Empire as it is now. . . . The change, more than of any other man, living or dead, was the work of James Monroe." John Quincy recalled how Monroe had scoffed at Congress for denying it had "the power of appropriating money for the construction of a canal to connect the waters of Chesapeake Bay with the Ohio."[6] He portrayed the "unspeakable blessings" of Monroe's vision of a transnational network of roads and canals. "Sink down, ye mountains!" John Quincy called out. "And ye valleys—rise!"

> Exult and shout for joy! Rejoice! that . . . there are neither Rocky Mountains nor oases of the desert, from the rivers of the Southern [Pacific] Ocean to the shores of the Atlantic Sea; Rejoice! that . . . the waters of the Columbia mingle in union with the streams of the Delaware, the Lakes of

Charles Francis Adams was the youngest child of John Quincy and Louisa Catherine Adams. Like his father, he was a Harvard graduate and lawyer. (NATIONAL PARKS SERVICE, ADAMS NATIONAL HISTORICAL PARK)

the St. Lawrence with the floods of the Mississippi; Rejoice! that . . . the distant have been drawn near . . . that the North American continent swarms with hearts beating as if from one bosom, of voices speaking with but one tongue, of freemen constituting one confederated and united republic of brethren, never to rise . . . in hostile arms . . . to fulfill the blessed prophecy of ancient times, that war shall be no more.[7]

After he had delivered his eulogy, John Quincy and Louisa learned to their delight that Charles Francis's wife, Abby, had given birth to their first child, a girl they named Louisa Catherine Adams. With John II's two daughters, John Quincy and Louisa now had three granddaughters, but they still awaited the birth of a grandson to carry the family name into the future.

By the time John Quincy and Louisa began their return to Washington for the opening of Congress in December 1831, his eloquence had resounded across the nation, with both his July 4 oration and eulogy to Monroe having been published in most American newspapers. Old political friends greeted him in New York. In Philadelphia, Albert Gallatin, his associate in Ghent, asked him to preside at the Literary Convention then in session and won his appointment to a committee drawing up plans for a National Library and Scientific Institution. By the time he reached Washington, his political enemies in Congress feared he was mounting a surreptitious campaign to recapture the presidency, and to prevent that possibility, they shunted him onto the least important committees. Instead of the Committee on Foreign Affairs—"the line of occupation in which all my life has been passed"—he found himself chairman of the Committee on Manufactures, "for which I feel myself not to be well qualified. I know not even enough of it to form an estimate of its difficulties."[8]

Although any member of the House could introduce a bill relating to anything he chose, by tradition, members limited the bills they proposed to matters within the purview of their own committees. To escape what he considered a procedural straitjacket, John Quincy decided to flaunt House tradition and use the right of every committee chairman to read citizen petitions on the House floor—regardless of their content.

On his first day in Congress, therefore, he hurled his first thunderbolt on the floor of the House, shocking both sides of the aisle with not one but fifteen petitions from Pennsylvania Quakers "praying for the abolition of slavery and the slave trade in the District of Columbia." Under rules adopted by the First Congress in 1790, the House had agreed to remain silent on the question of abolition—largely because of South Carolina's threat to walk out at the mention of abolition or slavery. The Capitol all but imploded under the tension of his words. "I was not more than five minutes on my feet but I was listened to with great attention, and when I sat down, it seemed to myself as if I had performed an achievement."[9]

He had indeed performed an achievement. Although most of the House rose as one to roar its disapproval, former President John Quincy Adams had burst open the doors of Congress to abolitionist voices for the first time in decades—voices that other congressmen had routinely ignored for years and would never be able to ignore again. Although Pennsylvania Quakers were not his constituents, he had proclaimed himself a representative of the whole nation, and the whole nation now took him at his word, inundating him with petitions they knew their own representatives would never accept.

It was not a good time to be a proponent of abolition in America, however. Only months before, a black preacher, Nat Turner, had led an insurrection in Virginia, killing fifty-seven white people, including eighteen women and twenty-four children. Only swift retaliation by U.S. marines prevented the insurrection from spreading into North Carolina. Although one hundred blacks had been killed and twenty were later executed, the specter of future black uprisings terrified southerners—and many northerners—and southern states were tightening their slave codes to curb black mobility. Some required blacks to carry special passes for travel; others banned all travel by blacks except to church meetings. Ten states were considering or had proposed changes in their state constitutions to ban voluntary emancipation of slaves by slaveholders.

Most House members responded to John Quincy's petitions for abolition with such hostility that he feared for the very future of the nation. He had entered Congress convinced "that this federative Union was to last for ages," but after his presentation, "I now disbelieve its duration for twenty years and doubt its continuance for five."[10]

In his self-appointed role as representative of the entire nation, John Quincy was determined to fulfill his obligation to his huge constituency by attending every session of Congress—from its first day on December 5, 1831, to its last, in March 1833—regardless of the weather or his own health. He threw his mind and soul into his new work, studying rules and proceedings of previous Congresses and reviewing his law texts and the language of laws. His work brought new joy into his life—and misery into Louisa's. Unlike his presidency, John Quincy's role as a congressman did not generate the need to entertain at home, thus leaving Louisa with so little to do that she took up fishing—and poetry writing. Even when John Quincy returned home, his mind, his heart, his soul remained in Congress. The only joy in her life came from caring for her two granddaughters.

As much as, and even more than, anything he had ever done in his life, John Quincy's work in Congress seemed to him the ultimate patriotic service he could perform for his country. "The forms and proceedings of the House," he exulted, were "a very striking exemplification of the magnificent grandeur of this nation and the sublime principles upon which our government is founded."

> The colossal emblem of the Union over the Speaker's chair, the historic muse at the clock, the echoing pillars of the hall . . . the resolutions and amendments between the members and the chair, the calls of ayes and noes, with the different intonations . . . from the different voices, the gobbling manner of the clerk in reading over the names, the tone of the Speaker in announcing the vote, and the varied shades of pleasure and pain in the countenances of the members on hearing it, would form a fine subject for a descriptive poem.[11]

As it had throughout his life, tragedy forced its way into his sublime existence when he returned to his home on F Street one evening to find John II in a drunken stupor, still another inheritor of the disease that had plagued his maternal forbears for generations. And then, on March 12, John Quincy's beloved younger brother, Thomas Boylston, died of the family affliction, leaving John Quincy the only surviving son of an American Founding Father. Thomas's death left John Quincy the sole support for his brother's spendthrift wife and their dysfunctional children.*

---

*Three of the sons joined the military not long after their father's death; two of them died of typhoid fever, and the third was lost at sea. Still, John Quincy supported Thomas's wife, Nancy, until her death in 1845.

Before long, John Quincy realized that Congress had not transduced his petitions for abolition into legislative proposals; although he kept presenting them, he knew he would need his committee's support to produce actual bills for enactment into laws. He soon mastered all the intricacies of American economics and manufacturing—especially cotton and woolen goods manufacturing—and discovered the intricate ties between manufacturing and a broad range of other issues, including foreign affairs, tariffs, and slavery. He now knew the way to broaden the scope of his committee proceedings, using the most obvious issue first: tariffs.

For a while, high tariffs on imported English cotton goods had protected small New England manufacturers against competition from British imports, but the tariffs that protected New England mills against British competition hurt southern cotton growers, who shipped more of their crop to the big British cotton mills than they did to New England. As high U.S. tariffs cut British textile sales to America, British mills bought less cotton from the American South and left planters with too many slaves to support for the amount of cotton they picked.

John Quincy proposed—and Congress approved—a compromise tariff bill that reduced duties on British goods with a high content of southern cotton, but the British mills resented the selective tariffs, saying they would not submit to a foreign government's dictating their sales policies. Responding to their British clients, southern planters demanded an end to the tariffs, and South Carolina's governor called a special Nullification Convention in November 1832, which declared federal tariff laws null and void in South Carolina, prohibited collection of federal tariffs in the state, and threatened South Carolina's secession from the Union if federal officials tried using force to collect tariffs. A week later, the South Carolina legislature authorized raising a military force and appropriated funds for arms. Civil war seemed imminent.

The state's declaration and mobilization shocked the nation and left even President Andrew Jackson, a champion of states' rights, aghast. "The nation will be preserved," he declared angrily. "Perpetuity is stamped upon the Constitution by the blood of our fathers. Nullification therefore means insurrection and war, and the other states have a right to put it down."[12]

South Carolinians responded with huge demonstrations in Charleston. South Carolina senator Robert Hayne resigned from the Senate to run for governor of his state and lead the fight for nullification. Vice President Calhoun resigned his post and won election as Hayne's replacement in the Senate, although rumors swept through Charleston that he intended returning to become first president of a Southern Confederacy.

On December 5, 1832, Jackson overwhelmed John Quincy's former secretary of state, Henry Clay, in the presidential election, with New York's Martin Van Buren winning the vice presidency. Former vice president Calhoun from South Carolina won reelection to the Senate. Five days after his reelection, Jackson issued a presidential proclamation declaring "the power to annul a law of the United States, assumed by one state, incompatible with the existence of the Union" and warning of "dreadful consequence" for the "instigators" of the South Carolina Nullification Act. "Disunion . . . is treason," he told the people of South Carolina. "On your unhappy heads will inevitably fall all raw evils of the conflict you force upon the government of your country."[13]

The summer recess postponed further congressional debate over nullification until fall, and during that time, Harvard University voted to grant President Jackson an honorary degree. Although firmly on Jackson's side in the battle against nullification, John Quincy refused to attend the ceremonies honoring the President. "As myself an affectionate child of our Alma Mater," he explained, "I would not be present to witness her disgrace in presenting her highest literary honors upon a barbarian who could not write a sentence of grammar and hardly could spell his own name."[14]

Although the summer began disagreeably, it ended in joy, when Charles Francis and his wife realized what had become one of John Quincy's cherished dreams—the birth of his first grandson. They named him John Quincy Adams II and ensured the preservation of the legendary Adams name in the United States for at least another generation. "There is no passion more deeply seated in my bosom," John Quincy exulted, "than the longing for posterity worthily to support my own and my father's name. . . . There is now one son of the next generation."[15]

John Quincy returned to Congress refreshed and ready to battle nullification, even if it meant strengthening ties to President Jackson. On January 16, 1833, with civil war threatening, Jackson asked Congress to grant him authority to use military force if necessary to crush the nullifiers and enforce revenue- and tariff-collection laws. Congress complied, with John Quincy voting in favor. Jackson signed the Force Bill into law on March 2 and frightened South Carolina's legislature into rescinding its Nullification Act.

After John Quincy had supported the President by voting for the Force Bill, he leaped back across the political fence to oppose efforts by Jacksonian Democrats to mollify the South by eliminating tariffs.

"Our slaves," explained Georgia's Democratic congressman Augustus Smith Clayton in arguing for tariff cuts, "are our machinery, and we have as good a right to profit by them as do the northern men to profit by the machinery they employ."[16]

John Quincy listened to Clayton's appeal in disbelief, the phrase "our machinery" resounding in his head until he exploded in outrage.

"That machinery," John Quincy roared in response, "sometimes exerts self-moving power!"[17]

With Nat Turner's insurrection still fresh in the minds of many northern as well as southern congressmen, the House all but shouted John Quincy down, while another South Carolina member, William Drayton, cried out, "The member from Massachusetts has thrown a firebrand into the hall."

"It is not I who have thrown the firebrand," John Quincy shouted back. "The Nullification Ordinance is the firebrand."[18]

In the end, northerners capitulated by voting for further tariff cuts, as did Henry Clay, who had originally based his American System on high tariffs but was now licking his wounds from the presidential race and seeking to court southern votes for the next election.

Before the presidential election of 1834, tragedy struck the Adams family again. In the autumn of that year, John II suffered a series of seizures—a consequence of alcoholism—and lapsed into a coma. By the time his father reached his bedside, he was close to death, and indeed, he died the next day, October 22, without recognizing his father. Besides his wife and two daughters, he left debts of $15,000 (which John Quincy paid). John Quincy and Louisa turned to each other for comfort, with John Quincy calling his wife "the dearest partner of my life." Both doted on their granddaughters, with John Quincy stopping at his dead son's house each day on the way to the Capitol to help the older girl learn her arithmetic. John Quincy would support his granddaughters and their mother as long as he lived.

In December 1835, President Jackson sent Congress a curious and unexpected message: an Englishman, James Smithson, had left a bequest of about $500,000 to the United States "to found at Washington, under the name of the Smithsonian Institution, an Establishment for the increase and diffusion of knowledge among men."[19] Son of the first Duke of Northumberland, Smithson had, ironically, been the half-brother of General Hugh Lord Percy, the British commander at the Battle of Lexington in 1775. Although both houses of Congress licked their collective chops at the possibilities for personal profits, the House acceded to John Quincy's fierce interest in science and named him chairman of the committee to determine how to disburse the money.

Besieged by schools and colleges for shares of the money, John Quincy ruled out disbursement of any of the principal, reserving it entirely to the government and limiting spending to interest generated. He intended combining George Washington's vision of creating "institutions for the general diffusion of knowledge" with his own vision of national astronomical observatories—the "lighthouses in the sky" that his political opponents had ridiculed when he was President. He called "the link between earth and heaven . . . the means of acquiring knowledge . . . therefore the greatest benefit that can be conferred upon mankind."[20] He was now prepared to fight his opponents in ways that had eluded him when he was President.

South Carolina senator John Calhoun, the former vice president, assailed John Quincy's proposal as federal intrusion in an area the Tenth Amendment reserved for the states. He pointed out correctly that the Constitutional Convention had twice rejected efforts to give the government powers to establish a national university. John Quincy countered, however, that there were no constitutional restrictions on establishing research institutions—nor did the framers restrict the national government from establishing any kind of institution in the District of Columbia. John Quincy won the day, with both houses deferring to his constitutional scholarship and approving his bill to establish the Smithsonian Institution as a public institution that remains in the hands of the American people to this day.

Despite President Jackson's proclamation that nullification was tantamount to treason, nullification fervor continued spreading in the South, and northerners responded with stepped-up demands for abolition. Peering into the future, John Quincy warned that "a dissolution of the Union for the cause of slavery would be followed by . . . a war between the two severed portions of the Union. It seems to me that its result must be the extirpation of slavery from this whole continent and desolating as this course of events . . . must be, so glorious would be its final issue, that, as God shall judge me, I dare not say that it is not to be desired."[21]

As petitions demanding an end to slavery increased, he found abolitionists as prepared as slavery proponents to dissolve the Union to further their cause. For several years, therefore, beginning with the debate over the Missouri Compromise, he had argued that the Constitution failed to give Congress any powers to interfere with slavery in any state or territory in which it already existed. It could prevent its establishment in states and territories where it did not exist but could not abolish it where it already did exist. Abolitionists argued, however, that Congress could at least eliminate slavery in the District of Columbia, where it had powers to legislate and govern, unrestricted by the Constitution.

In the wake of three House resolutions in 1836, however, John Quincy completely changed his stance on abolition. The first two resolutions declared Congress without constitutional powers to interfere in any way with slavery in any of the states and that it "ought not" do so in the District of Columbia. John Quincy voted for both, conceding that the Constitution offered no clear guidance on abolition in the District of Columbia. The third resolution, however, stepped beyond the abolition issue by clearly abridging free speech, and John Quincy all but exploded with rage as he listened:

> All petitions, memorials, propositions, or papers, relating in any way, or to any extent whatsoever, to the subject of slavery or the abolition of slavery shall, without being either printed or referred, be laid on the table, and that no further action whatever shall be had thereon.[22]

Although John Quincy shot to his feet for recognition, Speaker James K. Polk, a Tennessee slaveholder, ignored him and recognized only southern congressmen. John Quincy howled for recognition, but Polk looked the other way, and after southerners had finished their presentations, he put the third resolution to a vote. The House approved it 95–82, and the Speaker shut off all further debate, preventing John Quincy from saying a word.

"Am I gagged or am I not," John Quincy shouted in disbelief, inadvertently giving the new rule its historic name—the Gag Rule. Southerners tried shouting him down with cries of "Order! . . . Order!!" The Speaker called out over the din, "The motion is not debatable," and when John Quincy appealed to the House to overrule the Speaker, it sustained the Speaker 109–89. When the clerk called the Adams name, he stood: "If the House will allow me five minutes in time—"

"Order!" shouted southerners. "Order!"

"I hold the resolution—" John Quincy shouted above the roar, "I hold the resolution to be in direct violation of the Constitution of the United States, of the rules of this House, and of the rights of my constituents."[23]

The enmity he encountered in the House grew vicious—spiteful at times. When he asked the House to recognize the death of William Wirt, who had served the nation as attorney general for twelve years in the Monroe and Adams administrations, the House refused. John Quincy called the

*As Speaker of the House, James K. Polk of
Tennessee tried to silence John Quincy
Adams with the Gag Rule, which banned
mention of the word "slavery" and
presentation of citizen petitions to abolish
the institution.* (LIBRARY OF CONGRESS)

refusal mean-spirited. "I place in perpetual opposition to me and to everything that I propose or support," he growled, "twenty-nine members of the House and six of the Senate; and for all this and its consequences I have no compensation . . . but the bare consciousness of having done my duty."[24]

When he opposed Ohio's forcible takeover of disputed territory in Michigan, John Quincy reported that "the people in the territory of Michigan were grateful to me," but he predicted that "the people of Ohio, Indiana, and Illinois will hate me with perfect hatred for crossing their interests." Of his efforts in the House, he concluded, "Never in my life have I taken in public controversies a part more suicidal to my own popularity."[25]

The Gag Rule infuriated Americans across the North and parts of the West as much as it did John Quincy, however, and hundreds of thousands of petitioners rallied to his side, arguing that if the House could gag the reading of petitions against slavery, it could gag petitions against or for anything. Women's rights groups joined the protests and added their own petitions to the flood already inundating Congress. When Maryland's Benjamin Chew Howard objected to the "unseemliness" of women presenting a petition, John Quincy sharpened his tongue and leaped for the rhetorical kill:

"Why, does it follow," he boomed, "that women are fitted for nothing but the cares of domestic life, for bearing children and cooking the food of a family, devoting all their time to the domestic circle—to promoting the immediate personal comfort of their husbands, brothers, and sons?" Louisa had apparently taught her husband to alter his thinking if not his ways. "The mere departure of woman from the duties of the domestic circle, far from being a reproach to her, is a virtue of the highest order, when it is done from purity of motive, by appropriate means, and the purpose of good." He went on to read a petition opposing slavery from women in his constituency of Plymouth, Massachusetts. "Is this discreditable?" he asked, before thundering his oft-repeated conviction: "I do believe slavery to be a sin before the sight of God."[26]

Recognized by then as an authority on parliamentary rules, John Quincy kept finding ways around the Gag Rule, at one point asking for recognition to read the prayers of a group of Massachusetts women. When a House member objected, John Quincy responded by explaining that the women were not petitioning but simply praying for "the greatest improvement that can possibly be effected in the condition of the human race— the abolition of slavery."[27] The House exploded in collective anger at his flagrant violation of the ban on reading petitions against slavery and even uttering the word "slavery" in congressional debates. John Quincy smiled wryly, reiterating that he had not read a *petition* containing the word "slavery" (once more uttering the word) but a *prayer* of women who, like the members' own mothers, were offended by "the sinfulness of slavery [again, the forbidden word!] and keenly aggrieved by its existence in a part of our country over which—"

Choking with anger by then, South Carolina's Thomas Pinckney interrupted to charge John Quincy with reading a petition. "Point of order!"
Pinckney bellowed.

"—keenly aggrieved by its existence in a part of the country over which
Congress possesses exclusive jurisdiction in all cases whatever—"

"Order! Order!"

"—do most earnestly petition your honorable body—"

"Mr. Speaker! I rise on a point order!"

"—immediately to abolish slavery in the District of Columbia—"

"Mr. Speaker! A call to order!"

"Order! Order!"

"Take your seat!" the Speaker ordered John Quincy.

"—and," John Quincy began to sit, accelerating his words as he did,
"to-declare-every-human-being-free-who-sets-foot-upon-its-soil."[28]

Increasingly stifled by the Gag Rule and its proponents, John Quincy
finally ran out of parliamentary maneuvers and resorted to rhetorical trick-
ery to confuse, embarrass, and essentially emasculate his political enemies.
Early in February, he presented two petitions, one from nine unnamed
women and the other from actual slaves. As he knew they would, the
southerners erupted in collective fury, with one of them resolving that "infamous women . . . [and] slaves do not possess the right of petition secured
to the people of the United States by the Constitution." The same congressman resolved, as well, that any member who presents a petition from
slaves should be considered "unfriendly to the Union," and his third
resolution—its content almost comical—cited "the Hon. John Q. Adams"
as having "disclaimed all design of doing anything disrespectful to this
House." In effect, it accepted an apology from John Quincy that he had
never offered. To prolong the charade, John Quincy asked "for an opportunity for a full hearing in my defense." He insisted he had never apologized
and resented the accusation of having done so. After the laughter subsided,
even Gag Rule sponsors relented, recognizing that refusal to hear one of
their own colleagues might prevent each of them from defending themselves in the future.

Focusing on the constitutional right of petition rather than abolition, John Quincy asked, "Will you put the right of petitioning, of craving for help and mercy and protection on the footing of political privileges? . . . No despot of any age or clime has ever denied this humble privilege to the poorest or meanest of human creatures. . . . That would be a sad day, Sir . . . when a vote should pass this House that would not receive a petition from slaves. . . . When the principle is once begun of limiting the right of petition, where would it stop?"

John Quincy then accused the sponsor of the resolutions of having accused the nine unnamed women of prostitution.

"I did not say they were prostitutes," the congressman protested in his southern drawl. "I have not said I know those women!"

"I am glad to hear the honorable gentleman disclaim any knowledge of them," John Quincy smirked, "for I had been going to ask, if they were infamous women, who it was that had made them infamous. Not their color, I believe, but their masters! I have heard it said in proof of that fact . . . that in the South there existed great resemblances between the progeny of the colored people and the white men who claim possession of them. Thus, perhaps the charge of infamous might be retorted on those who made it, as reflecting on themselves."

As southerners exploded with rage, "Old Man Eloquent," as the press now called John Quincy, could shout touché. It was a rhetorical triumph like no other in congressional history at the time. Even the *Register of Debates* saw fit to note the response to John Quincy's words: "Great agitation in the House."[29]

Although the House voted down resolutions to censure John Quincy, it nonetheless voted to deprive slaves of the right to petition, thus eroding the sanctity of the Constitution and depriving most African Americans of the privileges and protections of the Bill of Rights.

"Vengeance is mine, say the South!" warned a printed sheet someone slipped under John Quincy's door. Beneath a drawing of a whip were the words, "Flog and Spare Not!" Another letter addressed him as "Sir" but warned that "your conduct . . . is such as to draw upon you the indignation of the South. . . . The rod is cut that will make your old hide smart for your insidious attempt on southern rights. . . . If ever you dare to vindicate abolition again you will be lynched . . . drawing you from your seat in the House by force. So be on your guard."[30]

Thousands of northerners, however, wrote to support him, calling him the "Sage of Quincy" and urging him to "fear not southern insolence. . . . We will defend and sustain you."[31]

The death threats terrified Louisa, and she, Charles Francis, and Charles Francis's wife, Abby, pleaded with John Quincy to retreat from his war with what he called the "slaveocracy." They could do nothing to dissuade him. At sixty-nine, he was on fire, breathing the flames of freedom his father had lit and that he believed he had to maintain. As they approached their fortieth wedding anniversary, it was Louisa, not John Quincy, who turned to poetry and prayer for solace:

> Grant, grant! O God a helping hand
> And save us when we call;
> Protect us 'gainst the murderer's hand;
> Support us lest we fall.[32]

"I walk on the edge of a precipice in every step I take," John Quincy admitted, but defying age, aching joints, and the deterioration of his body, he found renewed strength in battle. He had never been to war and had always personified the perfect diplomat, but he now seemed fearless, felt fearless—like a knight charging into battle.

He pursued his daily routine of walking vigorously—defiantly—to and from his house and the Capitol—and swimming the Potomac nude. Occasionally, he misjudged his physical strength and agility and tripped and fell, suffering cuts and bruises and even dislocating his shoulder once—but he never missed a session of Congress. He believed the future of the nation was at stake, and he returned day after day to fight his war against the "slaveocracy." And Quincy voters sent him back to Congress again and again. Louisa fretted about his health and safety, but she had lost all influence over him and could do nothing to restrain him. He was unstoppable—a meteor spiraling out of control in the political firmament. By 1836, Charles Francis and Abigail had given John Quincy and Louisa a second grandson, Charles Francis Jr., whose presence only added to his grandfather's determination to defeat injustice in the nation his grandchildren would inherit.

With each session, his opponents renewed the Gag Rule to try to silence his assault on slavery, but he sidestepped their obstructions and found another target: the admission of slave states into the Union. A fierce advocate of westward expansion when he was President—indeed, he had offered to buy Texas from Mexico—he now led the fight to block Texan appeals to join the Union. With a population of 30,000 American frontiersmen and 5,000 slaves, Texas had always stood apart from the rest of Mexico, and when the Mexican government abolished slavery in all Mexican territory including Texas, Texans declared independence and recruited an army that defeated Mexican forces. They then formed a government that restored slavery and applied for U.S. recognition as a first step toward joining the United States. With Mexico still claiming sovereignty over the territory, U.S. recognition of Texan independence would have meant war—not only with Mexico but with England and France, which had both outlawed slavery and the slave trade and pledged to stand by Mexico in enforcing the ban on slavery.

John Quincy shot out of his seat to oppose recognition of Texan independence, knowing it was a prelude to annexation and, therefore, an end to the slave-state/free-state balance worked out in the Missouri Compromise. Annexation of Texas, he knew, would give slave states a majority in both houses of Congress and end all hopes for emancipation in the United States.

In leading the fight against recognition of Texan independence, he also found a perfect weapon against the Gag Rule: "Mr. Chairman," he thundered. "Are you ready for all these wars? A Mexican war? A war with Britain, if not with France? A general Indian war? A servile war? And, as an inevitable consequence of them all, a civil war?" The South and South-west, he warned, would be "the battlefield upon which the last great conflict must be fought between slavery and emancipation."

> I avow it as my solemn belief that the annexation of an independent foreign power to this government would be *ipso facto* a dissolution of this Union. . . . The question is whether a foreign nation [Texas] . . . a nation damned to everlasting fame by the reinstitution of that detested system of slavery, after it had been abolished within its borders, should be admitted into union with a nation of freemen. For, Sir, that name, thank God, is still ours![33]

"Take your seat!" the Speaker ordered, trying to apply the Gag Rule, but John Quincy shouted back, "Am I gagged? Am I gagged?" He then appealed to the House membership, and it overruled the Speaker to ensure open debate on the Texas question—and once they opened the debate on Texas, they automatically reopened the debate on slavery. "The annexation of Texas," John Quincy thundered in response, "and the proposed war with Mexico are all one and the same thing."[34]

Humiliated by John Quincy's rhetorical tactics, southerners began to shout, "Expel him!" whenever he spoke. "Expel him!" they repeated, as he continued—sometimes prolonging his diatribes against slavery for hours and, in one instance, for parts of fifteen days.

John Quincy went beyond the halls of Congress to the American people and became a national presence, a force for justice and progress that he had never been before—even as President of the United States. Invited to speak throughout the Northeast and parts of the West, he used traditional July 4 orations, along with eulogies on the deaths of the Marquis de Lafayette and James Madison, to echo the words of George Washington and other Founding Fathers. Although silent on slavery, all had inveighed against involvement in foreign wars, and John Quincy now connected the two issues. John Quincy appealed to church leaders, calling slavery "a sin before the sight of God," and they, in turn, formed peace societies that inundated Congress and the White House with petitions signed by tens of thousands of Americans opposed to war with Mexico. State legislatures in Vermont, Michigan, Ohio, and Massachusetts passed resolutions supporting John Quincy's war against war—and against recognition of Texas. Southerners in Congress, however, proved too strong, and after both houses voted in favor of recognizing Texan independence, President Jackson agreed and appointed a chargé d'affaires. As John Quincy had predicted, a petition for U.S. annexation of Texas followed recognition, but, in the face of the growing antiwar movement, Jackson, nearing the end of his presidency, rejected it, refusing to risk certain war with Mexico.

By then, Andrew Jackson had decided to follow the precedent of earlier Presidents and cede his office after two terms, and the Democratic Party nominated Vice President Van Buren of New York as their candidate to succeed Jackson. Van Buren had used his presidency of the Senate to court antiabolition sentiment in Congress, and in December 1836, he scored an overwhelming victory over three other candidates, including Daniel Webster. John Quincy—by then towering over his House colleagues as champion of national interests—easily won reelection to the House without a party designation and without campaigning. Approaching seventy and feeling the effects of his age, he returned to Congress in 1837 determined to save his nation from destruction.

Having pledged to "tread . . . in the footsteps of President Jackson," President Van Buren confirmed Jackson's rejection of Texas's annexation, thus temporarily setting aside one of the major controversies facing the new Congress but ceding center stage to abolition again. The House immediately reinstituted the Gag Rule, and John Quincy struck back, presenting more than two hundred petitions remonstrating against the Gag Rule as a violation of the Constitution, of the rights of his constituents, "and of my right of freedom of speech as a member of this House." The House responded with what he described as "war whoops of 'Order!'"[35]

Day after day, the struggle continued. During the 1837–1838 session alone, the American Antislavery Society sent the House 130,200 petitions, with untold thousands of names, to abolish slavery in the District of Columbia; 32,000 petitions to abolish the Gag Rule; 21,200 to forbid slavery in U.S. territories; 22,160 against admitting any new slave states; and 23,160 to abolish the slave trade between states.[36] Whenever John Quincy tried to comment on a resolution, the Speaker interrupted: "The gentleman from Massachusetts," he shouted, "must answer aye or no and nothing else! Order!"

"I refuse to answer," John Quincy fired back, "because I consider all pro-ceedings of the House—"

Again, the Speaker interrupted him with shouts of "Order! Order!"

John Quincy slumped into his seat in response, but his voice persisted: "—a direct violation of the Constitution!"[37]

Around him came the cries, "Expel him! Expel him!" from southerners, whose numbers grew ever greater with the expansion of the slave popula-tion, which could not vote. Slaves had increased the number of southern members of the House by 35 percent—enough to expel John Quincy, and they now prepared to do just that.

CHAPTER 14

Freedom Is the Prize

Washington's oppressive summer heat forced Congress to recess before proceeding against John Quincy Adams in 1839, and he was able to return home to the cool breezes of Quincy Bay with Louisa and their two "angelic" granddaughters, the children of their son John II. What should have been a summer of joy, however, proved a season of heartbreak, when the older girl, nine-year-old Fanny, contracted diphtheria. Often shrieking from the pain gripping her throat, she spent weeks in agony before dying in the fall. Her death devastated John Quincy and left him pessimistic about his own future, as he faced expulsion from the House. "I fear I have done little good in the world," he moaned, "and my life will end in disappointment of the good I would have done had I been permitted."[1]

After burying Fanny, the Adamses returned to Washington and brought their surviving granddaughter and her mother to live in their house on F Street. Their presence brought new joy into Louisa's otherwise drab life and even sparked a smile or two on John Quincy's often dour face—especially when Mary Louisa turned to her "Grandpappa" for help in algebra and logarithms. He often encouraged her to copy poems—one of them a favorite of his by Scottish poet William Russell, whose "Ode to Fortitude"[2] asked, "Can noble things from base proceed?"

"Not so the lion springs," John Quincy often answered his grandchild, "not so the steed; Nor from the vulgar tenants of the grove, sublimed with pageant-fire, the strong-pounced bird of Jove."[3]

In addition to Mary Louisa, the Adamses had grandsons to fuss over. One of them, Charles Francis Adams II, would long remember his grandfather's continually herding the grandchildren through a canyon of books into his study, and his younger brother Henry Adams would remember his grandfather as "an old man of seventy-five or eighty who was always friendly and gentle, but . . . always called 'the President,'" while Louisa was "the Madam."

Author of the renowned autobiography *The Education of Henry Adams*, Henry Adams passed summers with his grandparents at Quincy until he was twelve years old and would remember throughout his life "the effect of the back of the President's head as he sat in his pew on Sundays."

> It was unusual for boys to sit behind a President grandfather and to read over his head the tablet in memory of a President great-grandfather who had pledged "his life, his fortune, and his sacred honor" to secure the independence of his country and so forth. . . . The Irish gardener once said, "You'll be thinkin' you'll be President too."[4]

When Congress reconvened in December 1839, elections had divided the House evenly, and disorder attended every effort to establish committee memberships. Deadlocked and facing legislative paralysis, Congress turned to the only man every member trusted, regardless of what they felt about his politics or him personally—and some genuinely hated him. But John Quincy Adams was the man who represented the whole nation, and above all else, they knew him to be that rarest of colleagues: an honest man and patriot. Astonished by the sudden—and almost universal— embrace, John Quincy accepted the invitation and served as Speaker pro tem long enough to work out committee memberships. When he suc-

John Quincy and Louisa Catherine Adams's grandson Henry Adams, seen here as a Harvard undergraduate, had warm memories of his grandparents that he related in his autobiography, The Education of Henry Adams. (NATIONAL PARKS SERVICE, ADAMS NATIONAL HISTORICAL PARK)

ceeded to everyone's satisfaction and stepped down from his leadership role, they immediately turned on him again, reimposed the Gag Rule, and overrode his angry demands to repeal it.

Just then, however, his friend Ellis Gray Loring, a prominent Massachusetts attorney and outspoken opponent of slavery, drew John Quincy's attention away from the turmoil in Congress with some startling legal documents. In January 1840, a federal district court in New Haven, Connecticut, was about to hear the case of thirty-six Africans who had been prisoners on the slave ship *Amistad* off the coast of Cuba. Led by a Congolese chief named Cinque, they had broken their chains, killed the captain and three crewmen, and overpowered the white crew. Knowing nothing of navigation, they ordered the white crew to sail them to Africa, and by day the crew complied. At night, however, the crewmen reversed course and eventually sailed

Killing of the captain of the Amistad *by a band of free Africans kidnapped by slavers and transported to Cuba to be sold as slaves. John Quincy Adams pleaded for their freedom before the U.S. Supreme Court.* (LIBRARY OF CONGRESS)

into American waters, where an American frigate seized the ship and took it to New London, Connecticut. Officials there arrested the Africans and charged them with piracy and murder, but a number of legal questions complicated the case: Were the Africans property—that is, slaves—to be returned to their owners? Or were they people, to be released on habeas corpus and later tried for piracy and murder? And finally, did the United States have jurisdiction? Or should U.S. authorities release the prisoners to Spanish authorities to do with as they wished under Spanish law?

The district court pronounced the Negroes to have been free men, whom slavers had kidnapped and transported to Cuba illegally—under Spanish as well as American law. It deemed the killings justified as legitimate acts of self-defense against the kidnappers and ordered the Africans turned over to the President of the United States for transport back to their native land at American government expense.

Having already alienated southerners by rejecting Texas annexation, President Van Buren was unwilling to provoke his southern constituency further and ordered the district attorney to appeal the lower court order to the circuit court. The circuit court upheld the district court and forced government prosecutors to take the case still higher to the U.S. Supreme Court. By then, however, abolitionists who had paid for the legal defense of the *Amistad* Africans ran out of funds, and all but two attorneys quit. Only Loring and Roger Sherman Baldwin, grandson of Revolutionary War hero Roger Sherman, agreed to remain on the case pro bono. They turned to John Quincy to join their appeal to the Supreme Court—also without a fee—and he agreed.

"Gracious heavens, my dear Sir," an outraged Virginian exclaimed in reaction to John Quincy's embrace of the Africans' defense. "Your mind is diseased on the subject of slavery. Pray what had you to do with the captured ship? . . . You are great in everything else, but here you show your weakness. Your name will descend to the latest posterity with this blot on it: Mr. Adams loves the Negroes too much, *unconstitutionally*."[5]

Before the case reached the Supreme Court, seventy-three-year-old John Quincy won reelection to the House by a two-to-one majority, while sixty-eight-year-old General William Henry Harrison, hero of the Indian wars, defeated President Martin Van Buren in the presidential election.

"The life I lead," John Quincy grumbled to his diary as he returned to Washington for double duty in Congress and before the Supreme Court, "is trying to my constitution and cannot be long continued."

> My eyes are threatening to fail me. My hands tremble like an aspen leaf. My memory daily deserts me. My imagination is fallen into the sear and yellow leaf and my judgment sinking into dotage. . . . Should my life and health be spared to perform this service . . . then will be a proper time for me to withdraw and take my last leave of the public service.[6]

Before the *Amistad* appeal began, John Quincy received a letter from one of his new African clients, a member of an obscure tribe, the Mendi. He had had no knowledge of English before languishing in Connecticut jails for two years:

"Dear Friend Mr. Adams," the letter began.

> I want to write a letter to you because you love Mendi people and you talk to the Great Court. We want you to ask the court what we have done wrong. What for Americans keep us in prison. Some people say Mendi people crazy dolts because we no talk American language. Americans no

Congolese chief Cinque masterminded the killing of the Amistad
*captain but knew too little about navigation to prevent the crew from
sailing into American waters, where the Africans on board were
captured and brought to trial as escaped slaves.* (LIBRARY OF CONGRESS)

talk Mendi. Americans crazy dolts? . . . Dear friend Mr. Adams you have
children and friends you love them you feel very sorry if Mendi people
come and take all to Africa. . . . All we want is make us free.[7]

On February 22, 1841, John Quincy walked from his house to the Supreme Court, which sat in the east wing of the Capitol beneath the Senate
floor. It was George Washington's birthday—the Founding Father whom
John Quincy most revered after his own father and who had launched John
Quincy's career in public service. Uncompromising southern slaveholders
made up the majority of the nine judges, and John Quincy knew them all.
In the minority were Joseph Story of Massachusetts, a former Harvard law
professor, and Chief Justice Roger B. Taney, a Maryland slaveholder who
would later free his slaves. After the prosecution demanded that the government return the *Amistad* Negroes to the Spanish minister for restoration to
their "owners," Roger Baldwin argued for the defense: "The American

people," he declared, "have never imposed it as a duty upon the government of the United States to become actors in an attempt to reduce to slavery men found in a state of freedom by giving extraterritorial force to a foreign slave law." The prosecuting attorney replied that slaves "released from slavery by acts of aggression" do not lose their status as the property of their rightful owners "any more than a slave becomes free in Pennsylvania who forcibly escapes from Virginia."[8]

The next day, February 24, John Quincy rose to address the court. "The courtroom was full, but not crowded," he noted, "and there were not many ladies. I had been deeply distressed and agitated till the moment when I rose, and then my spirit did not sink within me. With grateful heart for aid from above . . . I spoke four hours and a half, with sufficient method and order to witness little flagging of attention by the judges."[9]

"Justice," he began, "as defined in the Institutes of Justinian nearly 2,000 years ago . . . is the constant and perpetual will to secure every one his own right."

> I appear here on behalf of thirty-six individuals, the life and liberty of every one of whom depend on the decision of this court. . . . Thirty-two or three have been charged with the crime of murder. Three or four of them are female children, incapable, in the judgment of our laws, of the crime of murder or piracy or, perhaps, of any other crime. . . . Yet they have all been held as close prisoners now for the period of eighteen long months.[10]

John Quincy told the justices of his distress in prosecuting the government of his own nation before the nation's highest court and, indeed, "before the civilized world." But, he said, it was his duty. "I must do it."

> The government is still in power. . . . The lives and liberties of all my clients are in its hands. . . . The charge I make against the present executive administration is that in all their proceedings relating to these unfortunates, instead of that justice which they were bound not less than this

honorable court itself to observe, they have substituted sympathy!—sympathy with one of the parties in this conflict and antipathy to the other. Sympathy with the white; antipathy to the black—and in proof of this charge, I adduce the admission and avowal of the secretary of state himself.[11]

John Quincy went on to read the letter from Secretary of State John Forsyth of Georgia to the Spanish minister in America, citing the owners of the *Amistad* as "the only parties aggrieved"—that all the right was on their side and all the wrong on the side of their surviving, self-emancipated victims.

"I ask your honors, was this justice?"[12]

Far from any "flagging of attention," the judges sat transfixed for more than four hours—until other needs forced them to adjourn until the next day. That night, however, one of the justices died, and Chief Justice Taney postponed resumption of John Quincy's argument for a week.

The court reconvened on March 1, with John Quincy summarizing his previous argument, then standing for three more hours, reiterating the argument that the *Amistad* Negroes had been free men, seized against their will on their native soil, abducted onto a ship, where they defended themselves and, in doing so, killed their kidnappers. "What . . . would have been the tenure by which every human being in this Union, man, woman, and child, would have held the blessing of personal freedom? Would it not have been by the tenure of executive discretion, caprice, or tyranny . . . at the discretion of a foreign minister, would it not have disabled forever the effective power of *habeas corpus*?"

Then he came to the end of his presentation. Eschewing secular, legalistic appeals, "Old Man Eloquent" reached into his rhetorical reservoir for spiritual principles he believed he shared with every decent human being. In a moment that ensured his standing in the history of Congress and the Supreme Court, John Quincy Adams told the court that "more than thirty-seven years past, my name was entered and yet stands recorded on both the rolls as one of the attorneys and counselors of this court."

I appear again to plead the cause of justice, and now of liberty and life, in behalf of many of my fellow men. . . . I stand before the same court, but not before the same judges. . . . As I cast my eyes along those seats of honor and of public trust, now occupied by you, they seek in vain for one of those honored and honorable persons whose indulgence listened then to my voice.[13]

After a dramatic pause, John Quincy turned his eyes toward the heavens, calling out the hallowed names of the court's early justices—John Marshall, Bushrod Washington, and Thomas Todd of Virginia, William Cushing of Massachusetts and Samuel Chase of Maryland, William Johnson of South Carolina, and Henry Livingston of New York. "Where are they?" he cried out, turning to focus on the faces of each of the justices. "Where?" he paused before lowering his voice to a near whisper.

Gone! Gone! All Gone! Gone from the services which . . . they faithfully rendered to their country. . . . I humbly hope, and fondly trust, that they have gone to receive the rewards of blessedness on high. In taking leave of this bar and of this honorable court, I can only . . . petition heaven that every member of it may . . . after a long and illustrious career in this world, be received at the portals of the next with the approving sentence, "Well done, good and faithful servant; enter thou into the joy of the Lord."[14]

As tears flowed down spectators' faces, the prosecuting attorney shook his head in disbelief. He had no idea what John Quincy's closing had to do with the facts of the case, but members of the court understood that by recalling the names of the legendary justices who had helped establish the nation's federal judiciary and, indeed, the nation itself, John Quincy was asking them to abide by standards higher than man's law. Accordingly, the court voted unanimously to give its senior member, Joseph Story, the honor of reading their monumental decision on March 9:

"There does not seem to us to be any ground for doubt that these Negroes ought to be free."[15]

"Glorious!" Roger Sherman Baldwin congratulated John Quincy. "Glorious not only as a triumph of humanity and justice, but as a vindication of our national character from reproach and dishonor."[16]

John Quincy was equally elated and wrote to his last surviving son, describing his courtroom triumph as one of the most notable events in the family's illustrious history: "The signature and seal of Saer de Quincy to the old parchment [the Magna Carta]," John Quincy told his son, "were . . . almost my only support and encouragement, under the pressure of a burden upon my thought that I was to plead for more, much more than my own life."[17] John Quincy's plea for the freedom of the *Amistad* captives marked more than six centuries during which he and his forbears had led man's quest for freedom. "Well done, good and faithful servant," he said to himself.

A flood of anonymous hate mail awaited John Quincy when he returned home. "Is your pride of abolition oratory not yet glutted?" asked a Virginian. "Are you to spend the remainder of your days endeavoring to produce a civil and servile war? Do you . . . wish to ruin your country because you failed in your election to the Presidency? May the lightening of heaven blast you . . . and direct you . . . to the lowest regions of Hell!"[18]

While John Quincy continued his daily walks and public swims unmolested, abolitionists paid the price for sending the *Amistad* captives back to their homeland. After they left, a shipload of 135 slaves mutinied aboard the ship *Creole*, bound from Hampton Roads, Virginia, to New Orleans. After killing one of the owners, they directed the crew to sail to Nassau, where British authorities hanged those identified as murderers and freed the rest.

Although John Quincy had promised himself that if his life and health were spared to defend the men of the *Amistad,* he would "take my last leave of the public service," his Supreme Court triumph so elated him that he decided the time had not yet come to keep his promise. "Fifty years of incessant active intercourse with the world," he now said to himself,

has made political movement to me as much a necessary of life as atmospheric air. This is the weakness of my nature, which I have intellect enough left to perceive, but not energy to control. And thus, while a rem-

*President John Tyler of Virginia was a slaveholder
who defended slavery as a quintessential American
institution and supported efforts in the House to
censure and expel John Quincy Adams.* (LIBRARY OF
CONGRESS)

nant of physical power is left to me to write and speak, the world will
retire from me before I retire from the world.[19]

A few days later, on April 4, 1841, President William Henry Harrison
died of pneumonia after only a month in office. Vice President John Tyler,
a fervent defender of states' rights from Virginia and champion of slavery,
succeeded to the presidency. With Tyler's warm approval, slaveholders in
the House prepared to censure and expel John Quincy Adams.

Too elated by his Supreme Court triumph to notice the puerile antics
of his congressional enemies, John Quincy pursued his interests in the sciences, using his chairmanship of the committee on the Smithson bequest to

promote establishment of astronomical observatories—his famous "light-houses of the sky." He not only ignored the ridicule of political foes but gave his alma mater, Harvard, $1,000 to help build its own observatory and loaned $13,000 of his own money to Columbian College, the institution "for the general diffusion of knowledge" that George Washington had helped found with a bequest in his will. It would grow to become George Washington University.

His constant glorification of the benefits of astronomical observatories to expand man's knowledge encouraged the Navy Department, the University of North Carolina, Williams College, Western Reserve College, Miami College (Ohio), and the United States Military Academy to build observatories. Even Philadelphia's high schools built one—the Philadelphia High School Observatory, which opened a John Quincy Adams "Light-house of the Sky" to the citizens of the city. Ridiculing those who had scoffed at John Quincy's advocacy of such observatories, enlightened communities across the nation turned his vision into reality.

John Quincy's broad interest in science included insatiable curiosity about every new invention. As a boy, he had witnessed the first balloon flights in Paris and public demonstrations of Franz Mesmer's then new technique, mesmerism, later known as hypnotism. In 1839, another French inventor, Louis-Jacques-Mandé Daguerre, a scene painter for the Paris opera, developed a process that used sunlight to make permanent pictures on metal plates. By 1842, John Plumbe Jr., a civil engineer, had opened the Daguerrian Gallery in Boston, which John Quincy visited in September 1842, becoming the first American President ever to be photographed live. Unfortunately, the Plumbe photos of John Quincy were lost, with much of that pioneering photographer's works, but the following year, engraver Philip Haas opened another daguerreotype studio, and John Quincy Adams asked him to take another photograph. By then, sixteen portrait artists, five sculptors, and one medalist had captured John Quincy's likeness. Haas produced the first surviving photograph.[20]

The *Amistad* case touched John Quincy in ways different from any previous experience, pushing him firmly into the abolitionist camp. Although

*Daguerreotype of John Quincy Adams is the
first surviving live photograph of an American
President. Taken by Philip Haas, a pioneer in
the process.*

they had failed to organize a full-fledged political party, northern abolitionists had nonetheless formed a powerful Select Committee on Slavery
and rejoiced when John Quincy accepted their long-standing invitation to
join. He did so on condition that they accept his leadership in matters
concerning the House of Representatives, and the first thing he made
them do was change their name to the Committee of Friends of the Right
of Petition. The change cloaked their divisive abolitionist goal in the man-
tle of constitutional rights and broadened their appeal to defenders of the
Bill of Rights by calls to defend the rights of all Americans to petition and
to free speech.

When Congress convened in January 1842, John Quincy hoped his
Supreme Court victory had covered him—and the Constitution—with

enough laurels to convince the House to repeal the Gag Rule. As he had at the beginning of every session since its imposition six years earlier, he opened the January 1842 session of Congress by assailing the Gag Rule as a clear violation of his own constitutional right to free speech and the right of his constituents to petition government for redress of grievances. To these, he added the questionable constitutional right of uninterrupted free debate in Congress.

In renewing the Gag Rule, each session of Congress had extended its scope, so that instead of simply banning the mention of the word "slavery," the rule now stated, "No petition, memorial, resolution or other paper, praying for the abolition of slavery in the District of Columbia, or any other state or territory, or the slave trade between the states and territories of the United States where it exists shall be received by this House, or entertained in any way whatsoever." The increased strictures offended many congressmen unopposed to slavery in the South but concerned only with its spread into other states and territories. The new Gag Rule seemed too restrictive. Far from the overwhelming majority that had instituted the rule in 1836, it passed by only four votes in 1841, and John Quincy sensed victory near as he honed his rhetorical weapons for 1842. He picked what he knew "would set them in a blaze"—a petition from "the citizens of Haverhill, in the Commonwealth of Massachusetts . . . that you will immediately adopt measures peaceably to dissolve the Union of these States."[21]

As he knew it would, the parliamentary lynch mob from the South gathered about him, with cries of "Order!" "Stop him!" He raised his voice and continued above the din.

"Old Nestor," said an eyewitness at the scene, "lifted up his voice like a trumpet, till slaveholding, slave trading, and slave breeding absolutely quailed and howled. . . . The old man breasted the storm and dealt blows upon the head of the monster. Scores . . . of slaveholders [strove] constantly to stop him by . . . screaming at the top of their voices, 'That is false!' . . . 'I demand that you shut the mouth of that old harlequin.'"[22]

Kentucky congressman Thomas Marshall, a nephew of the deceased chief justice John Marshall, moved to censure John Quincy for having "committed high treason when he submitted a petition for the dissolution of the Union."

"Sir," John Quincy shot back, "what is high treason? The Constitution of the United States says what high treason is. . . . It is not for the gentleman from Kentucky, or his puny mind, to define what high treason is and confound it with what I have done." John Quincy then ordered the clerk to read the first paragraph of the Declaration of Independence. When the clerk hesitated, John Quincy repeated his demand, shouting, "The first paragraph!"

"When in the course of human events it becomes necessary for one people to dissolve the political bands which have connected them with another and to assume among the powers of the earth, the separate and equal station to which the Laws of Nature and of Nature's God entitle them, a decent respect to the opinions of mankind requires that they should declare the causes which impel them to the separation—"

"Proceed!" John Quincy thundered. "Proceed! Down to 'right' and 'duty'!"

The clerk continued: "It is their right, it is their duty, to throw off such government."

"Now, Sir, if there is a principle sacred on earth and established by the instrument just read, it is the right of the people to alter, to change, to destroy, the government if it becomes oppressive to them. There would be no such right existing if the people had not the power in pursuance of it to petition for it. . . .

"I rest that petition on the Declaration of Independence!" John Quincy boomed.

When the House had quieted down, he then challenged its right to charge him with high treason, a crime for which, he said, "I could only be tried by a regular circuit court, by an impartial jury."[23]

Virginia's Henry Wise stood to contradict John Quincy but made the tactical mistake of talking too much and digressing into a defense of "the principle of slavery" as "a leveling principle . . . friendly to equality. Break down slavery and you would with the same blow destroy the great democratic principle of equality among men." Wise had built a reputation as a staunch defender of slavery, which he said was "interwoven in our political existence . . . guaranteed by our Constitution . . . resulting from our system of government."[24]

After catcalls from northern congressman subsided, Wise got back on track, pretending to mourn John Quincy's having "outlived his fame. . . . To think of the veneration, the honor, the reverence with which he might have been loved and cherished. . . . I thank God that the gentleman, great as he was, neither has nor is likely to have sufficient influence to excite a spirit of disunion throughout the land. . . . The gentleman is politically dead."[25]

Far from politically dead, John Quincy found new life across the nation, as tens of thousands in the North and parts of the West rallied to his side. "When they talk about his old age and venerableness and nearness to the grave," Ralph Waldo Emerson responded, "he is like one of those old cardinals who, as quick as he is chosen Pope, throws away his crutches and his crookedness and is as straight as a boy. He is an old roué, who cannot live on slops, but must have sulphuric acid in his tea."[26]

When the time came for John Quincy's final defense against the attempt to quiet him, he challenged the southern parliamentary lynch mob, daring them to punish him for having presented the Haverhill petition. "If they say that they will punish me, they must punish me. If they say that in grace and mercy they will spare my expulsion, I disdain and cast their mercy away. . . . I defy them. I have constituents to go to who will have something to say if this House expels me. Nor will it be long before gentlemen will see me here again."[27]

John Quincy then turned and pointed to Virginia's Henry Wise, whom the House had blandly readmitted after his participation in a duel that was tantamount to murder. Crack shots and swordsmen from the South had used dueling as a weapon to silence political opponents who lacked shooting skills and feared uttering even the slightest criticism that a southerner might interpret as an insult and thus grounds for a challenge. John Quincy's son had faced just such a challenge, and Wise had been a second in such a duel between two other congressmen. When both had survived the first round and would normally have left the field with their honor—and bodies—intact, Wise insisted that they keep firing, until the third round left one duelist dead. John Quincy Adams was so outraged at the spectacle that he sponsored a landmark bill—the Prentiss-Adams Law—to ban dueling in the District of Columbia. In proposing the ban, John Quincy called dueling a form of slavery that allowed trained killers to blackmail the less skilled marksman or swordsman into suicidal combat or face a loss of honor.

"That far more guilty man," John Quincy pointed at Wise, "came into this House with his hands and face dripping . . . reeking with the blood of murder." Turning, he then pointed at Kentucky's Thomas Marshall, urging him to "go to some law school and learn a little of the rights of the citizens of these states and the members of this House."[28] John Quincy's public scolding sent Marshall scurrying back to Kentucky humiliated, with his intellectual tail between his legs, never again to return to national politics.

With John Quincy luring more House members to his side, one southerner offered to withdraw the petition of censure if John Quincy would withdraw the Haverhill petition for disunion.

"No! No! I cannot do that," John Quincy replied in the deepest tones he could find to add to the drama of the moment. "That proposition comes to the point and issue of this whole question . . . the total suppression of the right of petition to the whole people of this Union. . . . If I withdraw this petition, I would consider myself as having sacrificed . . . every element of liberty that was enjoyed by my fellow citizens. . . . Never more would the House see a petition presented from the people of the Union expressing their grievances in a manner that might not be pleasing to the members. . . . *There* is the deadly character of the attempt to put me down."[29]

The debate continued for two weeks, with John Quincy's eloquence stirring the nation to petition Congress. Day after day, he held the floor, as petitions flew through the door protesting congressional attempts to censure him. On February 7, he tried holding back a smile as he announced he would need another week to complete his defense, to which a member of the Virginia delegation moved to table the censure motion and end the matter. When the House agreed, John Quincy responded by presenting two hundred more petitions and addressing the House with one of the most momentous speeches he would ever deliver. Indeed, his words would later serve as the constitutional basis for Abraham Lincoln's Emancipation Proclamation.

"Under this state of things," he spoke, staring at the southerners, "so far from its being true that the states where slavery exists have the exclusive management of the subject, not only the President of the United States but the commander of the army has power to order the universal emancipation of the slaves."[30]

Years later, Henry Wise would characterize John Quincy as the "acutest, astutest, archest enemy of southern slavery that ever existed . . . and his prophecies have been fulfilled . . . far faster and more fearfully . . . than ever he anticipated."[31]

John Quincy's triumph in the House provoked the usual hate mail, but the number of his supporters swelled across the nation, with one Pennsylvanian writing, "You are honored, old man—the hearts of a hundred thousand Pennsylvanians are with you." Another called him "the only public man in the land who possesses the union of courage with virtue." Poet John Greenleaf Whittier prayed, "God bless thee, and preserve thee."[32] Even those who had opposed the aggressive tactics of abolitionists now wrote, "I am no abolitionist, yet I am in favor of the emancipation of the colored race."[33]

His popularity exceeded that of the President, and had he defended his beliefs as aggressively when he was President, he would certainly never have suffered the humiliation of defeat in his run for reelection. Few Americans knew or understood him as President; almost every American now knew and understood him—indeed, revered him—after his battle in Congress, and millions now listened to every word of the Sage of Quincy. Hundreds lined up to see him, to hear his words, to try to talk to him as he walked about Washington, striding to and from the Capitol each day. Luminaries from all parts of the United States, Britain, and Europe called at his home. Charles Dickens and his wife stopped for lunch, and Dickens asked for

John Quincy's autograph before leaving. John Quincy had emerged as one of the most celebrated and beloved personages in the Western world.

In 1843, his son Charles Francis, by then a member of the Massachusetts state legislature, introduced a resolution calling for a constitutional amendment abolishing the right of slave states to count five slaves as equal to three white men in determining representation in the House of Representatives. With deep pride, John Quincy in turn introduced his son's amendment in the House—which ignored it. After he won reelection in 1844, however, the House could not ignore his resolution abolishing the Gag Rule. Indeed, it passed it immediately, 105–80, ending the great battle he had fought for freedom of debate in Congress, freedom of speech generally, and the right of citizens to petition their government. It was the first victory the North would win against the South and the slaveocracy.

"Blessed, ever blessed be the name of God," John Quincy exulted afterwards.[34]

Riding his wave of popularity, he set off to promote national interest in science and education by accepting an invitation to speak at ceremonies laying the cornerstone of the Cincinnati Astronomical Society's observatory. It was an arduous trip for an old man, but one with opportunities to promote science education—especially his "lighthouses of the sky"—across a broad territory.

He had no sooner received his invitation to speak in Cincinnati when another invitation arrived—this one to attend the long-anticipated completion of the Bunker's Hill Monument, commemorating the battle he had witnessed as a seven-year-old with his mother in 1775. When, however, he learned that President John Tyler "and his cabinet of slave-drivers" would also attend, he refused. "How," he asked, "could I have witnessed this without an unbecoming burst of indignation or of laughter? John Tyler is a slave-monger."

> With the association of the thundering cannon, which I heard, and the smoke of burning Charlestown, which I saw on that awful day, combined with this pyramid of Quincy granite and John Tyler's nose, with a shadow

Celebration at the completion of the Bunker's Hill Monument in Charlestown in June 1843. Invited to be the principal orator, John Quincy Adams refused to attend because of the presence of President John Tyler, a Virginia slaveholder and fierce opponent of abolition. (LIBRARY OF CONGRESS)

outstretching that of the monumental column, I stayed at home and visited my seedling trees and heard the cannonades, rather than watch the President at dinner in Faneuil Hall swill like swine and grunt about the rights of man.[35]

Shortly after the Bunker's Hill ceremonies, John Quincy left for Cincinnati, fulfilling his every lust to experience the latest scientific advances in transportation—steam-driven trains to Albany, New York, and across New York State to Buffalo, then steamboats across Lake Erie to Cleveland and down the Ohio Canal to Columbus. At every stop, cheering crowds welcomed him as a hero. The "firing of cannon, ringing of bells . . . and many thousand citizens" greeted him in Schenectady, New York; thousands more—and the governor—waited in Albany. A torchlight parade led his way through Utica, New York, climaxing with a photographer taking a daguerreotype of him with General Tom Thumb. "Multitudes of citizens" cheered in Cleveland, and in Columbus, he confessed, he had never witnessed "so much humanity." In Dayton, two military companies awaited to escort him, along with "an elegant open barouche in which I took a seat and thus in triumphal procession we entered the city," where "a vast multitude" awaited. He reached Cincinnati on November 8 and, to his enormous satisfaction, learned that the city had named the hill on which its new observatory would stand Mount Adams.

His last major stop was in Pittsburgh, which gave him a "magnificent reception" before he helped lay the cornerstone for still another astronomical observatory "to promote the cause of science." He returned to Washington in November, after traveling across Pennsylvania, with brass bands, public officials, and huge crowds cheering his visit in every community. Speaking at every stop, however, took its toll, and he contracted a debilitating cold, complete with sore throat, cough, and other symptoms.

"My strength is prostrated beyond anything that I ever experienced before," he moaned. It was, after all, his first "campaign." He had refused to campaign in 1824 and 1828 when he ran for the presidency, and now that he was not even contemplating that office, he finally learned what campaigning was like—and he rather enjoyed it.

After President Tyler declined to run for a second term, former Speaker James K. Polk of Tennessee won the Democratic nomination for President in 1844 and the presidency itself, defeating the perennially ambitious Henry Clay. As loser, Clay nonetheless shared one distinction with his winning opponent: news of the presidential election results had, for the first time in history, traveled over the wires of a new invention, the telegraph.

During his last month in office, President Tyler asked Congress again to approve annexation of Texas, and although John Quincy had blocked two earlier attempts, the House finally approved it in February 1846. As John Quincy had predicted, war with Mexico followed Polk's assumption of power. Only ten members of the House joined John Quincy in voting against the war.

In November 1846, John Quincy suffered a stroke while visiting his son Charles Francis in Boston. Rendered speechless and confused, his right side paralyzed, he seemed close to death; his doctors gave Louisa little hope for her husband's recovery. As she kept vigil in his room each day, however, he gradually recovered his speech, then his mind and memory, and by early December, he laughed off his illness, snapping at his friends that he had suffered only vertigo. But when he tried to stand and walk, he fell; he could no longer support himself.

By Christmas, however, he was talking about returning to Congress, and on New Year's Day, he set out for a ride in his carriage. A month later, on Sunday, February 7, sheer willpower held him upright as he walked from his son's house to both morning and afternoon church services to take communion. Despite protests from his wife and son, he and they, and a nurse, left for Washington the next day, reaching the Adamses' F Street home in February 1847, in time to celebrate Louisa's seventy-second birthday. The following morning he walked slowly, but magisterially, onto the floor of the House, and as he took his seat, the members rose as one—North, South, East, and West—to cheer him. Among those celebrating his return was a tall, lanky, unkempt freshman congressman from Springfield, Illinois—Abraham Lincoln. During his short tenure in the House, Lincoln would prove one of John Quincy's strongest supporters—not just in the cause of abolition but regarding Adams's proposals for federal initiatives in highway and canal construction and other forms of national expansion. Echoing the words of James Monroe and John Quincy Adams, Lincoln asserted that "Congress has a constitutional authority . . . to apply the power to regulate commerce . . . to make improvements."[36]

After Congress recessed in 1847, John Quincy insisted on returning to Quincy for the summer. Friends and relatives staged a gala eightieth birthday party for him on July 11, and two weeks later, they feted John Quincy

*Congressman Abraham Lincoln won election to the
House of Representatives in 1847 and served during John
Quincy Adams's last days in Congress. He is seen here in
a daguerreotype probably taken in Springfield, Illinois,
in 1847.* (LIBRARY OF CONGRESS)

and Louisa's golden wedding anniversary. John Quincy overwhelmed Louisa by giving her a beautiful bracelet that his son Charles Francis had purchased for him.

On November 1, Louisa and Charles Francis took John Quincy back to Washington, but the trip exhausted him—left him palsied, his entire body shaking. Too weak to speak audibly or to write, he walked unsteadily; he was nearly blind. He nonetheless insisted on taking his seat at the opening of the House on December 6, and Louisa conceded, "The House is his only remedy."[37]

Although he gave up all but one of his committee obligations and rode instead of walking to the House, he appeared for every roll call every day thereafter. He cast one of only four votes in favor of a resolution to withdraw U.S. troops from Mexico. Even Lincoln voted against it. And his face, if not his body, came to life when he heard a resolution supporting a Spanish government demand that the United States pay the *Amistad*'s owners $50,000 for the loss of their ship and its "cargo," which the Spanish minister characterized as a band of assassins. Although he lacked the spring that once shot him to his feet, he nonetheless accomplished the same result and assailed the Spanish minister for having wanted the *Amistad* captives "tried and executed for liberating themselves."

"There is not even the shadow of a pretense for the Spanish demand," John Quincy growled after the laughter subsided. "The demand, if successful, would be a perfect robbery committed on the people of the United States. Neither these slave dealers, nor the Spanish government on their behalf, has any claim to this money whatever."[38] The House agreed and rejected the proposal. He then presented two petitions for peace with Mexico, and the House rejected them both.

By mid-December, he had grown too weak to continue writing in the diary he had kept for sixty-eight years, and, indeed, he had to refuse a treasured invitation to speak at the laying of the cornerstone of the Washington Monument on December 10.

On New Year's Day, he wrote to his only surviving son, Charles Francis, and, with an unsteady hand, wished him "a stout heart and a clear conscience, and never despair."[39] On February 21, 1848, President Polk sent the Senate a treaty of peace with Mexico for ratification. In the House, supporters of the war proposed sending the thanks of Congress to the American generals for their victory. When the echoes from the roar of "ayes" had faded, a single, shrill voice startled the Congress. In a last, desperate effort to punish those engaged in what he called that "most unrighteous war,"[40] John Quincy Adams sounded a firm, unmistakable "No!" It was his last word to the Congress he cherished.

When the clerk read the next resolution and called his name—his was third on the alphabetical roll—he tried to stand, his right hand gripping

The death of John Quincy Adams in the Capitol he loved, with, presumably, his former secretary of state Henry Clay holding his right hand. (FROM A NATHANIEL CURRIER LITHOGRAPH, LIBRARY OF CONGRESS)

his desk as he rose. Then he slumped to his left—fortunately, into the arms of a fellow congressman who had been watching him.

"Mr. Adams is dying," cried a congressman nearby. "Mr. Adams is dying." The words passed from member to member. Other members found a couch that they brought onto the House floor and helped their stricken colleague stretch out. Someone thought to ask for a formal adjournment. Both the Senate and Supreme Court followed suit when they learned of John Quincy's collapse. A group of congressmen carried the sofa and its occupant into the rotunda to give John Quincy more air, but they eventually moved it into the Speaker's office, where they barred every one but physicians, family, and close friends. John Quincy revived enough to thank those around him and to ask for Henry Clay, who arrived weeping. He clasped his old President's hand, unable to say a word before he finally left, inconsolable.

"This is the end of earth, but I am composed," John Quincy whispered, then lapsed into a coma. Louisa arrived with a friend and looked down at her husband, but his eyes showed no sign of consciousness. Eighty-year-old John Quincy lay in a coma for the next two days, and at 7:20 p.m., on February 23, 1848, he died in the Capitol he adored.

The next day, House members appointed a committee with one member from each state to escort John Quincy home to Massachusetts for burial. In the Senate, one of his bitter political foes, Thomas Hart Benton, stood to proclaim, "Whenever his presence could give aid and countenance to what was useful and honorable to man, there he was. . . . Where could death have found him but at the post of duty?"[41]

The nation mourned as it had not since the deaths of George Washington and Benjamin Franklin. John Quincy lay in state in a committee room in Congress for two days after his death; thousands filed by silently, often not knowing why exactly, but somehow realizing they had lost a champion of their rights—a representative of no single constituency, state, or region but of all Americans and of the whole nation. He was an aristocrat of an earlier generation, raised in an age of deference, who spoke a rich language that ordinary people could seldom fathom, but in the end, they sensed that he spoke for their greater good and to protect their rights and freedoms.

A single cannon blast awakened Washington on Saturday morning, February 25; another boom shook the city a minute later and every minute until noon. Again, the multitude reappeared, filling the streets like a great river flowing to the Capitol. At 11:50, the bell on Capitol Hill began to toll, and the President of the United States led the justices of the Supreme Court, high-ranking members of the military, the diplomatic corps, and members of the Senate into the House chamber. John Quincy lay in a silver-framed coffin on an elevated platform in front of the rostrum, his eloquence still resounding in the silent chamber:

My cause is the cause of my country and of human liberty . . . the fulfillment of prophesies that the day shall come when slavery and war shall be banished from the face of the earth.[42]

With the President seated at the Speaker's right, the vice president at his left, and the portraits of Washington and Lafayette looking down on them all, the chaplain of the House prayed and set off what Charles Francis Adams called "as great a pageant as was ever conducted in the United States." Choirs sang to the gods, and orators lifted their voices to men, repeating the appeal for John Quincy's precious "Union." When the assembly had intoned its final hymn, pallbearers carried the former President out of the Capitol to a silent multitude that stretched to the edge of the city. The great casket emerged from the Capitol, surrounded by an official committee of escort and followed by Charles Francis Adams and his wife, then John Quincy's closest friends from the legislature. In the procession that followed, the Speaker of the House led members of that body, the Senate, then President Polk, justices of the Supreme Court, the diplomatic corps, and an interminable line of military officials, state officials, college students, firemen, and members of craftsmen's organizations and literary societies. . . . It was endless—a collective outpouring of love and veneration the nation had rarely seen.

John Quincy lay in rest at the Congressional Cemetery for a week before the congressional committee of escort—a member from each state—came to take him aboard a train to Boston. Thousands lined the tracks northward to bow their heads as the train passed slowly, one car draped in black bearing John Quincy's coffin. The train stopped at various stations and crossings to allow citizens to climb aboard and say their good-byes as they filed past him. Churches sang his praises; newspapers expounded his glory and cited and published his oratory and poetry. Thousands awaited his arrival in Boston, filling the streets and all but blocking passage for his coffin to Faneuil Hall for a massive funeral ceremony before members of the state legislature and other prominent citizens. With the end of the eulogy and last prayer, the congressional committee delivered the body of their colleague, John Quincy Adams, to Mayor Josiah Quincy, John Quincy's cousin and former president of Harvard, for transport to the family vault in Quincy. A lifetime of friends and neighbors had gathered with his relatives and family to place John Quincy beside his father. As they laid John Quincy to rest, a small troop fired rifles in a last salute from nearby Penn's Hill, where John Quincy and his mother, Abigail, had watched the Battle of Bunker's Hill and the beginning of the Revolution that spawned a new nation.

> *Day of my father's birth, I hail thee yet.*
> *What though his body moulders in the grave,*
> *Yet shall not Death th' immortal soul enslave;*
> *The sun is not extinct—his orb has set.*
> *And Where on earth's wide ball shall man be met,*
> *While time shall run, but from thy spirit brave*
> *Shall learn to grasp the boom his Maker gave,*
> *And spurn the terror of a tyrant's threat?*
> *Who but shall learn that freedom is the prize*
> *Man still is bound to rescue or maintain;*
> *That nature's God commands the slave to rise,*
> *And on the oppressor's head to break his chain.*
> *Roll, years of promise, rapidly roll round,*
> *Till not a slave shall on this earth be found.*
>
> —JOHN QUINCY ADAMS,
> THE WHITE HOUSE, 1827.[43]

* * *

A little more than twelve years after John Quincy died—on December 24, 1860—South Carolina's legislature proclaimed without dissent that "the union now subsisting between South Carolina and the other States, under the name of the 'United States of America,' is hereby dissolved." Early in 1861, ten other states followed suit, and in April 1861, the civil war that John Quincy Adams had predicted was under way, eventually costing the lives of more than 275,000 Americans.

* * *

Louisa Adams died four years after John Quincy, on May 15, 1852, in Washington, DC.

She and her husband now lie together next to John and Abigail Adams in a granite crypt in the church in Quincy, Massachusetts, where Charles Francis had them all transferred after escorting his mother's body from the capital. Although no subsequent members of the Adams family ever followed John or John Quincy Adams to the presidency, no American family ever surpassed the Adamses in accession to national prominence in so many fields. Beginning with his son Charles Francis Adams, who served as American ambassador to Britain and twice ran unsuccessfully for vice president, John Quincy Adams spawned an august line of American scholars, teachers, historians, authors, legislators, jurists, diplomats, lawyers, doctors, business leaders, and other professionals who upheld—and uphold—the principle of their distinguished ancestor:

> You must have one great purpose of existence . . . to make your talents and your knowledge most beneficial to your country and most useful to mankind.
> —JOHN QUINCY ADAMS, "TO MY CHILDREN."[44]

Notes

Explanatory note: John Quincy Adams kept his diary from November 1779 to December 1847, accumulating a total of 14,000 pages. The early diaries, from November 1779 to December 1788, were published in book form as *Diary of John Quincy Adams* (Cambridge, MA: Belknap Press of Harvard University Press, 1981). The rest of the diary—fifty-one volumes in all—is only available digitally, over the Internet, by logging on to "The Diaries of John Quincy Adams: A Digital Collection," on the website of the Massachusetts Historical Society (www.masshist .org/jqadiaries). In this book, notes referring to extracts from the first two published volumes of the diary will show the appropriate volume and page numbers. When extracted from the Internet, the notes will simply show the appropriate date and the initials MHS (Massachusetts Historical Society).

Abbreviations:

AA   Abigail Adams
AP   Adams Papers
AFC   *Adams Family Correspondence*
JA   John Adams
JM   James Monroe
JQA   John Quincy Adams
LCA   Louisa Catherine Adams
MHS   Massachusetts Historical Society

EPIGRAPH

1. Charles Francis Adams, ed., *Memoirs of John Quincy Adams, Comprising Portions of His Diary from 1795 to 1848*, 12 vols. (Philadelphia: J. B. Lippincott, 1874), 7:164 (hereafter *Memoirs*). Mistakenly published in his *Memoirs* as written on October 30, 1826. In his old age, JQA had slipped the undated poem at random between pages of his diary bearing the 1826 date, and his son, Charles Francis, in compiling his father's *Memoirs* for publication, assumed that was the date on which his father had written it.

CHAPTER 1

1. L. H. Butterfield, ed., *The Adams Papers: Diary and Autobiography of John Adams*, 4 vols. (Cambridge, MA: Harvard University Press, 1961), 4:6–7.

2. Ibid.

3. Ibid., 12.

4. Ibid.

5. *Memoirs*, 1:4.

6. Increase Mather, in Samuel Eliot Morison, *Three Centuries of Harvard, 1636–1936* (Cambridge, MA: Belknap Press of Harvard University Press, 1936), 35.

7. Phyllis Lee Levin, *Abigail Adams: A Biography* (New York: Thomas Dunne Books, 2001), 5.

8. Ibid.

9. Boston Sons of Liberty to John Wilkes, November 4, 1769, in *Papers of John Adams*, ed. Robert J. Taylor, 10 vols. (Cambridge, MA: Belknap Press of Harvard University Press, 1983), 1:233.

10. Ibid.

11. William M. Fowler Jr., *The Baron of Beacon Hill: A Biography of John Hancock* (Boston: Houghton Mifflin, 1980), 181.

12. *Memoirs*, 1:5.

13. Abigail Adams to Mary Cranch, October 6, 1766, in John Ferling, *John Adams: A Life* (New York: Henry Holt, 1992), 53.

14. Worthington Chauncey Ford, ed., *Journals of the Continental Congress*, 34 vols. (Washington, DC: U.S. Government Printing Office, 1904–1936), 2:77–78.

15. AA to JA, May 24, 1775, in *Adams Family Correspondence*, ed. L. H. Butterfield et al., 10 vols. (Cambridge, MA: Belknap Press of Harvard University Press, 1963–2007), 1:204–206 (hereafter AFC).

16. JA to AA, May 29, 1775, and June 2, 1775, in ibid., 206–209.

17. Charles Francis Adams, ed., *The Works of John Adams, Second President of the United States*, 10 vols. (Boston: Little, Brown, 1856), 2:416–417 (hereafter Adams, *Works*).

18. John Hancock to Joseph Warren, June 18, 1775, in Herbert S. Allan, *John Hancock: Patriot in Purple* (New York: Beechhurst Press, 1953), 196.

19. Abigail Adams, *My Dearest Friend: Letters of Abigail and John Adams*, ed. Margaret A. Hogan and C. James Taylor (Cambridge, MA: Belknap Press of Harvard University Press, 2007), 65–68.

20. Ibid.

21. AA to JA, June 18, 1775, in AFC, 1:222.

22. Ibid.

23. *Memoirs*, 1:6.

24. AA to JA, June 25, 1775, in AFC, 1: 230–233.

25. *Memoirs*, 1:5.

26. AA to JA, June 22, 1775, in AFC, 1:225–226.

27. Ibid.

28. JA to AA, August 29, 1774, in AA, *My Dearest Friend*, 39–41.

29. JA to AA, June 23, 1777, in ibid., 183–184.

30. *Memoirs*, 1:7.

31. JA to AA, June 23, 1777, in AA, *My Dearest Friend*, 183–184.

32. John Quincy Adams, *Diaries of John Quincy Adams*, September 24, 1829, MHS (hereafter JQA *Diaries*).

33. JA to AA, May 22, 1776, in AFC, 1:412–413.

34. AA to JA, July 21, 1776, in AA, *My Dearest Friend*, 132–133.

35. JA to AA, December 3, 1775, in AA, *My Dearest Friend*, 91–92.

36. AA to JA, May 7, 1776, in AFC, 1:375, 387; 2:13–16.

37. JA to AA, in AFC, 2:50–51.

38. JA to AA, December 3, 1775, in AA, *My Dearest Friend*, 91–92.

39. JQA to JA, June 2, 1777, in *Memoirs*, 1:7–8.

40. Butterfield, *Diary and Autobiography*, 4:1.

41. James Lovell to JA, November 28, 1777, in Adams, *Works*, 5:337–338.

42. AA to John Lovell, December 15, 1777[?], in AFC, 2:370–371.

43. AA to Lovell, December 15, 1777, in AFC, 2:370–371.

44. AA to JQA, June [10?] 1778, in AFC, 3: 37–39.

45. Page Smith, *John Adams*, 2 vols. (Garden City, NY: Doubleday, 1962), 1:352.

46. Ibid., 12.

47. Ibid.

CHAPTER 2

1. Butterfield, *Diary and Autobiography*, 2:272.

2. Ibid., 276–277.

3. Ibid.

4. Ibid., 277.

5. Ibid.

6. Ibid., 276.

7. Ibid., 272.

8. Ibid., 272–273.

9. Ibid., 273.

10. Ibid., 284.

11. Ibid., 293–294.

12. Ibid., 295–296.

13. Ibid., 296.

14. Ibid., 307.

15. JQA to AA, September 27, 1778, in *Memoirs*, 1:8–9.

16. Butterfield, *Diary and Autobiography*, 2:305.

17. Ibid., 367.

18. Jonathan Sewell to [?], 1787, in Adams, *Works*, 1:56n–58n.

19. Butterfield, *Diary and Autobiography*, 2:314.

20. Ibid., 385.

21. John Adams, *The Revolutionary Writings of John Adams* (Indianapolis, IN: Liberty Fund, 2000), Part 10, "The Report of a Constitution or Form of Government for the Commonwealth of Massachusetts," 298.

22. AA to JA, November 14, 1779, in AA, *My Dearest Friend*, 229.

23. JA to AA, November 13, 1779, in ibid.

24. AFC, 3:233.

25. *Diaries*, MHS, November 12, 1779.

26. *Diary*, 1:25.

27. Butterfield, *Diary and Autobiography*, 2:226.

28. AA to JQA, September 29, 1778, in AFC, 3:97–98.

29. Butterfield, *Diary and Autobiography*, 4:243.

30. JA to JQA, December 20, 1780, in AFC, 38–39.

31. AA to JQA, January 21, 1781, in AFC, 3: 67–68.

32. AA to JQA, May 26, 1781, in ibid., 136–137.

33. *Tragedy of Cato*, by Joseph Addison, 3:v.

34. *Diary*, 1:89.

CHAPTER 3

1. Ibid., 92, 96.

2. Ibid., 99.

3. JQA to John Thaxter, September 8–19, 1781, in AFC, 4:214; JQA to JA, August 21, 1781, in AFC, 4:206–207.

4. *Diary*, 1:105–106.

5. JA to JQA, December 15, 1781, in AFC, 4:264.

6. JA to JQA, February 5, 1782, in ibid., 282–283.

7. JA to JQA, May 13, 1782, in ibid., 322–323.

8. JQA to JA, February 21–March 4, 1782, in ibid., 286–287.

9. JQA to Alexander H. Everett, August 19, 1811, Everett-Peabody Papers, MHS.

10. AA to JA, November 11, 1783, in AA, *My Dearest Friend*, 294–297.

11. February 10–11, 1783, in JQA *Diaries*, 1:170.

12. JA to AA, November 20, 1783, in AA, *My Dearest Friend*, 299–301; July 26, 1783, in AFC, 5:218.

13. AA to JQA, November 20, 1783, in AFC, 5:272–275.

14. *Diary*, 1:176ff.

15. August 16, 22, 23, 27, 1783, in JQA *Diaries*, 1:184–188.

16. September 20, 1783, in ibid., 1:192.

17. AA to JA, July 23, 1784, in ibid., 397–399.

18. JA to AA, July 26, 1784, in ibid., 399–400.

19. AA to Mary Smith Cranch, July 6–July 30, 1784, in ibid., 382.

20. Ibid.

21. AA to JA, July 30, 1784, in ibid., 408–409.

22. JA to Thomas Jefferson, January 22, 1825, in Adams, *Works*, 10:414.

23. *Diary*, 1:242.

24. Ibid., 236–256.

25. Ibid., 224.

26. AA to Lucy Cranch, September 5, 1784, in AFC, 5:436–439.

27. *Diary*, 1:256–257.

28. Morison, *Three Centuries of Harvard*, 136. A legendary Harvard professor of history, Morison was graduated from Harvard in 1908 and won two Pulitzer Prizes for biographies of Christopher Columbus and John Paul Jones. Among many other works, he wrote the monumental fifteen-volume *History of the United States Naval Operations in World War II, The Oxford History of the American People*, and *The Intellectual Life of Colonial New England.*

29. JA to Benjamin Waterhouse, December 13, 1784, in Worthington Chauncey Ford, ed., *Statesman and Friend: The Correspondence of John Adams with Benjamin Waterhouse, 1784–1822* (Boston: Little, Brown, 1927), 6.

30. *Diary*, 1:266.

31. Thomas Jefferson to John Adams, May 25, 1785, AP MHS.

32. *Diary*, 1:289.

33. Ibid., 290.

34. Ibid., 296.

35. Ibid., 299.

36. JQA to "Nabby," in AFC, 6:251–256.

37. *Diary*, 1:312.

38. Mary Smith Cranch to AA, August 14, 1785, in AFC, 6:268–275.

39. *Diary*, 1:317.

CHAPTER 4

1. Ibid., 406.

2. Ibid., 334.

3. Ibid., 383.

4. Ibid., 378.

5. Ibid., 335, 339.

6. Ibid., 390.

7. Ibid., 410.

8. Ibid., 2:28–29.

9. JA to JQA, May 26, 1786, in AFC, 7:205–206.

10. *Diary*, 2:2.

11. AA to JQA, July 21, 1786, in AFC, 7:274–277.

12. Paul C. Nagel, *John Quincy Adams: A Public Life, a Private Life* (Cambridge, MA: Harvard University Press, 1997), 53.

13. JQA to AA, December 30, 1786, in AFC, 7:417–420.

14. *Diary*, 2:337–338.

15. Ibid., 361.

16. April 8, 1788, in *Diaries*, MHS.

17. Ibid., 2:343.

18. March 29, April 6, and April 11, 1789, in *Diaries*, MHS.

19. JQA to AA, November 20, 1790, in AFC, 9:146–149.

20. JQA to AA, December 14, 1790, in ibid., 161–162.

21. JA to JQA, December 13, 1790, in ibid., 160.

22. *Letters of Publicola* in *The Selected Writings of John and John Quincy Adams,* ed. Adrienne Koch and William Peden (New York: Alfred A. Knopf, 1946), 227.

23. Dumas Malone, *Jefferson and the Rights of Man* (Boston: Little, Brown, 1951), 214.

24. George A. Peek Jr., ed., *The Political Writings of John Adams* (New York: Liberal Arts Press, American Heritage Series, 1954), 194.

25. Ron Chernow, *Alexander Hamilton* (New York: Penguin Press, 2004), 459.

26. *Memoirs*, 1:25.

27. JQA to JA, February 10, 1793, in AFC.

28. AA to JA, February 22, 1793, in AA, *My Dearest Friend,* 341–342.

29. Douglas Southall Freeman, *George Washington: A Biography,* completed by John Alexander Carroll and Mary Wells Ashworth, 7 vols. (New York: Charles Scribner's Sons, 1957), 7:36.

30. Meade Minnigerode, *Jefferson, Friend of France 1793: The Career of Edmond Charles Genet* (New York: G. P. Putnam's Sons, 1928), 207.

31. Alexander DeConde, *Entangling Alliance* (Durham, NC: Duke University Press, 1958), 181; Dumas Malone, *Jefferson and the Ordeal of Liberty* (Boston: Little, Brown, 1962), 97.

32. JQA to JA, February 10, 1793, in *Writings,* 1:79–86.

33. George Washington to Thomas Jefferson, April 12, 1793, in *The Papers of George Washington, Presidential Series, September, 1788–May 1793,* ed. W. W. Abbott, Dorothy Twohig, Philander D, Chase, and Theodore J. Crackel, 12 vols. (Charlottesville: University Press of Virginia, 1987–2005, 16 vols. [in progress]), 12:448–449.

34. *Columbian Centinel,* April 24, 1793.

35. Harlow Giles Unger, *Noah Webster: The Life and Times of an American Patriot* (New York: John Wiley & Sons, 1998), 71, 183.

36. John Adams to Thomas Jefferson, June 30, 1813, in *The Adams-Jefferson Letters: The Complete Correspondence Between Thomas Jefferson and Abigail and John Adams,* ed. Lester J. Cappon (Chapel Hill: University of North Carolina Press, 1959), 346–347.

37. Minnigerode, *Jefferson,* 184.

38. Archives des Affaires Étrangères, Ministère des Affaires Étrangères, Quai d'Orsay, Paris, France, vol. 38, Dossier "Correspondence Consulaire: Genet."

39. Koch and Peden, *Selected Writings,* 238.

40. *Memoirs,* 1:28.

41. Minnigerode, *Jefferson,* 362.

42. JA to JQA, April 23, 1794, in AFC, 10:150–152.

43. JA to JQA, May 26, 1794, in ibid., 192–193.

44. JA to JQA, May 29 and 30, 1794, in ibid., 197–200.

45. JA to JQA, May 30, 1794, in ibid., 199.

46. AA to Martha Washington, June 20, 1794, in ibid., 206.

47. Michel Poniatowski, *Talleyrand aux États-Unis, 1794–1796* (Paris: Presses de la Cité, 1967), 375.

48. AA to JQA, July 20, 1794, in AFC, 10:215.

49. JA to JQA, August 24, 1794, in ibid., 227–228.

50. JA to John Quincy Adams and Thomas Boylston Adams, September 14, 1794, in ibid., 230.

CHAPTER 5

1. *La grande encyclopédie* (Paris: Librairie Larousse, 1973), 3895.

2. Felix Maurice Hippiel, *Napoleon* (New York: New American Library of World Literature, 1963), 27.

3. *Memoirs,* 1:80.

4. Thomas Boylston Adams to AA, October 20, 1794, in AFC, 10:237–239.

5. JA to JQA, December 2, 1794, in AFC, 10:284–285; AA to JQA, November 26, 1794, in AFC, 10:274–275.

6. AA to JQA, November 26, 1794, in AFC, 10: 274–275.

7. *Memoirs*, 1:42–43.

8. Ibid.

9. Ibid., 48–49.

10. Ibid., 1:61.

11. Ibid., 76–77.

12. JQA to Sylvanus Bourne, December 24, 1795, in *Writings*, 1:478.

13. JA to JQA, April 26, 1795, in AFC, 10:422–424.

14. JQA to AA, May 16, 1795, in ibid., 434–438.

15. JQA to JA, October 31, 1795, reel 380, AP MHS.

16. December 1, 1795, reel 380, in *Diaries*, AP MHS.

17. Ibid.

18. JA to AA, January 5, 1796, in AA, *My Dearest Friend*, 398.

19. AA to JA, February 20, 1796, in ibid., 404. A dissipated clergyman most of his life, Charles Churchill (1731–1764) had been a schoolmate of Cowper and acquired notoriety and fame as a poet and satirist during the last four years of his life. He was a strong supporter and ally of London's John Wilkes, the radical activist who supported America's War of Independence. Besides "Gotham" (1764), his most famous poems were "The Rosciad" (1761), "The Ghost" (1762–1763), "The Duelist" (1764), "The Candidate" (1764), and "The Times" (1764).

20. *Memoirs*, 1:162.

21. December 26, 1795, in *Diaries*, MHS.

22. Cited as AA to JQA, May 20, 1796, in Samuel Flagg Bemis, *John Quincy Adams and the Foundations of American Foreign Policy* (New York: Alfred A. Knopf, 1950), 80, 80n.

23. JA to AA, March 9, 1796, in AA, *My Dearest Friend*, 408–410.

24. JQA to AA, February 8, 1797, reel 383, AP MHS.

25. AA to JQA, November 29, 1796, reel 382, AP MHS.

26. JA to JQA, May 19, 1797, reel 384, AP MHS.

27. May 27, 1795, in *Diaries*, MHS.

28. June 30, 1796, in ibid.

29. July 31, 1796, reel 382, in ibid.

30. *Memoirs*, 2:51.

31. JA to JQA, November 11, 1796, reel 382, AP MHS.

32. Malone, *Jefferson and the Ordeal of Liberty*, 288.

33. Harlow Giles Unger, *The French War Against America* (Hoboken, NJ: John Wiley & Sons, 2005), 189.

34. Ibid., citing *American Minerva*, April, 11, 1794, 190.

35. JQA to AA, November 14, 1796, in *Writings*, 1:284.

36. George Washington to the vice president, February 20, 1797, in *The Writings of George Washington, from the Original Manuscript Sources, 1745–1799*, ed. John C. Fitzpatrick, 39 vols. (Washington, DC: U.S. Government Printing Office, 1931–44), 35:394.

37. JA to JQA, March 31, 1797, reel 385, AP MHS.

38. JQA and LCA to JA and AA, July 28, 1797, reel 385, AP MHS.

CHAPTER 6

1. LCA autobiographical sketch: "The Adventures of a Nobody," begun July 1, 1840, reel 269, MHS.

2. Boston's *Independent Chronicle*, May 29, June 1, July 4, and September 18, 1797.

3. *Philadelphia Aurora*, June 8, 1797.

4. AA to B. F. Bache, March 17, 1798, Bache Papers, American Philosophical Society, Philadelphia, cited in James Tagg, *Benjamin Franklin Bache and the "Philadelphia Aurora"* (Philadelphia: University of Pennsylvania Press, 1999), 124–125; JQA to Charles Adams, August 1, 1797, in *Writings*, 2:196–197.

5. *Memoirs*, 1:203.

6. Ibid., 216.

7. JQA to JA, December 6, 1797, in ibid., 219–220.

8. LCA, "Adventures," 63.

9. Ibid., 74–75.

10. Alexander DeConde, *The Quasi-War: The Politics and Diplomacy of the Undeclared War with France, 1797–1801* (New York: Charles Scribner's Sons, 1966), 23.

11. Notes of conversation as drafted by French emissary, "Monsieur Bellamy," in Michel Poniatowski, *Talleyrand et le directoire, 1796–1800* (Paris: Librairie Académique Perrin, 1982), 554–555; Albert J. Beveridge, *The Life of John Marshall*, 4 vols. (Boston: Houghton Mifflin, 1916–1919), 2:267.

12. Poniatowski, *Talleyrand et le directoire*, 559.

13. DeConde, *Quasi-War*, 53.

14. Ibid., 145.

15. JQA to Timothy Pickering, January 15, 1798, in *Writings*, 2:236–240.

16. JQA to Timothy Pickering, June 18, 1798, in ibid., 2:303–309.

17. JQA to Timothy Pickering, June 25, 1798, in ibid., 2:321–322.

18. JQA to William Vans Murray, July 7, 1798, in ibid., 2:332–335.

19. JQA to William Vans Murray, July 17, 1798, in ibid., 2:339–342.

20. AA to Mercy Warren, April 25, 1798, in *Warren-Adams Letters, Being Chiefly a Correspondence among John Adams, Samuel Adams, and James Warren, 1743–1814*, ed. Worthington C. Ford, 2 vols. (Boston: Little, Brown, 1917–1925), 2:336.

21. JA to Congress, June 21, 1798, Adams, *Works*, 9:158–159.

22. JQA to George Washington, October 29, 1798, in *Writings*, 2:377–378.

23. JQA to JA, September 25, 1798, in ibid., 367–369.

24. Talleyrand to JA, September 28, 1798, in Adams, *Works*, 8:690–691.

25. December 31, 1800, in *Diaries*, MHS.

26. Boston's *Independent Chronicle*, Merrill Jensen, John P. Kaminski, Gaspare Saladino, Richard Leffler, and Charles H. Schoenleber, eds., *The Documentary History of the Ratification of the Constitution*, 22 vols. to date (Madison: State Historical Society of Wisconsin, 1976–[in progress]), 13:154–155.

27. JQA to JA, November 25, 1800, reel 399, AP MHS.

28. Dumas Malone, *Jefferson the President: First Term, 1801–1805* (Boston: Little, Brown, 1970), 20.

29. April 12, 1801, in *Diaries*, MHS.

30. May 4, 1801, in ibid.

31. May 5, 1791, in ibid.

32. AA to JQA, September 23, 1801, reel 401, AP MHS.

33. *Memoirs*, 1:261.

34. April 1802, in *Writings*, 2:7.

35. January 28, 1802, in *Memoirs*, 1:249.

CHAPTER 7

1. Anne Hollingsworth Wharton, *Social Life in the Early Republic* (Williamstown, MA: Corner House Publishers, 1970), 161.

2. W. P. Cresson, *James Monroe* (Chapel Hill: University of North Carolina Press, 1946), 201.

3. Ibid., 202, citing Henry Adams, *History of the United States of America During the Administrations of Jefferson and Madison, 1801–1817,* 9 vols. (New York: Charles Scribner's Sons, 1889–1891), 2:351.

4. Ibid., citing Helen Nicolay, *Our Capital on the Potomac* (New York: Century Company, 1924), 70.

5. October 21, 1803, in *Diaries*, MHS.

6. October 31, 1803, in *Memoirs*, 1:269.

7. John Dickinson to the Committee of the Whole, June 7, 1787, in James Madison, *Notes of Debates in the Federal Convention of 1787* (New York: W. W. Norton, 1987), 82 (first published in volumes 2 and 3 of *The Papers of James Madison* [Washington: Langtree O'Sullivan, 1840]).

8. Alexander DeConde, *The Affair of Louisiana* (New York: Charles Scribner's Sons, 1976), 178, citing Fabricus, in Boston's *Columbian Centinel,* July 13, 1803.

9. Ibid., 184, citing Livingston to Madison, June 25, 1803; *American State Papers: Foreign Relations* (Washington, DC: U.S. Government Printing Office, 1897–1933), 2:566.

10. JQA to AA, June 30, 1811, reel 411, AP MHS.

11. Stephen Higginson in *Letters of Stephen Higginson*, in *Annual Report of the American Historical Association*, ed. J. F. Jamieson (Washington, DC: U.S. Government Printing Office, 1896), 1:839–840; Worcester, Massachusetts, *Aegis*, December 4, 1803.

12. *Philadelphia Aurora*, December 1, 1803.

13. December 3, 1803, in *Diaries*, MHS.

14. JQA to Ezekiel Bacon, November 17, 1808, in *Writings*, 3:250.

15. JA to Thomas Jefferson, May 3, 1812, in Cappon, *The Adams-Jefferson Letters,* 302–304.

16. January 27, 1804, in *Diaries*, MHS.

17. January 10, 1804, in ibid.

18. December 31, 1803, in ibid.

19. *Annals of Congress*, 9th Cong., 2d Sess., 1806–1807, 77.

20. November 1, 1803, in *Memoirs*, 1:270.

21. John F. Kennedy, *Profiles in Courage* (New York: HarperCollins, 1955), 41.

22. AA to JQA, December 18, 1804, reel 403, AP MHS.

23. March 24, 1806, reel 404, AP MHS.

24. December 3, 1803, reel 402, AP MHS.

25. LCA to JQA, April 17, 1804, reel 403, AP MHS.

26. *The Complete Poems of John Donne* (Digireads.com Publishing, 2002), 73.

27. Richard B. Morris, *Encyclopedia of American History* (New York: Harper & Brothers, 1953), 133.

28. *American Citizen*, January 6, 1804.

29. November 5, 1804, in *Diaries*, MHS.

30. November 16, 1804, in ibid.

31. Malone, *Jefferson the President: First Term*, 466.

32. March 1, 1805, in *Diaries*, MHS.

33. March 3, 1805, in ibid.

34. March 4, 1805, in ibid.

35. JQA to LCA, July [?], 1806, reel 404, AP MHS.

36. JQA to LCA, December 8, 1806, reel 404, AP MHS.

37. *Memoirs*, 1:454.

38. JQA to LCA, February 14, 1807, reel 237, AP MHS.

39. LCA to JQA, February 17, 1807, reel 405, AP MHS.

40. Kennedy, *Profiles*, 44.

41. Ibid.

42. February 1, 1808, in *Memoirs*, 1:510.

43. Sullivan to Jefferson, June 3, 1808, in Dumas Malone, *Jefferson the President: Second Term, 1805–1809* (Boston: Little, Brown, 1974), 594, citing Library of Congress, Jefferson Papers, 31525.

44. Autobiographical sketch to Skelton Jones, April 17, 1809, in Koch and Peden, *Selected Writings*, 261–267.

45. JA to JQA, January 8, 1808, in *Writings*, 3:189n.

CHAPTER 8

1. Adams, *Works*, 6:280.

2. July 5, 1809, in *Memoirs*, 1:549.

3. JQA to Charles W. Upham, February 2, 1837, cited in Bemis, *John Quincy Adams and the Foundations*, 152n63.

4. John Quincy Adams, *Lectures on Rhetoric and Oratory Delivered to the Senior and Junior Sophisters in Harvard University,* 2 vols. (Boston: Hillard and Metcalf, 1810).

5. Ibid.

6. JQA to Thomas Boylston Adams, August 7, 1809, reel 408, AP MHS.

7. AA to granddaughter Caroline Amelia Smith, August 5, 1809, in ibid.

8. August 5, 1809, in *Memoirs,* 2:3.

9. JQA "To My Children," September 18, 1809, reel 408, AP MHS.

10. Ibid.

11. JQA to the secretary of state, October 4, 1809, in *Writings,* 4:3.

12. Ibid.

13. Stuart Gerry Brown, ed., *The Autobiography of James Monroe* (Syracuse, NY: Syracuse University Press, 1959), 209.

14. Bemis, *John Quincy Adams and the Foundations,* 161.

15. Ibid.

16. Ibid., JQA to the secretary of state, November 6, 1809.

17. Louisa Adams, "Adventures," reel 269, AP MHS, 144–145.

18. JQA to AA, March 22, 1811, reel 411, AP MHS.

19. Louisa Adams, "Adventures," reel 269, AP MHS, 147.

20. *Memoirs,* 2:193.

21. Ibid.

22. Nagel, *John Quincy Adams,* 198.

CHAPTER 9

1. JQA to Thomas Boylston Adams, April 10, 1811, reel 411, AP MHS.

2. Louisa Adams, "Adventures," reel 269, AP MHS.

3. Ibid.

4. JQA to Thomas Boylston Adams, April 28, 1812, in Letters from John Quincy Adams to Thomas Boylston Adams, Special Collections, MHS.

5. JQA to George Washington Adams, September 8, 1811, reel 411, AP MHS.

6. JQA to Thomas Boylston Adams, April 28, 1812, in Letters from John Quincy Adams to Thomas Boylston Adams, Special Collections, MHS.

7. September 15, 1812, in *Diaries,* AP MHS.

8. September 17, 1812, in ibid.

9. JQA to Robert Fulton, November 27, 1812, reel 414, MHS.

10. JQA to AA, December 31, 1812, in ibid.

11. JQA to Thomas Boylston Adams, November 24, 1812, in ibid.

12. Dispatch from Oliver Hazard Perry aboard U.S. Brig *Niagara* to General William Henry Harrison, September 10, 1813, in *Bartlett's Familiar Quotations*, 398:1.

13. JQA to LCA, July 22, 1814, reel 418, and August 19, 1814, reel 419, AP MHS.

14. JQA to the British commissioner, September 9, 1814, reel 419, AP MHS.

15. JQA to LCA, September 27, 1814, in ibid.

16. JQA to LCA, November 25, 1814, in ibid.

17. JQA to AA, December 24, 1814, in ibid.

18. *Memoirs*, 3:126.

19. JQA to LCA, December 30, 1814, reel 420, AP MHS.

20. Robert V. Remini, *The Life of Andrew Jackson* (New York: Penguin Books, 1988), 1.

21. Ibid., 2.

22. JQA to LCA, December 16, 1814, reel 420, AP MHS.

CHAPTER 10

1. JQA to LCA, December 27, 1814, in ibid.

2. LCA, *Narrative of a Journey from Russia to France 1815*, 20–21, AP MHS.

3. Ibid., 6–7.

4. Ibid., 13.

5. Ibid., 31–32.

6. May 25, 1815, in *Diaries*, AP MHS.

7. *Memoirs*, 3:241.

8. Talleyrand to JA, September 28, 1798, in Adams, *Works*, 8:690–691.

9. *Memoirs*, 3:242–243.

10. JQA to JA, February 24, 1816, reel 429, AP MHS.

11. *Memoirs*, 3:286–288.

12. Ibid., 257.

13. JQA to JA, May 29, 1816, in *Writings*, 6:38.

14. *Memoirs*, 3:333.

15. Ibid.

16. JQA to AA, April 23, 1817, reel 430, AP MHS.

17. JA to JQA, August 27, 1815, reel 426, AP MHS.

18. October 16, 1816, in *Diaries*, MHS.

19. John Quincy Adams, "The Wants of Man," in *Poems of Religion and Society, with Notices of His Life and Character by John Davis and T. H. Benton* (New York: William H. Graham, 1848), 15.

20. March 13, 1817, reel 436, in *Diaries*, MHS.

21. JA to JQA, March [?], 1817, in ibid.

22. AA to JQA, March 12, 1817, in ibid.

23. Thomas McKean to John Adams, November 20, 1815, in Bemis, *John Quincy Adams and the Foundations*, 243.

24. JQA to AA, April 23, 1817, reel 436, AP MHS.

25. JA to JQA, August 10, 1817, in ibid.

26. AA to JQA, August 10, 1817, in ibid.

27. AA to Harriet Welsh, August 18, 1817, reel 438, AP MHS; see also Charles Francis Adams, *Charles Francis Adams* (Boston: Houghton Mifflin, 1900), 10.

28. Levin, *Abigail Adams*, 482.

29. *Memoirs*, 4:62–63.

30. Bemis, *John Quincy Adams and the Foundations*, 261, citing E. F. Ellet, *Court Circles of the Republic from Washington to Grant* (Hartford, CT: Hartford Publishing, 1869), 123.

31. JM to JQA, June 30, 1829, reel 491, AP MHS.

32. *Memoirs*, 4:8.

33. Ibid.

34. Ibid., 45–46.

35. Ibid., 64.

CHAPTER 11

1. Ibid., 1:170; Bemis, *John Quincy Adams and the Foundations*, 174.

2. *Memoirs*, 2:252.

3. JM to Andrew Jackson, December 28, 1817, in ibid., 118–119.

4. Remini, *Andrew Jackson*, 120.

5. Andrew Jackson to JM, June 18, 1818, in Remini, *Andrew Jackson*, 123–124.

6. Ibid.

7. *Memoirs*, 4:42.

8. Ibid., 157–158.

9. JQA to JA, November 2, 1818, reel 445, AP MHS.

10. Stanislaus Murray Hamilton, ed., *The Writings of James Monroe: Including a Collection of His Public and Private Papers and Correspondence Now for the First Time Printed*, 7 vols. (Washington, DC: Government Printing Branch, U.S. Department of State, 1898–1903; reprint edition, New York, AMS Press, 1969), 54–61.

11. Koch and Peden, *Selected Writings*, 300.

12. Ibid.

13. Ibid.

14. Ibid., 300–301.

15. Remini, *Andrew Jackson*, 127.

16. February 22, 1821, in *Diaries*, MHS.

17. Ibid.

18. Lord Castlereagh to Sir Charles Bagot, January 2, 1819, Public Records Office, British Foreign Office, London, 115/34, cited in Bemis, *John Quincy Adams and the Foundations*, 328n.

19. *Memoirs*, 4:502, 529.

20. March 3, 1820, in *Diaries*, MHS.

21. JM to Dr. Charles Everett, March 23, 1812, in Hamilton, *Writings of James Monroe*, 5:201–202.

22. Samuel Flagg Bemis, *John Quincy Adams and the Union* (New York: Alfred A. Knopf, 1956), 369–370.

23. *Memoirs*, 4:530.

24. Ibid., 531.

25. February 14, 1821, in *Diaries*, MHS.

26. January 8, 1821, in ibid.

27. James Monroe Message to Congress on South American Affairs, March 8, 1822, in Hamilton, *Writings of James Monroe*, 6:207–211.

28. March 9, 1821, in *Diaries*, MHS.

29. *Memoirs*, 6:190.

30. Ibid., 163.

31. JM to JQA in Noble E. Cunningham Jr., *The Presidency of James Monroe* (Lawrence: University Press of Kansas, 1996), 156.

32. Harry Ammon, *James Monroe: The Quest for National Identity* (Newtown, CT: American Political Biography Press, 1971), 481–482, citing Adams memo in Monroe Papers, New York Public Library; also see *Memoirs*, 6:185, and Bradford Perkins, *Castlereagh and Adams: England and the United States, 1812–1823* (Berkeley: University of California Press, 1964).

33. Seventh Annual Message, December 2, 1823, in Hamilton, *Writings of James Monroe*, 6:325–342.

34. December 4, 1823, in *Diaries*, MHS.

35. *Massachusetts Centinel*, July 19, 1817.

36. Samuel L. Gouverneur to Secretary of the Navy Samuel L. Southard, September 3, 1831, in Ammon, *James Monroe*, 543–544, citing Southard Papers, Princeton, New Jersey.

37. JM to James Madison, May 10, 1822, in ibid., 284–291.

38. Henry Adams, *The Education of Henry Adams: An Autobiography* (Boston: Houghton Mifflin Company, 1918), 32.

39. Joseph Hopkinson to LCA, January 1, 1823, reel 458, AP MHS.

40. LCA to JQA, June 28, 1822, AP MHS.

41. JQA to Joseph Hopkinson, January 23, 1823, reel 458, AP MHS.

42. December 12, 1822, reel 456, LCA diary, AP MHS.

43. February 21, 1823, reel 458, in ibid.

44. Ibid.

45. September 30, 1821, in *Diaries*, MHS.

46. *Memoirs*, January 1823, AP MHS.

CHAPTER 12

1. Daniel Coit Gilman, *James Monroe* (Boston: Houghton Mifflin, 1898), 221.

2. *Memoirs*, 8:546.

3. Wharton, *Social Life*, 212–217.

4. Ibid., 213–216, citing as author "Mr. Agg."

5. *Memoirs*, 6:415.

6. January 9, 1825, in *Diaries*, MHS.

7. Cokie Roberts, *Ladies of Liberty: The Women Who Shaped Our Nation* (New York: William Morrow, 2008), citing Sara Gales Seaton, February 24, 1825, 393.

8. JQA to JA, February 9, 1825, reel 467, AP MHS.

9. JA to JQA, February 18, 1825, in ibid.

10. Remini, *Andrew Jackson*, 153.

11. Andrew Jackson to John Overton, February 14, 1825, in ibid., 155.

12. Ibid., 153.

13. March, 4, 1825, in *Diaries*, MHS.

14. Inaugural address, March 4, 1825, in Koch and Peden, *Selected Writings*, 353–360.

15. Paul C. Nagel, *The Adams Women: Abigail and Louisa Adams, Their Sisters and Daughters* (New York: Oxford University Press, 1987), 216.

16. Harlow Giles Unger, *Lafayette* (Hoboken, NJ: John Wiley & Sons, 2002), 32.

17. June 13, 1825, in *Diaries*, MHS.

18. Ibid.

19. JQA First Annual Address, December 6, 1825, in Koch and Peden, *Selected Writings,* 360–367.

20. Ibid.

21. Nathaniel Macon to B. Yancey, December 8, 1825, in Edwin M. Wilson, *The Congressional Career of Nathaniel Macon* (Chapel Hill: University of North Carolina Press, 1900), 76.

22. Remini, *Andrew Jackson,* 160, citing Edward P. Gaines to Andrew Jackson, 1826, Jackson Papers, Library of Congress.

23. Ibid., citing Andrew Jackson to John Branch, March 3, 1828, Branch Family Papers, Southern Historical Collection, Chapel Hill, North Carolina.

24. LCA, autobiographical sketch, "Record of a Life, or My Story," begun July 23, 1825, reel 265, AP MHS.

25. Nagel, *Adams Women*, 215.

26. Wharton, *Social Life,* 210.

27. July 15, 1820, in *Diaries,* MHS.

28. July 13 and 14, 1826, in ibid.

29. May 13, 1827, in ibid.

30. Wharton, *Social Life,* 225.

31. Ibid., 233.

32. May 31, 1828, in *Diaries*, MHS.

33. July 4, 1828, in ibid.

34. Ibid.

35. Wharton, *Social Life,* 232–233.

36. February 28, 1829, in *Diaries,* MHS.

CHAPTER 13

1. June 11, 1829, in ibid.

2. September 24, 1829, in ibid.

3. Wharton, *Social Life,* 242–245.

4. November 7, 1830, in *Diaries,* MHS.

5. Morris, *Encyclopedia,* 130.

6. John Quincy Adams, "Life of James Monroe," a eulogy delivered in Boston, July 4, 1831, in Koch and Peden, *Selected Writings,* 373–379.

7. John Quincy Adams, *The Lives of James Madison and James Monroe, Fourth and Fifth Presidents of the United States* (Rochester, NY: Erastus Darrow; Buffalo: G. H. Derby, 1850), 288–289.

8. December 12, 1831, in *Diaries,* MHS.

9. Ibid.

10. February 2, 1832, in *Diaries,* MHS.

11. February 20, 1832, in ibid.

12. Andrew Jackson to Joel Poinsett, November 29, 1832, in Remini, *The Life of Andrew Jackson,* 235.

13. J. D. Richardson, *Compilation of Messages and Papers of the President,* 20 vols. (Washington, DC: U.S. Government Printing Office, 1908), 2:1203–1217.

14. June 18, 1833, in *Diaries,* MHS.

15. *Memoirs,* 9:18.

16. *Register of Debates,* 22, Pt. 2, 1583, February 2, 1833.

17. Ibid., 1609–1615, February 4, 1833.

18. Ibid., 1639–1651, February 7, 1833.

19. William J. Rhees, ed., *Smithsonian Miscellaneous Collections: Documents Relating to the Origins and History of the Smithsonian Institution* (Washington, DC: Smithsonian Institution, 1880), 1–2.

20. Report of Mr. John Q. Adams from the Select Committee of the House of Representatives on the *Smithsonian Bequest,* in the House of Representatives, December 21, 1835, and published in the *National Intelligencer,* February 17, 1836.

21. November 29, 1820, in *Diaries,* MHS.

22. *Register of Debates*, 12, Pt. 3, 3758–3778, May 18–19, 1836.

23. *Memoirs*, 10:199–200.

24. Ibid., 9:222.

25. March 18, 1835, in *Diaries*, MHS.

26. Bemis, *Union*, 369–370.

27. Ibid., 341.

28. *Register of Debates*, 13, Pt. 1, 1314–1339, January 8, 1837.

29. Ibid., Pt. 2, 1586–1735.

30. "Dirk Hatteraik" to JQA, February 10, 1837, AP MHS.

31. "Justice" to JQA, April 28, 1837, AP MHS.

32. Jack Shepherd, *The Adams Chronicles: Four Generations of Greatness* (Boston: Little, Brown, 1975), 332.

33. *Register of Debates*, 12, Pt. 4, 4046–4047.

34. *National Intelligencer*, December 16, 1837.

35. December 21, 1837, in *Diaries*, MHS.

36. Statistics obtained from Bemis, *Union*, 340.

37. December 14, 1838, in *Diaries*, MHS.

CHAPTER 14

1. JQA to Reverend Charles W. Upham, February 2, 1837, AP MHS.

2. William Russell (1741–1793) was best known as a historian, having written *The History of America, from the First Discovery by Columbus to the Conclusion of the Late War* (1779) and the five-volume *History of Modern Europe* (1786). He wrote "Ode to Fortitude" in 1769.

3. "Ode to Fortitude," *Lloyd's Evening Post*, March 17, 1769.

4. Henry Adams, *Education of Henry Adams*, 15–16.

5. "A Virginian" to JQA, December 31, 1839, AP MHS.

6. November 11, 1840, in *Diaries*, MHS.

7. "Ka-le" to JQA, January 4, 1841, AP MHS.

8. Bemis, *Union*, 407–408.

9. February 24, 1841, in *Diaries*, MHS.

10. "Argument of John Quincy Adams Before the Supreme Court of the United States . . . ," History Central, http://www.historycentral.com/amistad/amistad.html (originally published by S. W. Benedict, 1841).

11. Ibid.

12. Ibid.

13. *Memoirs*, 10:436–437.

14. Ibid.

15. Bemis, *Union*, 410.

16. Roger S. Baldwin to JQA, March 12, 1841, AP MHS.

17. JQA to Charles Francis Adams, April 14, 1841, in ibid.

18. Anonymous (from Dumfries, Virginia) to JQA, June 15, 1841, in ibid.

19. March 23, 1841, in *Memoirs*, 10: 450–451.

20. By 1845, Plumbe had opened a chain of twenty-five studios, and working out of his Washington studio in that same year, he became the first photographer to make a portrait of a sitting President, James K. Polk. His other subjects included Dolley Madison, Daniel Webster, Martin Van Buren, and John James Audubon. Although photographers took portrait shots of Andrew Jackson, Martin Van Buren, William Henry Harrison, John Tyler, and James K. Polk, all had photo-portraits; John Quincy Adams, although out of office, was the earliest American President ever to be photographed.

21. *Memoirs*, 11:71.

22. Bemis, *Union*, citing Theodore Weld to Angelina G. Weld and Sarah Grimké, January 23, 1842, *Weld-Grimké Letters*, January 23, 1842, 2, 899–1000, in Bemis, *Union*, 426.

23. *Memoirs*, 11:73–74.

24. *Register of Debates*, 11, Pt. 2, 1399.

25. Bemis, *Union*, 432.

26. Ibid., 56.

27. Bemis, *Union*, 434–435; *Congressional Globe*, 11:208.

28. *Congressional Globe*, 11:168–208.

29. *Congressional Globe*, 11:208.

30. Allan Nevins, ed., *The Diary of John Quincy Adams, 1794–1845* (New York: Charles Scribner's Sons, 1951), xxvii.

31. Barton H. Wise, *The Life of Henry Wise of Virginia, 1806–1876* (New York: Macmillan, 1899), 61–62, cited in Bemis, *Union*, 436–437.

32. Letters to JQA from Isaac Fisher (February 15, 1842), William Shinn (March 4, 1842), and John Greenleaf Whittier (January 31, 1842), AP MHS.

33. T. H. Brower to JQA, February 8, 1842, AP MHS.

34. *Memoirs*, 12:116.

35. Ibid., 11:383.

36. Abraham Lincoln Speech in the U.S. House of Representatives on Internal Improvements, June 20, 1848, in *Abraham Lincoln: Speeches and Writings, 1832–1858*, ed. Don E. Fehrenbacher (New York: Library of America, 1989), 187–198.

37. LCA to her niece Abigail Brooks Adams, December 9, 1847, reel 536, AP MHS.

38. *Congressional Globe,* 17:437–438.

39. *Memoirs,* 12:281.

40. Bemis, *Union,* 534.

41. *Token of a Nation's Sorrow: Addresses to the Congress of the United States and Funeral Solemnities on the Death of John Quincy Adams Who Died in the Capitol at Washington on Wednesday Evening, February 23, 1848* (Washington: J. and G. S. Gideon, 1848), in Bemis, *Union,* 538.

42. November 12, 1842, in *Diaries,* MHS.

43. *Memoirs,* 7:164, mistakenly published in his *Memoirs* as written on October 30, 1826. In his old age, JQA had slipped the undated poem at random between pages of his diary bearing the 1826 date, and his son, Charles Francis, in compiling his father's *Memoirs* for publication, assumed that was the date on which his father had written it.

44. JQA "To My Children," September 18, 1809, reel 408, AP MHS.

Bibliography and Research Resources

W. W. Abbott, Dorothy Twohig, Philander D. Chase, and Theodore Crackel, eds. *The Papers of George Washington, Presidential Series.* 16 vols. Charlottesville: University Press of Virginia, 1987–(in progress).

Abigail Adams. *My Dearest Friend: Letters of Abigail and John Adams*, edited by Margaret A. Hogan and C. James Taylor. Cambridge, MA: Belknap Press of Harvard University Press, 2007.

Charles Francis Adams. *Charles Francis Adams.* Boston: Houghton Mifflin, 1900.

———, ed. *Letters of John Adams Addressed to His Wife.* 2 vols. Boston: C. C. Little and J. Brown, 1841.

———, ed. *Memoirs of John Quincy Adams, Comprising Portions of His Diary from 1795 to 1848.* 12 vols. Philadelphia: J. B. Lippincott, 1874–1877.

———, ed. *The Works of John Adams, Second President of the United States.* 10 vols. Boston: Little, Brown, 1856.

Henry Adams. *The Education of Henry Adams: An Autobiography.* Boston: Houghton Mifflin, 1918.

———. *History of the United States of America during the Administrations of Jefferson and Madison, 1807–1817.* 9 vols. New York: Charles Scribner's Sons, 1889–1891.

John Adams. *The Political Writings of John Adams*, edited by George A. Peek Jr. New York: Liberal Arts Press, American Heritage Series, 1954.

———. *The Revolutionary Writings of John Adams.* Indianapolis, IN: Liberty Fund, 2000.

340 ▲ Bibliography and Research Resources

———. *Thoughts on Government*. Philadelphia: John Dunlop, 1776.

John Quincy Adams. *Diary of John Quincy Adams*. 2 vols. Cambridge, MA: Belknap Press of Harvard University Press, 1981.

———. *Lectures on Rhetoric and Oratory Delivered to the Senior and Junior Sophisters in Harvard University*. 2 vols. Boston: Hillard and Metcalf, 1810.

———. *The Lives of James Madison and James Monroe, Fourth and Fifth Presidents of the United States*. Rochester, NY: Erastus Darrow; Buffalo: G. H. Derby, 1850.

———. *Poems of Religion and Society, with Notices of His Life and Character by John Davis and T. H. Benton*. New York: William H. Graham, 1848.

———. *The Writings of John Quincy Adams*, edited by Worthington Chauncey Ford. 7 vols. New York: Macmillan, 1913–1917.

Herbert S. Allan. *John Hancock: Patriot in Purple*. New York: Beechhurst Press, 1953.

———. *American State Papers: Foreign Relations*. 38 vols. Washington, DC: U.S. Government Printing Office, 1832–1861.

Harry Ammon. *The Genet Mission*. New York: W. W. Norton, 1973.

———. *James Monroe: The Quest for National Identity*. Newtown, CT: American Political Biography Press, 1971.

Irving H. Bartlett. *John C. Calhoun: A Biography*. New York: W. W. Norton, 1993.

Spencer Bassett, ed. *Correspondence of Andrew Jackson*. 6 vols. Washington, DC: Carnegie Institution, 1926–1933.

Samuel Flagg Bemis. *John Quincy Adams and the Foundations of American Foreign Policy*. New York: Alfred A. Knopf, 1950.

———. *John Quincy Adams and the Union*. New York: Alfred A. Knopf, 1956.

Albert J. Beveridge. *The Life of John Marshall*. 4 vols. Boston: Houghton Mifflin, 1916–1919.

Julian P. Boyd et al., eds. *The Papers of Thomas Jefferson*. 34 vols. Princeton, NJ: Princeton University Press, 1950–(in progress).

Irving Brant. *James Madison: Commander in Chief, 1812–1836*. Indianapolis: Bobbs-Merrill, 1961.

Richard Brookhiser. *James Madison*. New York: Basic Books, 2011.

Stuart Gerry Brown, ed. *The Autobiography of James Monroe*. Syracuse, NY: Syracuse University Press, 1959.

Nina Burleigh. *The Stranger and the Statesman: James Smithson, John Quincy Adams, and the Making of America's Greatest Museum.* New York: Harper-Collins, 2003.

L. H. Butterfield, ed. *The Adams Papers: Diary and Autobiography of John Adams.* 4 vols. Cambridge, MA: Harvard University Press, 1961.

L. H. Butterfield, et al. *The Adams Papers: Adams Family Correspondence.* 10 vols. Cambridge, MA: Belknap Press of Harvard University Press, 1963–2010.

Lester J. Cappon, ed. *The Adams-Jefferson Letters: The Complete Correspondence between Thomas Jefferson and Abigail and John Adams.* Chapel Hill: University of North Carolina Press, 1959.

Ron Chernow. *Alexander Hamilton.* New York: Penguin Press, 2009.

Lawrence A. Cremin. *American Education: The Colonial Experience, 1607–1783.* New York: Harper & Row, 1970.

W. P. Cresson. *James Monroe.* Chapel Hill: University of North Carolina Press, 1946.

Marcus Cunliffe. *The Nation Takes Shape, 1789–1837.* Chicago: University of Chicago Press, 1959.

Noble E. Cunningham Jr. *Jefferson and Monroe: Constant Friendship and Respect.* Monticello, VA: Thomas Jefferson Foundation, 2003.

———. *The Presidency of James Monroe.* Lawrence: University Press of Kansas, 1996.

George Dangerfield. *Awakening of American Nationalism.* New York: Harper & Row, 1965.

———. *The Era of Good Feelings.* New York: Harcourt, Brace, 1952.

Alexander DeConde. *The Affair of Louisiana.* New York: Charles Scribner's Sons, 1976.

———. *Entangling Alliance.* Durham, NC: Duke University Press, 1958.

———. *The Quasi-War: The Politics and Diplomacy of the Undeclared War with France, 1797–1801.* New York: Charles Scribner's Sons, 1966.

David W. Dent. *The Legacy of the Monroe Doctrine: A Reference Guide to U.S. Involvement in Latin America and the Caribbean.* Westport, CT: Greenwood Press, 1999.

Maurice Denuzière. *Je te nomme Louisiane: Découverte, colonisation et vente de la Louisiane.* Paris: Editions Denoël, 1990.

Alice Morse Earle. *Child Life in Colonial Days*. Stockbridge, MA: Berkshire House Publishers, 1993.

E. F. Ellet. *Court Circles of the Republic from Washington to Grant*. Hartford, CT: Hartford Publishing, 1869.

Joseph J. Ellis. *First Family: Abigail and John Adams*. New York: Alfred A. Knopf, 2010.

John Ferling. *John Adams: A Life*. New York: Henry Holt, 1992.

John C. Fitzpatrick, ed. *The Writings of George Washington*. 39 vols. Washington, DC: U.S. Government Printing Office, 1931–1944.

Paul Leicester Ford. *The Writings of Thomas Jefferson*. 10 vols. New York: G. P. Putnam's Sons, 1892–1899.

Worthington Chauncey Ford, ed. *Journals of the Continental Congress*. 34 vols. Washington, DC: U.S. Government Printing Office, 1904–1936.

———, ed. *Statesman and Friend: The Correspondence of John Adams with Benjamin Waterhouse, 1784–1822*. Boston: Little, Brown, 1927.

———, ed. *Warren-Adams Letters, Being Chiefly a Correspondence among John Adams, Samuel Adams, Jr., and James Warren, 1743–1814*. 2 vols. Boston: Little, Brown, 1917–1925.

———, ed. *The Writings of John Quincy Adams*. 7 vols. New York: Macmillan, 1913–1917.

William M. Fowler Jr. *The Baron of Beacon Hill: A Biography of John Hancock*. Boston: Houghton Mifflin, 1980.

Douglas Southall Freeman. *George Washington: A Biography*, completed by John Alexander Carroll and Mary Wells Ashworth. 7 vols. New York: Charles Scribner's Sons, 1948–1957.

Richard Frothingham. *The Life and Times of Joseph Warren*. Boston: Little, Brown, 1865.

Edith Gelles. *Abigail and John Adams: Portrait of a Marriage*. New York: Harper-Collins, 2009.

———. *Abigail Adams: A Writing Life*. New York: Routledge, 2002.

Daniel Coit Gilman. *James Monroe*. Boston: Houghton Mifflin, 1898.

John Steele Gordon. *An Empire of Wealth: The Epic History of American Economic Power*. New York: HarperCollins, 2004.

Stanislaus Murray Hamilton, ed. *The Writings of James Monroe: Including a Collection of His Public and Private Papers and Correspondence Now for the First*

Time Printed. 7 vols. Washington, DC: Government Printing Branch, U.S. Department of State, 1898. Reprinted by AMS Press, 1969.

David S. Heidler and Jeanne T. Heidler. *Henry Clay: The Essential American.* New York: Random House, 2010.

Ann Heinrichs. *Louisa Catherine Johnson Adams.* New York: Children's Press, 1998.

Donald R. Hickey. *The War of 1812: A Forgotten Conflict.* Urbana: University of Illinois Press, 1989.

Don Higginbotham. *The War of American Independence: Military Attitudes, Policies, and Practice, 1763–1789.* New York: Macmillan, 1971.

Felix Maurice Hippiel. *Napoleon.* New York: New American Library of World Literature, 1963.

Woody Holton. *Abigail Adams.* New York: Free Press, 2009.

Stanley J. Idzerda, Anne C. Loveland, and Marc H. Miller. *Lafayette, Hero of Two Worlds: The Art and Pageantry of His Farewell Tour of America, 1824–1825.* Flushing, NY: Queens Museum, 1989.

Andrew Jackson. *Correspondence of Andrew Jackson,* edited by John S. Bassett. 6 vols. Washington, DC: Carnegie Institution, 1926–1933.

Bernard Jaffe. *Men of Science in America.* New York: Simon & Schuster, 1958.

John P. Kaminski. *The Founders on the Founders: Word Portraits from the American Revolutionary Era.* Charlottesville: University of Virginia Press, 2008.

———. *James Madison: Champion of Liberty and Justice.* Madison, WI: Parallel Press, 2006.

———, ed. *The Quotable Jefferson.* Princeton, NJ: Princeton University Press, 2006.

———. *Thomas Jefferson: Philosopher and Politician.* Madison, WI: Parallel Press, 2005.

John Kaminski, Gaspare Saladino, Richard Leffler, and Charles H. Schoenleber, eds. *The Documentary History of the Ratification of the Constitution.* 22 vols. Madison: State Historical Society of Wisconsin, 1976–(in progress).

John F. Kennedy. *Profiles in Courage.* New York: HarperCollins, 1955.

Ralph Ketcham. *James Madison: A Biography.* Charlottesville: University of Virginia Press, 1990.

Margaret Brown Klapthor. *The First Ladies.* Washington, DC: White House Historical Association, 1985.

Bernhard Knollenberg. *Growth of the American Revolution, 1766–1775*. New York: Free Press, 1975.

Adrienne Koch and William Peden, eds. *The Selected Writings of John and John Quincy Adams*. New York: Alfred A. Knopf, 1946.

Auguste Lavasseur. *Lafayette in America in 1824 and 1825: Journal of a Voyage to the United States*. Manchester, NH: Lafayette Press, 2006. Originally published in 1829 and translated from the French by Alan R. Hoffman.

Phyllis Lee Levin. *Abigail Adams: A Biography*. New York: Thomas Dunne Books, 2001.

James Madison. *Notes of Debates in the Federal Convention of 1787*. New York: W. W. Norton, 1987.

Dumas Malone. *Jefferson and the Ordeal of Liberty*. Boston: Little, Brown, 1962.

———. *Jefferson and the Rights of Man*. Boston: Little, Brown, 1951.

———. *Jefferson the President: First Term, 1801–1805*. Boston: Little, Brown, 1970.

———. *Jefferson the President: Second Term, 1805–1809*. Boston: Little Brown, 1974.

William R. Manning, ed. *Diplomatic Correspondence of the United States Concerning the Independence of Latin American Nations*. 3 vols. New York: Oxford University Press, 1925.

David McCullough. *John Adams*. New York: Simon & Schuster, 2001.

Jon Meacham. *American Lion: Andrew Jackson in the White House*. New York: Random House, 2008.

William Lee Miller Jr. *Arguing about Slavery: John Quincy Adams and the Great Battle in the United States Congress*. New York: Vintage Books, 1995.

Meade Minnigerode. *Jefferson, Friend of France 1793: The Career of Edmond Charles Genet*. New York: G. P. Putnam's Sons, 1928.

———. *Some American Ladies: Seven Informal Biographies*. New York: G. P. Putnam's Sons, 1926.

James Monroe. *The Autobiography of James Monroe*, edited by Stuart Gerry Brown. Syracuse, NY: Syracuse University Press, 1959.

Chase C. Mooney. *William H. Crawford, 1772–1834*. Lexington: University Press of Kentucky, 1974.

Samuel Eliot Morison. *Three Centuries of Harvard, 1636–1936*. Cambridge, MA: Belknap Press of Harvard University Press, 1936.

Richard B. Morris. *Encyclopedia of American History.* New York: Harper & Brothers, 1953.

Paul C. Nagel. *The Adams Women: Abigail and Louisa Adams, Their Sisters and Daughters.* New York: Oxford University Press, 1987.

———. *John Quincy Adams: A Public Life, a Private Life.* Cambridge: Harvard University Press, 1997.

Allan Nevins, ed. *The Diary of John Quincy Adams, 1794–1845.* New York: Charles Scribner's Sons, 1951.

Helen Nicolay. *Our Capital on the Potomac.* New York: Century Company, 1924.

John Niven. *John C. Calhoun and the Price of Union.* Baton Rouge: Louisiana State University Press, 1988.

Michael O'Brien. *Mrs. Adams in Winter.* New York: Farrar, Strauss and Giroux, 2010.

Lynn Hudson Parsons. *The Birth of Modern Politics: Andrew Jackson, John Quincy Adams and the Election of 1828.* New York: Oxford University Press, 2009.

———. *John Quincy Adams.* Lanham, MD: Rowman & Littlefield, 1998.

George A. Peek Jr., ed. *The Political Writings of John Adams.* New York: Liberal Arts Press, American Heritage Series, 1954.

Bradford Perkins. *Castlereagh and Adams: England and the United States, 1812–1823.* Berkeley: University of California Press, 1964.

Michel Péronnet. *Le XVIIIe siècle (1740–1820): Des lumières à la Sainte-Alliance.* Paris: Hachette Livre, 1998.

Merrill D. Peterson. *The Great Triumvirate: Webster, Clay, and Calhoun.* New York: Oxford University Press, 1987.

Michel Poniatowski. *Talleyrand aux États-Unis, 1794–1796.* Paris: Presses de la Cité, 1967.

Robert V. Remini. *Henry Clay: Statesman of the Union.* New York: W. W. Norton, 1991.

———. *John Quincy Adams.* New York: Henry Holt, 2002.

———. *The Life of Andrew Jackson.* 3 vols. New York: Harper & Row, 1977–1984. Subsequently published as a one-volume paperback: *The Life of Andrew Jackson.* New York: Penguin Books, 1988.

William J. Rhees, ed. *Smithsonian Miscellaneous Collections: Documents Relating to the Origins and History of the Smithsonian Institution.* Washington, DC: Smithsonian Institution, 1880.

J. D. Richardson. *Compilation of Messages and Papers of the Presidents.* 20 vols. Washington, DC: U.S. Government Printing Office, 1908.

Cokie Roberts. *Ladies of Liberty: The Women Who Shaped Our Nation.* New York: William Morrow, 2008.

Robert R. Rutland et al., eds. *The Papers of James Madison.* 16 vols. Charlottesville: University Press of Virginia, 1984–1989.

William H. Seward. *Life and Public Services of John Quincy Adams, Sixth President of the United States, with the Eulogy Delivered before the Legislature of New York.* New York: C. M. Saxton, 1859.

Jack Shepherd. *The Adams Chronicles: Four Generations of Greatness.* Boston: Little, Brown, 1975.

Page Smith. *John Adams.* 2 vols. Garden City, NY: Doubleday, 1962.

Donald H. Stewart. *The Opposition Press of the Federalist Period.* Albany: State University of New York Press, 1969.

Dirk J. Struik. *The Origins of American Science.* New York: Cameron Associates, 1948.

James Tagg. *Benjamin Franklin Bache and the "Philadelphia Aurora."* Philadelphia: University of Pennsylvania Press, 1999.

Robert J. Taylor, ed. *The Adams Papers, Diary of John Quincy Adams, November, 1779–March, 1786.* 2 vols. Cambridge, MA: Belknap Press of Harvard University Press, 1981.

———, ed. *Papers of John Adams.* 10 vols. Cambridge, MA: Belknap Press of Harvard University Press, 1983.

Alexis de Tocqueville. *Democracy in America.* New York: Bantam Dell, 2000. First published in 1835 as *De la democracie en Amérique* and translated into English in 1838.

Margaret Truman. *First Ladies: An Intimate Group Portrait of White House Wives.* New York: Fawcett Columbine, 1995.

Jean Tulard, Jean-François Fayard, and Alfred Fierro. *Histoire et dictionnaire de la Révolution Française.* Paris: Éditions Robert Laffont, 1987.

Harlow Giles Unger. *The French War Against America.* Hoboken, NJ: John Wiley & Sons, 2005.

———. *Lafayette.* Hoboken, NJ: John Wiley & Sons, 2002.

———. *The Last Founding Father: James Monroe and a Nation's Call to Greatness.* Philadelphia: Da Capo Press, Perseus Books Group, 2009.

————. *Noah Webster: The Life and Times of an American Patriot.* New York: John Wiley & Sons, 1998.

Warren-Adams Letters: Being Chiefly a Correspondence among John Adams, Samuel Adams, and James Warren. 25 vols. Boston: Massachusetts Historical Society, Collections, 1917.

Anne Hollingsworth Wharton. *Social Life in the Early Republic.* Williamstown, MA: Corner House Publishers, 1970.

Francis Wharton, ed. *The Revolutionary Diplomatic Correspondence of the United States.* 6 vols. Washington, DC: U.S. Government Printing Office, 1889.

Joseph Wheelan. *Mr. Adams's Last Crusade: John Quincy Adams's Extraordinary Post-Presidential Life in Congress.* New York: Public Affairs, 2008.

Edwin M. Wilson. *The Congressional Career of Nathaniel Macon.* Chapel Hill: University of North Carolina Press, 1900.

Barton H. Wise. *The Life of Henry Wise of Virginia, 1806–1876.* New York: Macmillan, 1899.

MANUSCRIPT COLLECTIONS

The Adams Family Papers
Adams Family Correspondence
Boston Athenaeum
Bostonian Society
Boston Public Library
The Diaries of John Quincy Adams: A Digital Collection
Houghton Library, Harvard University
Library of Congress
Massachusetts Historical Society, Boston
Massachusetts State Archives
New England Historical and Genealogical Society
New York Historical Society
New York Public Library
Smithsonian Institution

NEWSPAPERS

American Citizen
Boston Evening Post
Boston Gazette
Boston *News-Letter*
Columbian Centinel
Congressional Globe
Independent Chronicle (Boston)
Massachusetts Centinel
Massachusetts *Spy*
National Intelligencer
New England Chronicle
Philadelphia *Aurora*

GENERAL REFERENCES

Bartlett's Familiar Quotations
Dictionary of American Biography
The Encyclopedia of American Education
The Encyclopedia of American History
Encyclopedia Britannica
La grande encyclopédie
Webster's American Biographies
Webster's New Biographical Dictionary

Index

Abolition/slavery, 48, 187, 211–215,
    273–283
    and *Amistad* case, 287–295, 296, 308
    and Committee of Friends of the Right
        to Petition, 297
    and free speech, 273, 274, 282, 297,
        298, 303
    and Gag Rule, 274, 275–281,
        282–283, 287, 298, 303
    and petition, right of, 266–267, 269,
        273–274, 276–278, 282–283,
        297–302, 303
    and petitions from Pennsylvania
        Quakers, 266–267
    and union, dissolution of, 273,
        298–302
Adams, Abigail "Abby" (née Brooks; wife
    of Charles Francis Adams), 261, 279
    and birth of daughter (Louisa
        Catherine Adams), 265–266
    and birth of first son (John Quincy
        Adams II), 270–271
    and birth of second son (Charles
        Francis Adams Jr.), 280
    marriage of, 260
Adams, Abigail "Nabby" (daughter of
    John Adams), 23, 54–55, 56,
    57 (photo)
    birth of, 9–10
    illness of, 162
    marriage of, 67
Adams, Abigail (née Smith; wife of
    John Adams; mother of John
    Quincy Adams), 9 (photo)
    and Adams, Louisa Catherine,
        relationship between, 189
    and black cockade, 113
    and Bunker's Hill, Battle of, witnessing
        of, 14–17
    burial place of, 313
    children of (*see* Adams, Abigail
        "Nabby"; Adams, Charles; Adams,
        John Quincy; Adams, Thomas
        Boylston)
    death of, 206
    education of, 9
    and education of son, 18, 19
    in England, 54–55
    family of, 1, 8–9
    and family reunion after eight years,
        192–193
    forebears of, 1
    and French Revolution, 77–78, 79
    as grandparent, 148, 189, 192–193
    and household, dominant role
        in, 23
    and husband, separation from, 20–21,
        23–24, 39–40

Adams, Abigail (continued)
and husband and son's trip to France,
23–25
in Paris, 55, 56
and sons, separation from, 85
and trip home to Boston from Great
Britain, 70–71
Adams, Charles Francis, II (grandson of
John Quincy Adams), 286
Adams, Charles Francis, Jr. (grandson of
John Quincy Adams), 280
Adams, Charles Francis (son of John
Quincy Adams), 149, 241, 261,
265 (photo), 307
as ambassador to Great Britain, 313
birth of, 142
and birth of daughter (Louisa
Catherine Adams), 265–266
and birth of first son (John Quincy
Adams II), 270–271
and birth of second son (Charles
Francis Adams Jr.), 280
and death of father, 311
and death threats against father, 279
education of, 193
and family reunion after eight years
abroad, 193
and family reunion after six years
abroad, 182–183
and father's disappointment in,
225–226
and father's return to politics, dismay
regarding, 262
and Harvard College, conditional
admission to, 225
marriage of, 261
as member of Massachusetts
legislature, 303
in St. Petersburg, 154
and trip from St. Petersburg to France,
180–182
Adams, Charles (son of John Adams), 23,
40, 45–46
birth of, 11
death of, 120
education of, 42

at Harvard College, 61, 67, 70, 71
at University of Leyden, 43–44
Adams, Elihu (brother of John Adams),
20
Adams, Fanny (granddaughter of John
Quincy Adams), 285
Adams, George Washington (son of John
Quincy Adams), 136, 148, 234
(photo)
and alcoholism, 234, 259
birth of, 120
death of, 259–260
and death of grandfather, 252
education of, 188–189, 193
and family reunion after eight years
abroad, 192–193
and family reunion after six years,
182–183
and father's disappointment in,
225–226
at Harvard College, 225
as overseer of family affairs, 233–235
Adams, Henry (grandson of John Quincy
Adams), 223, 286, 287 (photo)
The Education of Henry Adams, 286
Adams, John, II (son of John Quincy
Adams), 136, 148, 241, 249
(photo), 260, 261
and alcoholism, 268, 272
birth of, 123
death of, 272
and death of grandfather, 252
and duel challenge, by Jarvis,
248–249
education of, 188, 193
and family reunion after eight years
abroad, 192–193
and family reunion after six years,
182–183
and father's disappointment in,
225–226
and Harvard College, 225
and Harvard College, expulsion
from, 226
and humiliation of father, 244
marriage of, 253

Adams, John (father of John Quincy
    Adams), 13 (photo), 104 (photo)
accomplishments of, 1–2
and Alien and Sedition Acts, 263
as ambassador to France, 39, 43
as ambassador to Great Britain, 56
in Amsterdam, 43–44
birthplace of, 10 (photo)
and British orders to arrest, 12
and British rule, anger over, 10–11
burial place of, 313
congressional leadership of, 20
and Continental Army, 14
at Continental Congress, 12
death of, 252, 264
and Declaration of Independence, 21
education of, 8
and education of son, 18–19
as emissary to France, 23–24
and expulsion from Boston, 11
and family reunion after eight years,
    192–193
as farmer, in retirement, 226–227
and France, threat of war with,
    110–113
and Franklin, Benjamin, 36–37
and French Revolution, 73, 78
as grandparent, 148, 189, 192–193
and Great Britain, peace treaty (1783)
    with, 54
in Great Britain, 54
guardianship responsibilities of,
    31–34, 37
in The Hague, 54
and Harvard College, 67
and Harvard College, son's admission
    to, 58
as lawyer in Boston Massacre trial, 11
and Louisiana Purchase, 131
and Massachusetts Constitution
    of 1780, 39
as Massachusetts representative, 11
as minister plenipotentiary in
    The Hague, 51, 52
and nepotism, charges of, 103–105, 108
and nursing care, 234

in Paris, 33–37, 52, 55–56
personality of, 37
and presidency, succession to, 102
as president, and France, threat of
    war with, 110–113
as president, and nepotism, charges of,
    103–105, 108
as president, and Quasi-War,
    113–116, 117
and presidential election (1800),
    defeat in, 118–119
and presidential election victory
    of son, 238
and Quasi-War, 113–116, 117
retirement home of, 10 (photo), 140,
    141 (photo)
as secretary of war, 22–23
and Supreme Court nomination
    of son, 157
Thoughts on Government, 22
and trip home from France, 37–39
and trip home to Boston from Great
    Britain, 70–71
and trip to France with son, 5–6,
    23–27, 29–33, 39–40
as vice president, 71
and Washington's retirement as
    president, 97–98
and wife, separation from, 20–21,
    23–25, 39–40
Adams, John Quincy
and abolition/slavery, 48, 187,
    211–215, 273–283
and abolition/slavery, and *Amistad* case,
    287–295, 296, 308
and abolition/slavery, and Committee
    of Friends of the Right to
    Petition, 297
and abolition/slavery, and free speech,
    273, 274, 282, 297, 298, 303
and abolition/slavery, and Gag Rule,
    274, 275–281, 282–283, 287,
    298, 303
and abolition/slavery, and petition,
    right of, 266–267, 269, 273–274,
    276–278, 282–283, 297–302, 303

Adams, John Quincy *(continued)*
  and abolition/slavery, and petitions
    from Pennsylvania Quakers,
    266–267
  and abolition/slavery, and union,
    dissolution of, 273, 298–302
  accomplishments of, 1, 2–4
  and Adams Strip, 133, 134 (map)
  and Adams-Onis treaty, 209
  at age sixteen, 45 (photo)
  at age twenty-nine, 91 (photo)
  and Alexander I, 152–153
  and *Amistad* case, 287–295, 296, 308
  and Anglo-American reconciliation,
    185–188
  and Anglo-American treaty of
    commerce and maritime law,
    negotiations for, 183–185
  and Anglo-French War, 140–141,
    142–143
  and astronomical observatories,
    296, 305
  as attorney and counselor in U.S.
    Supreme Court, 132
  and bankruptcy in wife's family,
    107–108
  and bar exams, 71
  in Berlin, 116
  birth of, 10
  birthplace of, 10 (photo)
  in Boston, 61
  and boundaries, extension of western,
    to Pacific Ocean, 218
  and boundaries, fixing northern, with
    Canada, 133, 171, 174, 202
  and Bunker's Hill, Battle of, witnessing
    of, 14–17
  business venture of, 234–235
  and censure and/or expel, congressional
    attempts to, 278, 281, 283, 295,
    298–302
  as chairman of Committee on
    Manufacturers, 266, 269
  and Chase, Samuel, impeachment of,
    138–139
  and citizen committees, appointment
    to, in Boston, 74–75

  and civil war, prediction of, 273, 312
  cold and forbidding manner of, 251
  and congressional obstructionism,
    243–244, 248, 252
  as congressman, 261–283, 285–309
  as congressman, after stroke, 306–309
  as congressman, and attempts to
    censure and/or expel, 278, 281,
    283, 295, 298–302
  as congressman, and charges of treason
    against, 298–302
  as congressman, in later years, 289
  as congressman, popularity of,
    302–303, 305
  contacts of, 3
  death and burial of, 309–312, 309
    (photo)
  and death of daughter, 162–163
  and death of father, 252
  and death of granddaughter, 285
  and death of son, 259–260
  and death threats against, 278–279
  and Democrats as new party, 243
  depression of, 51, 226–227, 247,
    260–261
  Dermot MacMorrogh, 263
  descendants of, 313
  diary of, 3, 34–35, 40–41
  and dueling, ban on, 300–301
  education of, 18–20, 34, 42–43,
    66–68
  estate of, 193
  failed presidency of, and political
    inactivity, 247–251, 253–254
  and family reunion after eight years
    abroad, 192–193
  and family reunion after six years
    abroad, 182–183
  as "father of German studies in
    America," 117n
  and father's presidential defeat, 119
  and Federalist Party, abandonment
    of, 143
  as first American president to be
    photographed live, 296
  first political controversy of, 65–66
  and Floridas, acquisition of, 204–210

and Floridas, and Jackson, Andrew,
204–210
forebears of, 7–8
and foreign colonization in Americas,
217–218 (*see also* Monroe Doctrine)
and France, threat of war with,
111–112
and free speech, 139, 273, 274, 282,
297, 298, 303
and French Revolution, 77, 78,
79–80, 89
and Gag Rule, 274, 275–281,
282–283, 287, 298, 303
as grandparent, 265–266, 270–271,
272, 285–286
and Great Britain, military alliance
with, 216–217
and Great Britain, peace treaty (1783)
with, 54
in Great Britain, 54
in The Hague, as visitor, 52, 54
and Hamilton/Burr duel, and murder
indictment, 137–138
and Hammond, George, 97–98
and Harvard College, admission to, 66
and Harvard College, admission to,
arbitrary denial of, 63–64
and Harvard College, admission to,
preparation for, 63–64, 65
and Harvard College, entrance
examinations at, 66
and Harvard College, graduation
from, 68
and Harvard College, interview at,
61–62, 63
at Harvard College, as professor, 140,
147–148
at Harvard College, as student,
66–68
as head of commission to negotiate end
to War of 1812, 167, 169–174,
177–178, 180
and housing, in London, 188–189
and housing, in St. Petersburg,
155–156
and housing, in Washington, 193–194
inaugural address of, 239–241

and Jackson, Andrew, and Floridas,
204–210
and Jackson, Andrew, and honorary
degree, 270
and Jackson, Andrew, ridicule by,
244, 246
and Jay Treaty, 92–93, 96–97, 98
and Jefferson, Thomas, dinners with,
121, 131, 135, 140
and Jefferson, Thomas, newspaper
articles assailing, 72–74
and Lafayette, Marquis de, as guest at
White House, 241–243
language skills of, 34, 38–39
and Latin American independence
from Spain, 216
law practice of, 71–72, 72–73, 74,
145–146
and law study, in Newburyport, 69–70
Lectures on Rhetoric and Oratory, 147
Letters from Silesia, 116
Letters of Publicola, 72
and Louisiana Purchase, 126, 129–132
and Madison, James, chess games with,
125–126
marital engagement of, 99–101
marital estrangement of, 247, 252
and marriage, fiftieth anniversary of,
307
marriage of, 105–106
and Mexico, war with, 282–281,
306, 308
as minister in The Hague, 93–95
as minister plenipotentiary to Great
Britain, 167
as minister plenipotentiary to
Lisbon, 102
as minister plenipotentiary to Prussia,
108–109, 110–113
as minister plenipotentiary to Russia,
146–147, 148–150, 150–157, 164
as minister to Great Britain, 178,
182–190
as minister to Holland, 81–86
as minister to Lisbon, and nepotism,
charges of, 103–105
as minister to Prussia, 105

Adams, John Quincy *(continued)*
  and Monroe, James, eulogy for,
    264–265, 266
  and Monroe, James, reelection of, 215
  and Monroe Doctrine, 218–220
  and Napoléon I, and invasion of
    Russia, 164–165
  and national scientific institution,
    272–273
  and nepotism, charges of, 103–105,
    108
  and neutrality, 216
  and newspaper articles assailing Paine
    and Jefferson, 72–74
  and nomination to Supreme Court,
    refusal of, 159
  and nullification, 263–264,
    269–270, 271
  and Oregon coast, Russian claim to,
    217–218
  as out of touch with America, 244–247
  and Paine, Thomas, newspaper articles
    assailing, 72–74
  and parents'
    advice/criticism/expectations/praise,
    19–20, 22, 40, 43–44, 50–51,
    67–68, 80–81, 82–83, 85–86, 90,
    94, 135, 144, 191–192
  parents of *(see* Adams, Abigail;
    Adams, John)
  in Paris, 33–37, 52, 55–56
  and party affiliations, independent,
    227, 243, 261
  and patronage, 243
  and personal humiliation, 244
  and petition, right of, 266–267, 269,
    273–274, 276–278, 282–283,
    297–302, 303
  and Pickering, Timothy, father's
    dismissal of, 117
  poetry of, 69–70, 136, 142, 189
  and political dissent, right of, 138
  popularity of, as congressman,
    302–303, 305
  precociousness of, 44, 45, 52–53
  as president, 239–254, 240 (photo)

  and presidential campaign, refusal to
    actively participate in, 223,
    225, 227
  and presidential election (1824),
    229–235
  and presidential election (1824),
    and "corrupt bargain" charges,
    238–239, 243
  and presidential election (1824), Clay,
    Henry, and shift of votes to,
    235–236
  and presidential election (1824),
    victory in, 236–239
  and presidential election (1828),
    254–255
  and presidential election (1828), defeat
    in, 255–257
  and presidential reelection campaign
    (1828), 254–255
  and Quasi-War, 114, 115
  and religion, 117–118
  Report on Weights and Measures, 200
  as representative of whole nation, 227,
    261, 267, 286, 310
  and retirement, plans for, 226–227
  rhetorical tactics of, 277, 281
  salary of, 155, 155n, 195
  and scientific interests, 53, 295–296,
    304–305
  as secretary and translator for
    American minister Francis Dana, in
    St. Petersburg, 45–46, 48–51
  as secretary of state, 190–192,
    193–196, 198, 199–221,
    201 (photo)
  in semiretirement, 259–261
  and Shays's Rebellion, 68–69
  and silk worms, breeding, as
    president, 250
  and social life, at Harvard College, 67
  and social life, in Berlin, 117–118
  and social life, in London,
    188–189
  and social life, in New England,
    64–65
  and social life, in New York, 60

and social life, in St. Petersburg,
154–155, 155–156
and social life, in Sweden, 51–52
and social life, in Washington,
125–126, 199
as son of president, and nepotism,
charges of, 108
and sons, disappointment in scholastic
achievement and behavior of,
225–226
and sons, separation from, 148,
160–161
and son's duel challenge by Jarvis,
248–249
as Speaker pro tem, to organize
committee membership, 286–287
speech of, as basis for Emancipation
Proclamation, 302
and State Department Library, 200
in state senate, and anticorruption
campaign, 122
and stroke, 306–309
and studies in Holland, 95
and studies in London, 189
and studies in St. Petersburg, 50
and support for brother's wife and
children, 268
and support for son's wife and
children, 272
and Supreme Court, cases before,
145–146
and Supreme Court nomination,
refusal of, 157, 159
and Texas, annexation of, 282,
305–306
and Texas, independence of,
280–281, 282
and treason, congressional charges of,
298–302
and Treaty of Ghent, 175–176,
177–178
and trip home from France, 37–39,
58–59
and trip to England, 90–92
and trip to federal capital (New York),
59–60

and trip to federal capital
(Philadelphia), 72
and trip to France (as child), 5–6,
23–27, 29–33, 39–40
and trip to Quincy, to visit aging father,
226–227, 234
and trip to Quincy, to visit parents,
139–140, 210, 226–227
and trip to Russia, 148–150
and trip to Silesia, 116
and trip to St. Petersburg, 47–48
and union, dissolution of, 273,
298–302
at University of Leyden, 43–44
as U.S. senator, 122, 123–144
as U.S. senator, and disagreements with
colleagues, 126, 129–135, 137–139,
143–144
as U.S. senator, resignation of, 144
and War of 1812, 166, 167, 169–174,
177–178, 180
and Washington, George, retirement
of, 101–102
and weights and measures, system of,
200
and wife and family, separation from,
120–121, 135–137, 141–142
and wife's family, bankruptcy in,
107–108
and wife's presidential campaign work,
223–225
and XYZ dispatches, 112–113
and Yale College, 60–61
Adams, John Quincy, II (grandson of
John Quincy Adams)
birth of, 270–271
Adams, Joseph, III (son of Joseph
Adams Jr.), 8
Adams, Joseph, Jr. (great-grandfather of
John Quincy Adams), 8
Adams, Louisa Catherine (daughter of
John Quincy Adams)
birth of, 159–160
death of, 162–163
Adams, Louisa Catherine (granddaughter
of John Quincy Adams), 265–266

Adams, Louisa Catherine (née Johnson; wife of John Quincy Adams), 99–101, 100 (photo)
and Adams, Abigail, relationship between, 189
in Berlin, 116
as cabinet wife, 196–198
as cabinet wife, and Tuesday evening receptions, 199, 224–225
children of (*see* Adams, Charles Francis; Adams, George Washington; Adams, John, II; Adams, Louisa Catherine)
as congressional wife, 267–268
and cosmetics, husband's disapproval of, 109–110
death of, 313
and death of husband, 310
and death of son, 259–260
and death threats against husband, 279
and depression of husband, 247
and family bankruptcy, 105–106
and family reunion after six years abroad, 182–183
as first lady, 241, 247, 248 (photo), 250–251
as grandparent, 265–266, 272, 285–286
and housing, in Washington, 193–194
and husband, and disapproval of cosmetics, 109–110
and husband, and presidential campaign, 230–232
and husband, and presidential defeat, 255–256
and husband, and return to politics, dismay regarding, 262, 263
and husband, death of, 310
and husband, death threats against, 279
and husband, depression of, 247
and husband, private secretary to, 189
and husband, separation from, 120–121, 135–137, 141–142
illness of, 233, 239
and Johnson, Thomas, 108–109
marital estrangement of, 247, 252

and marriage, fiftieth anniversary of, 307
marriage of, 105–106
miscarriages of, 109, 116, 140
and presidential campaign work, 223–225
and silk worms, breeding, as first lady, 250–251
and social life, in London, 188–189
and social life, in St. Petersburg, 154, 155–157
and social life, in Washington, 125–126, 135, 196–198, 199, 224–225
and son, death of, 259–260
and sons, separation from, 148
in St. Petersburg, 153–154, 162
and support for sister's orphaned children, 226, 241, 253
and trip from St. Petersburg to France, 180–182
and trip home from St. Petersburg, 178
and trip to Russia, 148–150
and trip to Silesia, 116
and Tuesday evening receptions, as cabinet wife, 199, 224–225
and weekly receptions, as first lady, 250, 251 (photo)
Adams, Mary Louisa (granddaughter of John Quincy Adams), 285–286
Adams, Thomas Boylston (son of John Adams), 148
and alcoholism, 193, 210, 252
birth of, 11
death of, 268
and French Revolution, 89
in The Hague, as aid to brother, 85, 93, 102
at Harvard College, 67, 70, 71
Adams farm, 10 (photo)
Adams Strip, 133, 134 (map), 202. See *also* Boundaries
Adams-Onis Treaty (aka Transcontinental Treaty), 209, 210–211
Adet, Pierre August, 103
Alden, John, 7–8

Alexander I, 152–153, 164, 202, 202n
  and Johnson, Catherine "Kitty,"
    156–157, 162
  as mediator in War of 1812, 166
  and Oregon coast, 217–218
Alien and Sedition Acts, 263
American Revolution, 72–73, 87
  beginnings of, 6–7, 10–14
  and peace treaty (1783), 54,
    84–85
  See also Breed's Hill, battle at; Bunker's
    Hill, Battle of
Amistad case, 287–295, 288 (photo),
    296, 308
  justices of, 290
Anglo-American conflict, 161–162, 163,
    183–185
  and reconciliation, 185–188
Anglo-American treaty of commerce and
    maritime law, 183–185
Anglo-French War, 140–141, 142–143
  and Russia, 152–153
  See also France; Napoleonic Wars
Antoinette, Marie, 55
Articles of Confederation, 68, 69
Astronomical observatories, 296, 305

Babeuf, François Noël, 88
Bache, Benjamin Franklin, 34, 108,
    113, 130
Baldwin, Roger Sherman, 288–289,
    290–291, 294
Barbé Marbois, Marquis François de,
    38–39
Bayard, James, 170
Bellamy, Monsieur, 112
Bentham, Jeremy, 188
Benton, Thomas Hart, 310
Blanchard, Jean-Pierre, 56
Bonhomme Richard, 38, 38n
Boston Harbor, 15 (map)
Boston Massacre, 11
Boston Tea Party, 11
Boundaries
  extension of western, to Pacific
    Ocean, 218

fixing northern, with Canada, 133,
    171, 174, 202
  See also Adams Strip
Bourne, Sylvanus, 93
Boylston, Nicholas, 140
Boylston, Thomas, 7
Boylston, Zabdiel, 7
Breed's Hill, battle at, 14. *See also*
    American Revolution
Brooks, Abigail. *See* Adams, Abigail
    "Abby"
Bunker's Hill, Battle of, 14–17, 16
    (photo). *See also* American
    Revolution
Bunker's Hill Monument, 303, 304
    (photo)
Burr, Aaron, Jr., 119
  and Chase, Samuel, impeachment of,
    138–139
  and Hamilton, Alexander, duel
    with, and murder indictment,
    137–138
  as U.S. senator, resignation of, 139

Calhoun, John C., 212, 230 (photo)
  and Floridas, acquisition of, 203
  and Great Britain, military alliance
    with, 217
  and national scientific institution, 273
  and nullification, 264
  and presidential election (1824),
    229–230, 232
  as secretary of war, 194
  as U.S. senator, 270, 273
  as vice president, 243, 264
Canning, Stratford, 202–203
Castlereagh, Lord, 183–184,
    201, 210
  and Anglo-American reconciliation,
    186–187
Catherine II, 44
Chase, Samuel, impeachment of,
    138–139
Cinque (Congolese chief), 287, 290
    (photo)
Civil war, prediction of, 273, 312

Clay, Henry, 237 (photo)
  and Adams, John Quincy, death of,
      309
  and Adams-Onis treaty, 209
  and Anglo-American treaty of
      commerce and maritime law,
      negotiations for, 183, 185
  and Floridas, and Jackson, Andrew,
      205, 208, 210
  and Great Britain, military alliance
      with, 217
  and nullification, 271
  and presidential election (1824),
      229–230, 232, 235
  and presidential election (1824),
      and "corrupt bargain" charges,
      238–239, 243
  and presidential election (1824), and
      shift of votes to Adams, John
      Quincy, 235–236
  and presidential election (1828), 254
  and presidential election (1832), 270
  as secretary of state, 235, 239, 243
  as secretary of state, and leave of
      absence, 253
  as Speaker of the House, 194–195
  and War of 1812, commission to
      negotiate end to, 169–170, 177–178
Clayton, Augustus Smith, 271
Clinton, George, 59
  as vice president, 139
Colonization in Americas, 217–218
Committee of Friends of the Right to
      Petition, 297
Common Sense (Paine), 72
Congressional obstructionism, 243–244,
      248, 252
Continental Army, 14, 21
Continental Congress, 12, 68
Crawford, Susanna, 225
Crawford, William H., 212, 222 (photo),
      225
  and Monroe, James, rage against, 221
  and presidential election (1824),
      229–230, 232, 235
  as secretary of the Treasury, 194

The Crisis (Paine), 72
Crowninshield, Benjamin, as secretary
      of the navy, 194
Cushing, William, 157

Daguerre, Louis-Jacques-Mandé, 296
Dana, Francis, 40, 44–45, 47, 48–50,
      49 (photo), 149
Deane, Barnabas, 31
Deane, Jesse, 31–33, 34, 37, 42, 42n
Deane, Silas, 23–24, 31, 33, 42, 42n
Dearborn, Henry, 167
Decatur, Stephen, 166, 183
Declaration of Independence, 21
Democrats as new party, 243
Dermot MacMorrogh (John Quincy
      Adams), 263
Dickens, Charles, 302–303
Drayton, William, 271
Dueling, ban on, 300–301

The Education of Henry Adams
      (Henry Adams), 286
Emancipation Proclamation, 302
Embargo Act, 168
Emerson, Ralph Waldo, 300
Everett, Alexander, 149, 260, 261
Everett, Edward, 260, 260n, 261

Fauchet, Jean-Antoine-Joseph, 80
Federal capital (New York), 59–60
Federal capital (Philadelphia), 72
Federal capital (Washington). *See*
      Washington (capital city)
Ferdinand VII, 216
First Continental Congress. *See*
      Continental Congress
Fletcher, Robert, 146
Floridas, U.S. acquisition of, 203–210
Force Bill, 271
Forsyth, John, 292
France
  and Great Britain, war with, 75–76,
      77–79, 85
  and United States, and threat of war
      with, 110–113

See also Anglo-French War; French
Revolution; Napoléon I;
Napoleonic Wars
Franco-American alliance, 75
Franco-American treaty of 1778, 77
Franklin, Benjamin, 35 (photo), 39
and Declaration of Independence, 21
as emissary to France, 23
and Great Britain, peace treaty (1783)
with, 54
guardianship responsibilities of, 37
in Paris, 33–37, 52, 56
personal/social life of, 36–37
Frederick William II, 109
Frederick William III, 109, 120
Free speech, 139, 273, 274, 282, 297,
298, 303
French Revolution, 73–74, 75–80
and American support, erosion of, 96
and Napoléon I, 88–89
and Robespierre, Maximilian,
87–88
See also France
Fulton, Robert, 164

Gag Rule, 274, 275–281, 282–283, 287,
298, 303
Gaines, Edmund, 203, 245–246
Gales, Joseph, 219
Gallatin, Albert, 170, 266
and Anglo-American treaty of
commerce and maritime law,
negotiations for, 183, 185
and War of 1812, commission to
negotiate end to, 177–178
Gardoqui, Joseph, 42
Genet, Edmond, 75–76, 76 (photo),
78, 80
George II, and Jay Treaty, 98
George Washington University, 296
Gerry, Elbridge, 59, 111, 112
Ghent, Treaty of. *See* Treaty of Ghent
Great Britain, 73
and colonization in Americas, 218
and France, war with, 75–76,
77–79, 85

and French Revolution, 89
and United States, military alliance
with, 216–217
and United States, peace treaty (1783)
with, 54, 84–85 (*see also* Jay Treaty;
Treaty of Ghent)
and United States, unsettled issues
between, 200–203
See also American Revolution;
Anglo-American conflict;
Anglo-French War; War of 1812

Haas, Philip, 296
Hamilton, Alexander, 84
and Burr, Aaron, Jr., duel with,
137–138
and French Revolution, 74, 77
as inspector general and second in
command, 114
and presidential election (1800), 119
and whiskey rebellion, 89–90
Hammond, George, 96–98
Hancock, John, 14, 61, 70–71
Harrison, William Henry, 167, 179, 289
death of, 295
Hartley, David, 54
Harvard College, 8, 57, 64 (photo), 67
Hauteval, Lucien, 112
Haverhill petition, 298–302. *See also*
Petition, right of
Hayne, Robert, 270
Hellen, Nancy, 125
Hellen, Walter, 125
Holland, 75, 89
Hopkinson, Joseph, 223
Hottinger, Jean Conrad, 112
Howard, Benjamin Chew, 276

Jackson, Andrew, 180, 233 (photo)
and Adams, John Quincy, as president,
ridicule of, 244, 246
and congressional obstructionism,
243–244
and Floridas, acquisition of, 203–210
as governor of Florida, resignation
of, 221

Jackson, Andrew *(continued)*
  and Harvard University, honorary
    degree from, 270
  and national scientific institution, 272
  and New Orleans, Battle of, 172,
    176–177
  and nullification, 269–270, 271, 273
  as president, 269–270, 271, 282
  and presidential election (1824),
    229–233, 235
  and presidential election (1824),
    and "corrupt bargain" charges,
    238–239, 243
  and presidential election (1828),
    254–255
  and presidential election (1828),
    victory in, 255, 256
  and presidential election (1832), 270
  and Texas, independence of, 282
Jackson, Rachel, 254, 256
Jarvis, Russell, 248–249
Jay, John, 59, 70, 71
  and Great Britain, peace treaty (1783)
    with, 54, 84, 85 *(see also* Jay Treaty)
  in Paris, 52
Jay Treaty, 92–93, 96–97, 98
Jefferson, Thomas, 59, 72–73, 103,
    130 (photo)
  and Adams, John, death of, 252
  and Adams, John Quincy, 195
  and Adams, John Quincy, dinners
    with, 121, 131, 135, 140
  and Anglo-French War, 140–141,
    142–143
  and Chase, Samuel, impeachment of,
    138–139
  death of, 264
  and Declaration of Independence, 21
  and French Revolution, 73, 76–77
  and Great Britain, military alliance
    with, 217
  and Louisiana Purchase, 128, 131–132
  and Monroe, James, 195
  and nullification, 263
  in Paris, 55, 56
  as president, 119–120

  and presidential election (1800),
    victory in, 139
  resignation of, 80
  and Supreme Court, attempt to alter
    Federalist bias on, 138
Jenkinson, Charles (earl of Liverpool),
    176
Johnson, Catherine "Kitty," 37
  and Alexander I, 162
  marriage of, 162
Johnson, Catherine "Kitty" (sister of
    Louisa Catherine Adams [née
    Johnson]), 149, 156–157
Johnson, George, 235
Johnson, Joshua, 37, 98–99, 121
Johnson, Louisa Catherine. *See* Adams,
    Louisa Catherine
Johnson, Thomas, 37
  in Berlin, 108–109
Jones, John Paul, 38, 56
Jones, William, 167

Kennedy, John F., 4
Key, Francis Scott, 173
King, Rufus, 59
Kirkland, John, 225
Knox, Henry, 84

Lafayette, Adrienne, 55, 182
Lafayette, George Washington, 241
Lafayette, Marquis de, 55, 56, 59, 182,
    241, 242 (photo), 281
  as guest at White House, 241–243
Latin America, and independence from
    Spain, 216–217
Lavasseur, Auguste, 241
Lectures on Rhetoric and Oratory (John
    Quincy Adams), 147
Lee, Arthur, 23, 36
Lee, Richard Henry, 59–60
Letters from Silesia (John Quincy Adams),
    116
Letters of Publicola (John Quincy Adams),
    72
Lincoln, Abraham, 2, 260n, 302, 306,
    307 (photo), 308

Livingston, Robert, 21
Longfellow, Henry Wadsworth, 8
Loring, Ellis Gray, 287, 288–289
Louis XVI, 33, 55, 73, 75
Louis XVIII, 168, 216
Louisiana Purchase, 126, 127 (map),
    128–132
Lovell, James, 23
Luzac, Jean, 44
Luzerne, Chevalier de la, 38–39

Macon, Nathaniel, 245
Madison, Dolley, 250
Madison, James, 2, 281
    and Adams, John Quincy, chess games
        with, 125–126
    and Anglo-American conflict, 161–162
    and Anglo-French War, 140–141
    and Great Britain, military alliance
        with, 217
    and Louisiana Purchase, 128–129
    and nomination for presidency, 143
    and nullification, 263–264
    as president, 146, 147
    as secretary of state, 133
    and Treaty of Ghent, 174
    and War of 1812, 162, 163, 166,
        171–172
    and War of 1812, commission to
        negotiate end to, 170
Marshall, John, 111, 112, 241
    as chief justice of Supreme Court, 119
    as secretary of state, 117
Marshall, Thomas, 301
Maurepas, Comte de, 33
Merry, Anthony, 124
Mesmer, Franz, 296
Mexico, war with, 282–281, 306, 308
Missouri Compromise, 213, 214 (map),
    215, 273
Monroe, Elizabeth, 196–197, 250
Monroe, James, 2, 59, 98, 179, 229
    and abolition/slavery, 211, 212
    and Anglo-American conflict, 161–162
    and cabinet members as presidential
        aspirants, 220–221, 221–223

cabinet of, 194
death of, 264
eulogy for, 264–265, 266
and Floridas, acquisition of, 203–210
and New Orleans, Battle of, 177
as president, 190, 194, 195
reelection of, 215
as secretary of state, 161–162
as secretary of war and state, 180
and War of 1812, 167
Monroe Doctrine, 218–220
Montgolfier, Étienne, 53
Montgolfier, Joseph de, 53
Morison, Samuel Eliot, 57
Morris, Gouverneur, 124
Mullins, Priscilla, 8
Murray, William Vans, 112

Napoléon I, 88–89, 151 (photo)
    defeat of, 177
    as emperor, 151
    and escape from Elbe, 180–181, 182
    and exile to Elbe, 168
    and Louisiana Purchase, 126, 128
    and Quasi-War, 115, 116–117
    and Russia, 162
    and Russia, invasion of, 164–165
    surrender of, 167–168
    and Waterloo, 183
    See also Napoleonic Wars
Napoleonic Wars, 150–151, 163. *See also*
    French Revolution; Napoléon I
National scientific institution, 272–273
Nelson, Horatio, 115
Neutrality Proclamation, 95
New Orleans, Battle of, 172, 176–177
New York (federal capital), 59–60
Ney, Marshal Michel, 182
Noailles, Duc de, 33
Noël, Nicholas, 32, 33
Non-Importation Act, 143
Nullification, 263–264, 269–270,
    271, 273

Onis y Gonzales, Luis de, 205
Oregon coast, Russian claim to, 217–218

Paine, Thomas, 60, 72–74
  Common Sense, 72
  The Crisis, 72
  The Rights of Man, 73
Palais de Versailles, 36 (photo)
Parsons, Theophilus, 69
Paul I, 152
Peck, John, 145–146
Pennsylvania Quakers, petitions from,
  266–267
Percy, Hugh Lord, 272
Perry, Oliver Hazard, 167
Petition, right of
  and abolition/slavery, 266–267, 269,
    273–274, 276–278, 282–283,
    297–302, 303
  and Pennsylvania Quakers, 266–267
  and women, 276–278
Philadelphia (federal capital), 72
Pichegru, Charles, 93
Pickering, Timothy, 95–96, 126
  and Louisiana Purchase, 131
  and presidential election (1800),
    118–119
  and Quasi-War, 117
  as secretary of state, 195–196
  as secretary of state, dismissal of, 117
Pinckney, Charles Cotesworth
  and France, threat of war with,
    111, 112
  and presidential election (1800),
    defeat in, 139
Pinckney, Thomas, 96
  and Jay Treaty, 92
  and petition, right of, 277
Pius VII, 151
Plumbe, John, Jr., 296
Political dissent, right to, 138
Polk, James K., 274, 275n, 305, 308
  and Adams, John Quincy, death of,
    311
Prentiss-Adams Law, 301
Presidential election (1800), 118–119, 139
Presidential election (1824), 229–239
  and Clay, Henry, and shift of votes to
    Adams, John Quincy, 235–236

  and "corrupt bargain" charges,
    238–239, 243
  and inconclusive electoral votes, 235
Presidential election (1828), 254–257
Presidential election (1832), 270
Presidential election (1836), 282

Quasi-War, 113–116
  end of, 116–117
Quincy, John, 8, 74
Quincy, Josiah, 11, 311
Quincy, Massachusetts, 7, 10 (photo), 74
Quincy, Saer de (earl of Winchester), 7
Quincy Bay, 15 (map)
Quincy family
  forebears, 7–8
  origins of, 7n

Randolph, Edmund, 80, 84
Randolph, John, 95, 243
Report on Weights and Measures
  (John Quincy Adams), 200
Richardson, Rev. Joseph, 261
The Rights of Man (Paine), 73
Robespierre, Maximilian, 87–88
Rush, Richard, 201–202
Russell, Jonathan, 170
Russia
  and Anglo-French War, 152–153
  and Napoléon I, invasion of,
    164–165
  and Oregon coast, 217–218

Scott, Winfield, 167
Seaton, Sarah, 237
Second Continental Congress. *See*
  Continental Congress
Seminole War, 204
Shaw, Rev. John, 63–64
Shays, Daniel, 68–69
Shays's Rebellion, 68–69
Sherman, Roger, 21
Slavery. *See* Abolition/slavery
Smith, Abigail Quincy. *See* Adams,
  Abigail
Smith, Billy, 162

Smith, Robert, 149, 161
Smith, Samuel, 149
Smith, Mrs. Samuel Harrison, 256
Smith, Rev. William, 8
Smith, William, Jr., 8
Smith, William "Billy," 149
Smithson, James, 272, 295–296
Smithsonian Institution, 272–273
South America, and independence from Spain, 216–217
Southard, Samuel L., 221
Spain
    and Floridas, U.S. acquisition of, 203–210
    and French Revolution, 75
    and Latin American independence, 216–217
St. Petersburg, Russia, 48 (photo)
State Department Library, 200
Stevens, Joseph, 30
Stewart, Robert, 186
Stiles, Ezra, 60, 60n
Story, Joseph, 290, 293
Supreme Court, U.S., 145–146, 155n
    and Jefferson, Thomas, and attempt to alter Federalist bias on, 138
    slaveholders in, 290
    See also Amistad Case

Talleyrand-Perigord, Charles-Maurice de, 84, 110
    and France, threat of war with, 113
    and Quasi-War, 114, 115, 116–117
Taney, Roger B., 290, 292
Tecumseh (Shawnee chief), 167
Texas
    annexation of, 282, 305–306
    independence of, 280–281, 282
Thaxter, John, 18, 40, 42, 43
Thoughts on Government (John Adams), 22
Tillotson, John, 118
Transcontinental Treaty. *See* Adams-Onis Treaty
Treaty of Ghent, 174–177, 175 (photo), 177–178

Truxton, Thomas, 114
Turner, Nat, 267, 271
Tyler, John, 295 (photo), 305–306
    and abolition/slavery, 295, 303–304

Union, dissolution of, 273, 298–302

Van Buren, Martin, 239, 289
    and *Amistad* case, 288
    and presidential election (1836), victory in, 282
    and Texas, annexation of, 282
    as vice president, 270
Vattel, Emmerich von, 207
Vergennes, Comte de, 33, 43, 48–49
Vernon, William, 31–33
Versailles, Palais de, 36 (photo)

War of 1812, 162, 163, 165–167, 183
    commission to negotiate end to, 167, 169–174, 177–178, 180
    and New Orleans, Battle of, 172, 176–177
    and rockets, use of, 168–169, 169n
    and Treaty of Ghent, 174–177
    and Washington, burning of, 169
Warren, Joseph, 12, 14, 16–17
Washington, George, 49, 59, 81 (photo), 84, 272, 281, 290
    as commander in chief, 14, 114
    and Continental Army, 21
    and Continental Congress, 12
    death of, 118, 120
    and French Revolution, 74, 75, 80
    as general and commander-in-chief, 14
    and George Washington University, 296
    and Neutrality Proclamation, 95
    and nomination of Adams, John Quincy, as minister in The Hague, 81–82
    as president, 71, 72, 195
    as president, retirement of, 97–98
    and whiskey rebellion, 89–90
Washington, Martha, 72, 121, 250

Washington (capital city), 123–125,
    197 (photo)
  burning of, in War of 1812, 169
Waterloo, 183, 184, 186
Watson, Egbert R., 229
Wayne, "Mad" Anthony, 89
Webster, Daniel, 233
  and presidential election (1836), 282
Weights and measures, system of, 200
Wellington, Duke of, 183, 184, 186, 188
West, Benjamin, 54, 56
Wheate, Jacob, 60
Wheate, Lady, 60

Whiskey rebellion, 87, 89–90
Whittier, John Greenleaf, 302
Willard, Rev. Joseph, 58, 61–62, 63,
    66, 68
Wirt, William, 239, 274
  as attorney general, 194
Wise, Henry, 299–301, 302
Witherspoon, John, 60
Women, and petition, right of, 276–278

XYZ dispatches, 112–113

Yale College, 60–61